PALACE

**Neil Mackwood
and Bryan Renison**

ARROW BOOKS

Arrow Books Limited
62–65 Chandos Place, London WC2N 4NW

An imprint of Century Hutchinson Limited

London Melbourne Sydney Auckland
Johannesburg and agencies throughout
the world

First published by Robson Books Ltd 1986
Arrow edition 1987
Reprinted 1987

Printed and bound in Great Britain by
Anchor Brendon Limited, Tiptree, Essex

ISBN 0 09 953120 8

Contents

Prologue

EPISODE ONE: WINTER

EPISODE TWO: SPRING

EPISODE THREE: SUMMER

Prologue

The only signs of life in the vast white expanse of snow that covered Windsor Great Park were the tracks of roebuck, pheasant and badger. It had been snowing steadily since dawn on Christmas Day. Now, thirty-two hours later, the 4,800 acres of Royal parkland glistened luminously as the winter evening gathered in. Etched against the fading light, the majestic granite walls of Europe's oldest continuously inhabited castle, which had stood on this site since William the Conqueror, looked fearsome and impenetrable. Above the mighty stonework, high up on Jeffrey Wyatt's Round Tower, flapping in the glacial north-east wind, was the Royal Standard which proclaimed the presence of the sovereign family of the land. The only sign of life in this awesome fortress were the friendly lights that shone from the private apartments, where on the third floor of the Upper Ward quadrangle could be seen a lone figure, framed against the leaded-light window, in stark silhouette.

Castles in the air

Andrew, peering out into the darkening, snow-flurried night, scanned the castle battlements keenly. Brill, he thought. The Prince grinned mischievously to himself: absolutely bloody terrif.

This was his last night of luxurious captivity and he was determined to make sure it was a memorable one. Not that it was up to him. The slightest hiccup and the whole delicate, minutely-planned operation would result in an almighty cock-up. Shielding his eyes, Andrew pressed closer to the window and stared out attentively.

The last tourist had been shooed out of St George's Chapel twenty minutes before, and only the sodden Mars Bar wrappers and crumpled-up crisp packets scuttered back and forth before the chill eddies of wind. The grey castle walls glistened dully in the dim lamp light, and the echo of the hobnail boots of the lone Welsh guardsman was the only sound to reach the Royal apartments.

Prince Andrew, the Duke of York, glanced down at the

gold Rolex watch Sarah had given him for Christmas. It was only six-thirty. There was still plenty of time. Andrew sighed impatiently.

Christmas, for a high-spirited young serviceman, was strain enough, but a whole month with his family, strewth! And now that his wife was visiting her mother in the Argentine — a place that no other member of the Windsors could conceivably set foot — there was no one to share a laugh with. Dear old Granny insisting on playing charades every night, Auntie Margaret constantly blowing the smoke from her Sobranies into everyone's eyes, Father banging on about the problems of the black rhino (and blow the ruddy starving), while Charles — sweet, well-meaning Chas — just would bore the pants off everyone with his blatherings about the paranormal. Not to mention his godawful goon jokes. Grief, a whole month of Neddy Seagoon impersonations!

In the distance, beyond the castle walls, the Prince could make out the familiar string of multi-coloured lights that marked the Windsor Inn. Dashit, he'd much prefer to be in the pub right now, rather than preparing for the last formal supper with his family. Still, if he couldn't go out there for his fun, then he'd simply have to import it.

Princes, he mused, can't be choosers. He looked around his room, with its red brocaded walls, stuccoed ceiling put up by George III in a moment of sanity and good taste, and its Italianate marble fireplace, all cherubs, grapes and incongruous stags. It was exquisite. But it was a gilded cage.

Andrew, his hair still damp and tousled from his shower, turned to survey himself in the full-length inlaid mahogany mirror: with only a towel round his waist, he flexed his muscles and grinned appreciatively at his own reflection. Attaboy! From the adjacent room he could hear the muffled sound of a harsh male voice singing along, lungs bursting, with a classical recording. Andrew whipped off his towel with the flourish of a matador and let out a full-throated hunting yell. Yorrocks! He was going to take the castle by storm tonight.

More than meets the eye

From the massive three-foot high, silver-cornered Amtrax quad speakers came the vast rich sound of *The Marriage of Figaro*. The tweeters and woofers were quivering with every top C and low growling F. Sitting between the thundering speakers was the heir to the throne in a state approaching ecstasy. His royal blue eyes were misted over as if in a trance, and a faraway beatific smile relaxed his normally tense mouth as his outstretched arms wildly boxed the air in time to the intoxicating music. Some people took Mogadon; Charles took opera. Mozart was the Prince's tranquillizer, his restorative, a tonic to wipe away the formal cares of a day spent inspecting cheese whipples on a new assembly line in Pratt's Bottom and being unutterably nice to stout little men with chains around their necks.

> 'Se a casa madama la notte ti chiama,
> Dindin, dindin,
> In due passi da quella puoi gir.'

Charles's lungs gave forth in full uninhibited gusto:

> 'Vien poi l'occasione
> che vuolmi il padrone...'

Charles was transported. At such moments he felt in tune with the harmony of the universe — a spiritual experience he increasingly strove towards as an antidote to the everyday worldly cares of being the future king of England.

He cut an eccentric figure, sitting in the middle of the huge room in his favourite George III mahogany dining-chair, backed with Prince of Wales feathers. Charles had

4

always had a soft spot for his Hanoverian ancestor whose madness, he felt, had been much exaggerated, and who had been greatly maligned for the loss of the New World colonies. As a rule, the simple act of sitting in this chair made him curiously aware of the ancient line of succession and the ponderous responsibilities which one day would fall upon him.

But these cares were blissfully forgotten as Charles stared at his own operatic performance in the exquisite white and gilt Regency looking-glass, totally unaware of quite how bizarre his behaviour may have looked to a casual observer. So completely was he in a world of his own that he had forgotten the shimmering presence of the most beautiful woman in the kingdom who lay but ten feet behind him, curled up on the vermilion velvet chaise longue. Her slim, casually-draped body moulded softly into the pliant duck-down cushions. Her crossed,

long, tanned, waxed legs were as smooth as the velvet upon which she lay.

Diana languidly reached out, not taking her eyes for a moment from the book she was engrossed in, to pluck another of her Charbonnel et Walker chocolates. The Princess, too, was in her own dream world: she simply did not hear the volume of music that filled the room, bounced off the white and gold striped walls, and made the chandeliers tinkle gently. For she was wearing her faithful Sony Walkman personal stereo and through the earphones came the sounds, not of Wolfgang Amadeus, but the more strident, harsh dissonances of urban nihilism. Diana was getting into P-60.

> 'I don't know where I am going, babe,
> I don't know where I am coming from,
> But you have got me all wrong like...'

In synch with the rhythm of her favourite pop group she drummed her long, fine fingers on the mahogany occasional table. Yet where you would expect the sharp click of manicured nails on antique wood came no sound at all: for Diana, in a habit she had not yet conquered, had bitten her nails to the quick. She popped another hand-made chocolate into her mouth and she held it there, curling her tongue voluptuously round the confection, allowing it to melt slowly.

> 'Hey, hey you are my cornet,
> Yea, yea, lick me, boob-a-doob,
> I wanna sting you like a hornet...'

Diana paid no attention to the lyrics; she was idly flicking through a glossy coffee-table album of the Royal Wedding. Her attention was caught by the full-page engagement portrait by Snowdon.

Am-azing, thought Diana: how hugely inn-ocent I looked!

She smiled to herself at the charming but unsophisticated bobbed hairdo with its girlish fringe and the mousey brown tone of her mop. Her present style with its blonde highlights and full-bodied assertiveness was so much more glam, altogether more photogenic, well, simply more *her*.

At the other end of the room her husband suddenly ceased singing in mid-aria. Something had caught his eye in the looking-glass and, pulling down the lower lid of his left eye, he began to examine it closely. He stared for some moments in fascination at the contours and colours of his own iris.

'Do you know, darling, this iridology business is really rather intriguing,' said Charles, unaware that Diana was still lost in a world of her own. 'Eyes, y'know, aren't just for gazing into over candle-lit dinners... not just windows to the soul and all that stuff. You see, they can tell you exactly the state of your health and apparently by studying the iris one can diagnose a chap's mental and physical condition.' Charles chuckled. 'More to this than meets the eye, eh!'

He turned to see if his wife had got the joke. 'Popsicle,' he called out loudly with a hint of irritation. Diana lifted one earphone and Charles heard the metallic hiss and scratch of P-60. 'Darling...'

His words were cut off by a cry of horror from the recumbent Princess.

'Darling, what's the matter?' gasped Charles, alarmed. 'Too gross!' groaned Diana. 'Oh, no, no.' She closed her eyes as if in pain. 'Too, too horrid.'

'You alright, darling?'

'Ya,' replied Diana. 'But that tie...' She pointed an accusing finger. 'Hideous news. It's so... middle-aged. I thought I said, Charles, that it had to go.'

'Well, yes, I know that, sweetie, but...'

'But nothing.' Diana smiled demurely. 'People simply are not wearing kipper ties any more, Charles.'

'That's fishy,' laughed Charles uneasily. 'After all, Prince Michael does.'

'Exactly!' said Diana firmly. 'But you must stop dressing like your grandfather. Now where did *that* revolting thing come from again? Don't tell me it was your valet . . .'

'Ah,' hedged Charles, wishing he had worn one of the
dozen or so colourful silk Armani ties Diana had chosen
for him on their recent Italian tour. 'As a matter of fact,
poppet, Frisk did . . .'

There was a knock on the door.

'Aha!' exclaimed Charles in his silly Neddy Seagoon
voice. 'I have reason to believe that was a knock on the
door. Who could this portend? Knocker, reveal thyself!'

In minced Frisk.

The valet, thin-hipped and purse-lipped, was carrying
two identical pairs of standard black city lace-up shoes,
polished to perfection.

'Shall I draw your bath, Sir?' asked Frisk, pulling
himself up to attention before his master in a show of
the formal ceremony he so adored. 'Her Majesty is
expecting you for sherry in the red drawing-room at
eight.'

'Oh Lord,' murmured Diana, who had not taken her
eyes off the shoes dangling from his tiny, pale hands.
'Cringe factor ten!' Those were the very shoes, dull and
conventional, she had instructed Frisk to dispose of (to
charity, if they would not make a suitable Christmas
present for one of the servants).

'Mr Frisk,' she continued coolly, 'where are those
lovely Church's casuals?'

'The ones with tassels, Ma'am?' asked Frisk, with
barely-concealed distaste.

Charles, sensing they were about to embark on
another dispute over his personal wardrobe, placed the
needle back on the record.

> 'Se a casa madame la notte ti chiama.
> Din, din . . .'

Once again his favourite Figaro aria filled the room,
rendering further discussion impossible. Frisk, realizing
the Prince had come to his rescue, quickly laid down the
offending shoes in the adjacent room. As he returned,
Charles was humming the tune: Frisk, taking up a joke

he had long shared with the Prince, broke into the English rendition of the aria as he made for the door.

'My master wants me,
Dong, dong,
In three bounds I am ready to serve him.'

Diana fumed.

O! for a Muse of fire

Hard by the walls of Windsor Castle was the Windsor Inn. It was Boxing Day and only one drunk had ventured out into the inclement night to seek the meagre warmth of the public bar.He was slumped on the bench next to the miserable gas log fire. With his chin sunk on to his chest he tunelessly and repetitively intoned the first two lines of *Good King Wenceslas*.

The only other two customers, sitting in the opposite corner, glared resentfully at the droning inebriate. The portly and better-dressed of the two strangers finally exploded. 'Landlord,' he cried with a distinctive, fruity boom, 'kindly silence that infernal creature.'

The landlord was about to raise an objection when the thinner, more raffish stranger, who was wearing army fatigues, interjected: 'Look, governor, either you shut that bastard up — or I'll shove these delectable pickled eggs right down his gullet.'

The landlord, whose eyes had momentarily left the screen of the silent, flickering television, bellowed: 'Alf!' The singing trailed off.

'Sodding Christmas!' The smaller, dark-haired man pulled out a cheroot. 'By rights, I should be with Tracy and the kids, drinking Chivas Regal and wearing silly paper hats. Instead? Out on a bloody doorstep!'

His companion — sporting a curious combination of bow-tie, rosy pink complexion, owlish glasses and powerful Zeiss binoculars — might have given the impression he was an ornithologist. But birds were not the prey that Spalding stalked.

'Cheer up, Jerry old man,' he commanded. 'This is the season of good will and good cheer — what can I get you to drink?'

'Thanks, Nick. I'll have a Malibu and rum.'

Spalding grimaced. Photographers: God, sometimes he hated them almost as much as he hated his own news editor. Why, as an unrelenting law of nature, were news snappers such unregenerate proles? Cretures with no instincts for the finer things in life. Why, dear God, could he not, just once, be sent on assignment with Snowdon or Lichfield?

Spalding extended the sleeve of his candy-striped Turnbull and Asser shirt — the same bespoke Jermyn Street tailor as patronized by the Prince of Wales — to check the time on his chunky, matt black, multi-dialled, multi-buttoned Beitmeister Carmargue diver's watch, which was not only capable of computing the time from Tokyo to Murmansk, but could gauge the pressure at ten fathoms, act as a compass or stopwatch, and even display the altitude in a light aircraft. Not that Spalding, with his thinning hairline and over-indulged waistline, had ever called upon any of these facilities. The watch simply told him the time: it was 19.13 hours, 20 seconds.

He had forty-seven minutes to deadline. Three quarters of an hour to find, write and file that which his news editor, Ron Snitch, had been demanding: a page one Royal exclusive.

'Balding, m'boy,' Snitch had cried on returning, flushed, from lunch. 'This is the big one, laddie! One of my upper-class snouts tips me off that Diana has invited a mystery guest to the Palace to share a wee dram and some Christmas leftovers... you'll never guess who it is.' Snitch, smiling in triumph, bared his yellowing teeth. 'Joan Collins!' Snitch paused for effect and swayed perilously. 'On yer bike!' he barked.

After five frozen hours, during which he had staked out the castle gates, talked to passers-by, tried to wave down cars entering on official business in a futile attempt to interview the occupants, had paid an unproductive bribe to a royal corgi walker, in vain offered to buy the duty policeman a drink, made innumerable calls from drafty telephone kiosks to his various royal narks, including one frustrating and costly transatlantic call to Miss Collins's agent (he wasn't in), badgered the Buckingham Palace Press Office ('No comment'), rung the Windsor switchboard and asked to be put through to Miss Collins ('Who?'), and after being foiled in his attempt to enter the castle precincts disguised as a milkman, Spalding had his one stroke of luck. He chanced upon Frisk the valet, who announced breezily: 'Only one bitch here, dear. And her name isn't Joan.'

Disconsolate, Spalding and Jerry Sharpe retired to the Windsor Inn. The fact that once again a promising story turned out to be a figment of Snitch's lunchtime imaginings in the Albion would not save them from having to find a substitute story: the front page still waited for the enthralling, informative, crisp and compelling prose of the *Daily Disclosure's* star royal correspondent.

Thundering hooves

The Queen smiled dreamily.

The June sun reflected off the crisp white tents and marquees from wherein came the sound of bubbling laughter and the regular pop of liberated champagne corks. Across the Epsom Downs, opposite the Royal Box, the crowds stretched away to the horizon, from whence helicopters still buzzed in, like bees droning on a languid, clover-scented summer's day. Derby Day, for most of those in the exclusive marquees and private boxes, was an alfresco cocktail party: a time for hobnobbing, laughter, flirting, eating lobster and smoked salmon sandwiches, gossiping and having a modest flutter. But not for Her Majesty. Derby Day, for the Queen, was altogether a more important occasion.

Now it was about to reach its climax. Punters rushed to place last-minute bets for the big race as the horses came under starter's orders. A sudden expectant hush fell upon the course. They're off! Even the most hardened socializers had put down their glasses of Bollinger and taken up their field-glasses. Sixty-four hooves thundered past the grandstand, bunched together so closely that the jockeys' silks were just a smudge of colour. The crowd roared, and the sound rose to a crescendo as the familiar purple and gold braid of the Queen's colours nudged out in front.

This was her crowning moment. Her Most Excellent Majesty, by the Grace of God, of the United Kingdom of Great Britain and Northern Ireland and of her other Realms and Territories, Head of the Commonwealth and Defender of the Faith, was out of her chair, fists clenched, urging on her steed with yelps of encouragement. For one glorious moment her elevated status and imposing station were forgotten; she was just another racegoer cheering on her horse. And it was about to win!

'Come on, Golden Orb! Come *on!*'

'What's that, my dear?' said a brisk voice from the background.

The Queen turned.

Through the half-open door, in the next room, she could see the aquiline profile of her husband. He was seated with a towel spread over his evening trousers as he meticulously buffed up his pair of matching Purdeys in preparation for the next day's pheasant shoot.

'What are you gabbling about?' said Philip as he peered with satisfaction down the choke barrel of one of the guns.' Looks like a bit of a wind blowing up... that'll encourage some decent high-flying birds tomorrow.'

'Sounds nice, dear.' The Queen turned back, disappointed at having been woken from her reverie. She had been lost for the last twenty minutes in a glorious, transporting dream. She had been brought back to reality only seconds short of realizing her most cherished childhood ambition. Golden Orb had been about to cross the winning post and carry off the Derby.

Since the days when she used to sit on her rocking horse in the Royal nursery she had sustained this lingering fantasy that her horse would finally carry her colours home in the world's most famous race. Yet despite her wealth, and her passionate dedication to this end, it was a prize which still eluded her.

Philip's interjection had broken the spell, and now she looked out over the snow-blanketed Windsor Great Park, enveloped in darkness. The Queen's private suite, in the Queen's Tower, was situated on the south-eastern corner of the castle with a stunning view over the sweeping parklands: but now through the wintry gloom the only signs of life she could make out were the branches of the leafless trees as they bent lightly before the unfriendly north-east wind.

The apartment itself was light and airy. The living-

room had once been far more sombre, when it served as
Queen Victoria's Oak Dining Room; but in the 1920's
Queen Mary had completely redecorated it with the
fashionable gold and white Regency style popular at that
time. Queen Elizabeth had added her own homely touch,
and now the room had a far more cosy, informal, lived-in
look, with a 24-inch television in the corner, books and
magazines strewn over tables and chairs, while all
around the room, lending it the most distinctive aspect,
were statuettes of her favourite racehorses: the great
stallion Bustino, Special Leave, her favourite filly
Dunfermline, Pall Mall, Rhyme Royal. And in pride of
place, on her work desk, stood a 12-inch-high bronze of
the absolute royal champion, Edward VII's Derby
winner, the great Persimmon.

The Queen gazed intently at Persimmon. But she was
no longer dreaming as her thoughts returned once more
to the Derby; this time she would make it a reality: she
did not intend to let that much-desired trophy elude her
for one year longer.

Line of succession

'Gosh I'm bored,' sighed Edward for the third time that evening. 'Frankly I'll be glad to go back to Cambridge, won't you, Harborough?'

Edward tugged at the leather cuff of his houndstooth hacking jacket that, half a size too big for him and hanging baggily, gave him the misleading air of an earnest young don. He had to tug at his over-generous coat sleeve again to locate his Mickey Mouse watch. It had been a sweet thought of Sarah's; what a wacky sense of humour his sister-in-law had!

He sighed. Another hour to dinner.

It was not that he was hungry. The Royal Worcester tea service was still on the Sheraton side-table, with a plate of half-eaten Marmite and egg sandwiches, and chocolate Bath Olivers which were completely untouched.

But there was another whole sixty minutes to fill. Life, Edward sometimes thought, was just a protracted process of hanging around for the next official engagement.

And then, even worse, dinner en famille tonight would be the last time he would see his parents before returning to Jesus College, Cambridge. After a brief stint in the Marines, he was being sent back to University for a post-graduate course. He knew his father was bound to give him a pep talk about keeping his head down, nose to the grindstone, finger out, chin up and so on and so forth.

'Harborough?'

There was no reply.

Edward turned and saw that his detective was

stretched out on the chintz sofa, with his size twelve feet up, engrossed in a voluminously thick book.

'For heaven's sake, Harborough,' said Edward plaintively, 'you've been reading that for an hour!'

Alan Harborough looked up. 'Pardon, Sir?'

'I said, I'm bored, Sergeant. What on earth's that you're reading?'

'Broughton's *Poll Taxes in 18th-Century Rural Communities*, Sir.'

'I thought you were a Tory, Harborough.'

'Actually, it's on our reading list for next term, Sir.'

'Swotting early, eh? Good man.' Edward moodily paced up and down the room, hands clasped firmly behind his double-vented jacket. 'As a matter of fact, Alan, that's rather on my mind.'

'Eighteenth-century poll taxes, Sir?'

'No, Sergeant, exam results.'

'I see, Sir.'

'You don't at all, Sergeant.'

'Quite so, Sir.'

'Thing is, you see, my father...' Edward trailed off uncertainly.

'The Duke of Edinburgh...' prompted the detective.

'Of course,' replied Edward irritably. 'Who else could be under suspicion, for God's sake?'

Sergeant Harborough looked down at his shiny walking shoes, counted till ten, then looked up at the plaster whorls on the ceiling — which reminded him of the twirls on a Mister Softee ice-cream — and continued to a full count of thirty.

Being a personal bodyguard, Harborough always said, comprised being one quarter policeman, a quarter nanny, another quarter Father Confessor, while the rest was simply a matter of having the patience of a bloody Christian martyr. He waited for Edward, still striding up and down, to resume.

'You see, Harborough,' said the Prince finally, 'being the youngest son of the Windsors puts one under a terrible, terrible strain.'

'I can see that, Sir.'

'I mean, being the eldest is a piece of cake.' Edward stopped and swung round. 'You're our historical scholar, Sergeant — isn't that a fact?'

Harborough placed his toothpick on page 278, as a marker, and resignedly closed the book. 'I'm not quite sure of your drift, as we say in the force. Would you care to elaborate on this thesis, Sir?'

'Destiny, Harborough.'

'Ah.'

'Charles, being the first-born, has it all worked out for him. He's got it made. He knows what he's going to do.'

'What's that, Sir?'

'Really, Sergeant! Sometimes you are impossibly thick. He's going to be king, of course.'

'Quite right, Sir. I thought you were speaking existentially, as it were.'

Edward stared incredulously at his detective. 'You alright, Harborough?'

'Don't mind me, Sir. Carry on.'

'Well, the point that I am making, Sergeant, is that he has got it all charted out for him. He doesn't have to be clever, or knowledgeable, or talented . . . or even particularly good with his hands. In fact, he doesn't have to be any ruddy good at anything. It's all simply laid on for him.'

'I begin to perceive the line of your exposition, Sir.'

'And being the second son is even easier really.'

'How so, Sir?'

'Because they don't expect anything of you at all. In fact they jolly well expect you to be a chump, a wastrel or a playboy.'

'This is true, Sir.'

'I mean, it almost goes with the position, doesn't it? People would be disappointed if, as second in line, you weren't a bit of a scallywag.' Edward stopped pacing, and looked morosely out of the window. 'And then there's me.'

There was a long silence. Sergeant Harbourough coughed politely.

'So that leaves me,' muttered Edward eventually, still staring abstractedly out of the window into the night. 'But where does that leave me?'

'Sir?'

'Nowhere!'

'Nowhere?'

'Exactly, Sergeant! A man without a role, without a job, without expectations.' Edward began pacing nervously again. 'So what happens? People actually expect me to BE something.'

'I am not quite sure, Sir, what they could expect you to be.'

'Nor am I, Sergeant. And that, precisely, is the problem.' Edward stopped in his tracks and said plaintively: 'I think they expect me to be brainy or something.'

'Oh come, Sir. People don't expect that, Sir.'

'Well, anyway, Sergeant, that's why I am worried about tonight. I am sure Pater plans to deliver a bollocking about exam results and all that jazz.'

'Shouldn't worry about that, Sir. I well remember what your father told Prince Charles when he languished in the groves of academe.'

To comfort himself Edward picked up a half-eaten Marmite and egg sandwich — a taste acquired in nursery days — and swallowed it in one chomp.

'His Royal Highness said, if I am not mistaken,' continued Harborough in measured official tones as if submitting evidence, '"Look," he said, "I don't expect you to come top of the class. After all, that's showing off. And don't come bottom, because that is also drawing attention to yourself. Just come somewhere in the middle."'

'Really? Pater said that?'

'The very same, Sir.'

Edward wandered back to the window thoughtfully. He could just make out the fairy lights of the Windsor

Inn. He wondered what was going on inside the pub. He
had never dared set foot in there. Charles used to dress
up in all sorts of weird disguises, wigs and funny noses
and so on, to sneak out to pubs and that kind of thing.
And Andrew just used to saunter in with his chums, not
caring a fig, and even chatted up the local girls and got
boogalooed.

'Harborough,' said Edward with a sudden catch of
excitement in his voice, 'how about if you and I...'

'Sir?'

'Oh, forget it.' Edward lapsed into silence.

It was dangerous territory out there. Imagine if one
were to be caught with a G 'n' T in the tap room bar. The
scandal!

Sergeant Harborough coughed again. 'Beg pardon,
Sir.'

'What?'

'About the anomaly of your position, Sir.'

'Well?'

'In your reasoning about the, er, line of succession, Sir,
you omitted one very pertinent and important item.'

'What's that, Harborough?'

'Princess Anne, Sir.'

'Don't be silly, Sergeant,' sighed Edward, drawing the
Peter Rabbit-patterned curtains firmly. 'She's a girl. She
doesn't count.'

Thoughts of the turf

On the small, damask-draped desk in front of her, at which the Queen normally worked during the early evening, lay strewn dozens of computer read-outs in a confused jumble. They were not the State papers which had arrived shortly before from Downing Street in a battered red dispatch box, neither were they the briefings prepared for her nightly by her private secretary. Nor were they the reports from the Department of Social Security on the alarming rise of single-parent families and unemployment figures. The print-outs were of far more absorbing interest. Indeed, apart from Dick Francis, they were her favourite reading: the concertinaed reams of paper that littered her desk constituted the encyclopaedia of her bloodstock.

This definitive compilation contained every conceivable detail concerning her racehorses, all thirty of them — their breeding, bloodlines, potential, price at auction, condition, habits, quirks, weight, trainer, a resume of their track record, future projections and plans, progeny and breeding possibilities. In short, modern technology had provided the Queen with an exhaustive analysis of her stable. She studied it as intensely as a seminarian would study the scriptures.

Never had the monarch been more serious. She *was*, by God, going to win the Derby. Not since 1953, when Aureole had victory snatched from him in the last furlong, had she such an opportunity to win this classic of classics.

But she was not going to leave it to chance. This season she was going to devote herself, single-mindedly, to this one task.

She flicked over the page and found the entry for Golden Orb. Her racing manager, Lord Porchester, had done his homework. Golden Orb was eating well, drinking his daily pint of Guinness, and with six months to go was right on schedule to be at his peak on the great day.

Her racing manager wrote: 'Your Majesty, I humbly suggest that this three-year-old is the finest Derby prospect that has ever come to the Royal stables. He has that conviction and appetite for competition of a born winner, if ever I saw one. In his style and bearing he reminds me of Persimmon...'

The Queen's heart missed a beat. By thunder, she knew Golden Orb could do it.

There was a sharp, metallic click. The Queen froze. It was followed by another. She swung round.

Through the open doorway she saw Prince Philip standing upright in a familiar stance. Braced legs splayed, back ramrod straight, left arm outstretched, right arm crooked; he suddenly swept his Purdey with an arching upward swing as if following the flight of an unfortunate cock pheasant, and as he reached an eighty-five degree trajectory Philip let go with both barrels.

'Bam... Bam!' cried Philip.

Lowering his gun, he smiled across to his startled wife with evident satisfaction: 'Got 'em! Perfect shots... I can still make both barrels count, eh, Lilibet?'

The Queen smiled fondly back at him with that tolerant, kindly look she still sometimes gave her children when they became too boisterous and high spirited. She understood that Philip felt about his Purdeys the way she felt about Persimmon.

How well over the years Philip had managed to restrain his somewhat intemperate and impulsive nature. She watched as he braced himself once more to take out another brace of pheasant. She looked at the slim, proud figure in his elegant evening wear — starched white linen shirt, black bow tie — and thought how superbly fit he was for a man well into his sixties —

and what a sportsman! Perhaps, though, he had devoted himself too passionately to these manly pursuits; she sometimes worried it was her fault that she had not found a suitably fulfilling and challenging role for her energetic consort. Was being President of the World Wildlife Fund quite enough?

The plain, black, old-fashioned bakelite phone at her elbow rang. She picked it up.

'Yes?' she said softly.

It was Porchester. Her racing manager came straight
to the point. 'I thought you would like to know
immediately, Ma'am,' he explained briskly. 'I have just
this moment had some private intelligence from
Kentucky.'

'Yes...' The Queen knew from his tone that Porchy
was the bearer of bad news.

'One has heard astonishing rumours of a remarkable
young Arab grey.' Porchester paused. 'Sired by Blue
Grass out of Sirocco, from Arabesque by Scimatar.'

The Queen recognized these legendary names. But
now they had an ominous ring. 'Continue, Henry,' she
said with rising anxiety. 'Tell me the worst.'

'The grey was bought privately this afternoon for six
million by Sheik Mahoud al Mahoud. And from what I
hear, this beast is the only thing which could possibly
match Golden Orb.'

Her voice was barely audible. 'Yes?'

'The point, I'm afraid, Ma'am, is that the Sheik has his
sights on the Derby...'

Ferreting out the facts

Spalding eyed Jerry malevolently. Their deadline was hurtling towards them like an out-of-control locomotive. They had no story, and for the past half-hour Jerry had been retelling epic tales of how he got this or that sensational snap for the front page: Spalding had heard all these boasts a dozen times. Photographers, he devoutly believed, should have their vocal chords removed like pesky dogs. They were alright so long as they stared down a lens, but as conversationalists they were about as amusing as an Ansaphone.

Spalding, in contrast to his combat-jacketed photographer, adopted a flamboyant, somewhat showbiz style of dress, starting with the red-rimmed, over-size oval and pin-tinted Elton John glasses, an inexhaustible supply of large bow ties as colourful as tropical butterflies, and trendy up-to-the-minute three-piece designer-label lightweight suits that he bought from the same boutiques patronized by the more fashionable rock stars.

Before him on the bar lay his prim regulation reporter's notebook, the pages open and accusingly bare. Alas, they only reflected back the despairing blankness of his own mind. At his feet lay the crumpled-up balls of notepaper carrying his aborted attempts to concoct a story for tomorrow's edition. On each, before he could get to the end of the first paragraph, he had become paralyzed by the mental image of the large, loutish Snitch, his news editor, reading his efforts and bellowing with scorn as he tore them to shreds in front of the entire newsroom.

Sweet Madonna, groaned Spalding to himself, how was the remorseless, avenging Snitch to be appeased?

As Jerry's flat south London voice droned on in the
background Spalding began scribbling frantically again:
'The Queen, in a savage Christmas economy drive,
ordered her kitchen staff to leave the stuffing out of this
year's turkey, we can exclusively reveal.' Spalding had
written the same story last year, when in a similar jam,
and they had given it quite a reasonable show on page 5.
He wondered if everyone back at the office would still be
sufficiently well-oiled from their seasonal celebrations to
have forgotten. He ripped the page out and it joined the
crumpled mess at his feet.

To compose himself Spalding meticulously realigned
the stray, unruly wisps of receding blondish hair with
the flat of his palm, and then glanced at the Beitmaster
timepiece on his wrist: twenty minutes to deadline.

'Same again please, barman,' he shouted, for lack of any
other inspiration. The royal sleuth and his talkative
lensman were now effectively the only clients in the
Windsor Inn, the drunk having fallen asleep in his
corner.

'Make mine a Marbella Sunrise, squire,' ordered Jerry.
The barman, half asleep himself, looked at the ferret-
faced photographer blankly. Jerry smiled back pityingly,
and explained slowly as if to a half-witted country
bumpkin: 'That's three parts Tio Pepe, two parts
Tequilla, with a slug of Creme de Menthe.' Spalding
checked his watch: eighteen minutes to copytime.
Inconsequentially, he noticed it was four am in Adelaide
and four thirty pm in Caracas: he wished he was in either
of those faraway places. Anywhere rather than the
dingy Windsor Inn. He needed help. 'Landlord,' barked
Spalding. 'Make mine a vintage port.'

'Much as I am devoted to the Royal Family,' Jerry was
saying, 'international summits are better for expenses.
And no one expects us to crawl through the
undergrowth to get an off-guard pic of a prime minister
or president, know what I mean? Consequently us lads
have more time to get up to our own devices.' He
winked.

Spalding, with only the vengeful sound of Snitch's recriminations ringing in his ears, blinked. His distant, watery blue eyes focused on the mesmerizing goldfish movements of Jerry's slightly lopsided mouth.

'Take the Geneva jaunt,' resumed Jerry relentlessly. 'Well, on the first night, after the obligatory photo call of Ruskies smiling at the Yanks, all us Fleet Street snappers repaired with one accord to a house of pleasure known to Big Billy McNee of *The Chronicle*. Now the joke is, see, that all us lads nip up to watch Billy through a two-way mirror, and what do you know? Billy's got this absolutely tiny nudger.'

'Nudger?' repeated Spalding absently. 'What on earth, dear boy, is a nudger?'

His companion shook his head sadly. 'His pride and joy, Nick. His pogo-stick, his harmonium. Know what I mean? His blaster, double-barrelled shooter, pile driver.' Jerry's voice rose in exasperation. 'For God's sake, Nick, his winkle, plonker. His dongo!'

Spalding raised his port, and squinted through the richly-coloured liquid. This crude world, he found, looked better through rose-tinted glasses.

'Anyway, Big Billy's standing there starkers while this Swiss tart gawps at his minuscule nudger: "Oo do you think zat will satisfy?" says she scornfully. So Billy bangs his chest and growls: "Me!"'

The empty saloon bar of the Windsor Inn rang with the helpless laughter of Jerry Sharpe. Spalding watched his photographer disdainfully. 'Old man,' said Spalding finally, with exaggerated politeness, 'we have precious little time to deadline. In fact, if you don't mind my being pedantic we have,' he glanced at his wrist, 'precisely fourteen minutes and twenty seconds.'

Jerry shrugged. 'No problem. I've got a corker for you, Nick.'

A flutter of hope alighted in Spalding's breast. His heart beat a little faster.

'Y'know the Royals get together before lunch on Christmas day to exchange presents? Well, this year they was all there, from the Queen Mum to Prince Harry, when would you believe it . . .'

'What, Jerry, what?'

'In stumbles Princess Margaret, smashed . . .'

'Yes, yes . . .'

'And she crashed, blotto, at the feet of Her Maj.'

'Christ, Jerry.' Spalding's eyes shone feverishly. 'And then?'

'Her Majesty,' continued Jerry, 'acting as if nothing untoward had occurred, simply stepped over the slumped figure, and said to Philip: "Shall we adjourn to the dining-room, dear?"'

'Jerry, you're a genius!' Spalding gripped his photographer warmly by the arm. He would forgive him anything — his lack of connoisseurship, his cheap cigars, his endless chatter of light metre exposures and zoom lens apertures . . . even hanging on to this peach of a story till the eleventh hour. Jerry was his mate. Jerry was his mucker. They were a team, dammit. Spalding smiled fondly at his old pal: 'That, Jerry, as you say, is a corker. Where did you hear it?'

'I didn't.'

Spalding blinked. 'What?'

Jerry stifled a yawn. 'I just made that up.' The photographer watched curiously as Spalding, filled to bursting with the helium of hope only seconds before, deflated visibly. 'C'mon, Nick, better start scribbling. Ten minutes to deadline. Know what I mean?'

'I can't.'

'It's a rattling good yarn,' said Jerry, hurt.

'But, Jerry, it's simply not true.'

'So?'

Spalding shook his head mutely.

'Look, Nick, how's about . . . "Controversy rages over Queen's Christmas speech?"'

Spalding raised a querulous eyebrow. But Jerry, ever the optimist, was not to be deterred that easily. 'OK, then — a right Royal rift. Philip to spend most of the year away from Elizabeth on foreign freebies. I can see the headline now: "MY SINGLE BED AGONY, BY QUEEN".'

'Old story, old boy,' replied Spalding morosely. 'Stick to the pictures.'

'I've got it!' cried Jerry. 'Charles, after consulting his ouija board, wants to give away all his worldly possessions to East End dossers.' The photographer's determination to conjure a story rose in direct proportion to the increasing despair on Spalding's pale round face. 'Andrew and the birds, Nick. If all else fails you can't go wrong with that.'

'Don't you read the papers, matey? He's married, you know.'

'That's the point, numbskull,' replied Jerry. 'The angle is — "TWO-TIMING ANDY".'

'Back in your box, clutz.'

'Alright, we'll have Edward smuggle some crumpet into the castle then. "EAGER EDDY IN STEAMY SANTA SEX ROMPS"... no? How about two girls then?'

But Spalding was not to be consoled. 'If Snitch can't have Joan Collins,' he muttered darkly, 'he will be satisfied with nothing less than a fresh exclusive on Diana.'

The lapsed into silence.

Jerry lit up another powerful-smelling cheroot. Spalding, contemplating the bottom of his empty glass, ignored the thin, sallow-faced man in baggy blue overalls who had slipped in and begun quietly talking to the barman about his day's work at the castle. Jerry eyed the newcomer craftily.

'And what's your line of work, chum?' he asked casually. 'A liveried footman, are you?'

'Maintenance man.'

'Ever met any of them Royals then?'

'As a matter of fact I have exchanged words with the Duke of Edinburgh.'

'And what did the Duke say?' enquired Jerry, feigning indifference.

'Oh, very polite he was. A real gent.'

'But what did he say?'

'He said, "Good morning".'

Jerry offered him a drink. It was a cheap price to pay for the possibility of a story, as he continued to glean crumbs of information about life at the castle from the gullible boilerman.

Spalding, sunk in contemplation of Snitch's imminent fury, paid no attention till he felt a sharp, urgent kick on his ankle. 'Our pal here,' announced Jerry meaningfully, 'says Diana is particularly fond of bunny rabbits.'

'So was Alice in Wonderland,' said Spalding spitefully.

'But what is more, Nick, Diana was quite distraught to discover how these dear little bunnies were killed at Sandringham.'

'She told you that?' Spalding stared at the stranger ferociously. 'Diana told you that?'

'Well, not exactly.'

'What exactly?' snapped Spalding. 'Come on, man. Stop stalling. Spit it out.'

The small, lank-haired menial, used to the bark of authority, hurried to explain that he'd never actually heard this from Diana herself. Indeed he had never actually had the privilege of meeting the Princess. He had gathered this information from a friend of the cousin of the wife of the second gamekeeper at Sandringham, who had told his mother that Diana had apparently been upset to hear from the head gamekeeper that the rabbit population of Sandringham was kept down by ferrets.

'Ferrets? Upset!' Spalding leapt to his feet. The barman and the mechanic watched in amazement as he moved with surprising speed, for one so overweight, towards the outside phone.

'Give me copy,' rapped Spalding into the receiver with a crisp snap of authority. By the time he was back at the bar seven minutes later, ordering champagne for the astonished mechanic, Snitch held the three dictated folios of copy in his stubby fingers. His small, greedy eyes betrayed no sign of approval or otherwise as they rapidly scanned the blistering prose Spalding had rattled off from the top of his head. But he emitted several truffling, contented grunts of satisfaction.

'Get that political crap off the front page,' he ordered. 'We'll have a picture of Spalding, with the slug — "Another world exclusive: Royal retainer breaks silence over Sandringham savagery".'

'And the headline, chief?'

Snitch closed his eyes for a moment and smiled rapturously. '"DIANA LASHES QUEEN OVER WILDLIFE OUTRAGE".'

For what we are about to receive

The great brocade curtains, a legacy from Queen Victoria, were firmly drawn, lending the gilt state drawing-room almost a friendly family atmosphere, despite its vast and impersonal proportions. It was normally used on grand ceremonial occasions when the Queen received heads of government, presidents, prime ministers and African potentates. A homely apple log fire crackled in the marble fireplace.

The fireplace itself, with its assertive architectural decoration of flutes, columns, caryatids and scrolls, proclaimed those departed Victorian certitudes of progress, power, moral superiority and rectitude. Several bold embossed reliefs celebrated British victories; on the recent visit by the prickly French President the Queen had diplomatically stood in the way of the bas relief depicting the death agonies of French dragoons at the Battle of Waterloo.

But now the family clustered informally round the jolly fire. Slightly apart from the group was Prince Andrew, by the window, with a deep pewter tankard from which he heartily swigged his favourite best bitter. He would, frankly, have rather been at this very moment with his chums from the helicopter squadron down at the Crooked Billet, swopping jokes and getting squiffy. For Princess Sarah, after spending Christmas with them at Windsor, had departed in secret that morning to fly to Buenos Aires where her mother had been holidaying with her second husband, the swashbuckling Argentinian polo player Hector Barrantes.

Andrew surveyed the scene; no chance of a boisterous night here. He knew he had to mind his p's and q's tonight; the last time he had attended a formal occasion, a reception for the Sultan of Brunei, he had disgraced himself. During a lull in conversation between courses he had produced a wind-up willie. The clockwork plastic phallus, mounted on a pair of pink feet, had hopped and clattered its way across the table towards the Sultan, much to the appalled astonishment of the assembled dignitaries. The Queen was not amused.

A flurry of flunkies responded to an imperceptible signal from Her Majesty. They moved forward proffering silver trays of sherry, whisky and a long glass of orange pressé for Diana. His mother, Andrew noticed, accepted a third sherry; he was relieved to see that she was in an expansive mood tonight. Auntie Margaret was quick to pluck another single malt whisky, as did Granny.

Brother Charles was causing some discomfort to the Duke and Duchess of Kent by using them as posts for a game of peek-a-boo with Prince William. Diana, who was in polite conversation with dear old Princess Alice, watched her husband's antics out of the corner of her eye.

From this friendly babble Andrew heard talk of stock markets, commodities and the strength of the dollar between Prince Michael of Kent — what did he know? — Princess Alexandra and her amiable husband Angus.

Edward sidled up. 'Incidentally,' said Edward, 'that lovely watch Sarah gave me ... was it from you both?'

'Don't worry, I've not forgotten your prezzy!' grinned Andrew. 'It's rather special. I think you might be surprised — pleasantly I hope.'

'When I am going to get it?' Edward persisted.

'Get it you will. All good things come to those that wait — and believe me, little brother, it will be worth waiting for ...'

Baffled, Edward wandered off.

On the periphery of the gathering loomed the tall, handsome, imposing and self-conscious figure of the woman who had created so much public controversy and family dissension; the imperious Princess Michael of Kent. Tonight, when the Windsor women were not on show and wore their more informal and well-used dresses, the haughty Princess, as ever, stood out — she looked positively regal. Her luxuriant locks were piled in an elaborate concoction, which Andrew thought looked like whipped meringue, and from her ears hung large cultured pearls, which were echoed in a fabulous choker of five strands of pearls clasped together by an outsize silver and diamond catch. Who bought her that, Andrew wondered?

From the middle of the room came an agonized yelp followed by an ill-tempered snarl. It was Smokey, one of the Queen's favourite corgis, whose little bobbed tail had been given a sharp and playful yank by the boisterous Prince William. Everyone stopped talking and the concerned voice of Charles rang across the room. 'Willie, darling, doggies have feelings as well. You mustn't pull doggies' tails.'

'That's right,' said the Queen Mother sweetly, 'otherwise doggie-woggie will bite off your nosey-wosey.'

Smokey retreated, abashed and with what little tail he had between his legs, beneath the sofa occupied by the Duke and Duchess of Gloucester, who had the good fortune to be among the least recognized of The Firm. How terribly ordinary they looked, thought Andrew, just like an architect and his wife — which is precisely what they were.

'How terribly common,' he heard Princess Margaret remark to no one in particular. She was looking hard in the direction of Princess Michael who was intently examining the bottom of a Sèvres china vase.

As he drained his pint he spied through the glass bottom of the tankard the forlorn figure of his younger brother, who was having his ear chewed off by Prince Philip. Andrew felt a sense of relief; his disciplinarian father had obviously decided to give one of his 'get-your-finger-out' lectures to Prince Edward. That was one of the perks of being married; one tended to be treated as a responsible member of the community rather than as a wastrel or scoundrel.

Now Charles had moved next to Prince Michael of Kent and appeared to Andrew to be getting a speck out of his cousin's eye. 'I say, Michael, have you got any trouble with your left knee?' said Prince Charles in his most concerned and caring voice, which Andrew recognized as the one his brother reserved for audiences with ethnic minorities. 'A sort of sharp, stabbing pain?' Prince Michael, never the quickest to grasp a new concept, was lost for words. Charles, oblivious of Michael's discomfort, continued. 'The thing about this iridology business is, Michael, that it is absolutely conceptionally revolutionary...'

Prince Michael, trapped, stared back, somewhat out of his depth. With his neatly-trimmed beard and his slightly-lost expression he reminded Andrew of the doomed Czar Nicholas II; a kind, ineffectual man, who carried round with him the perpetually melancholy air of someone who sensed that before too long he would end up blindfolded in the face of a proletarian firing squad — or, in the case of poor Michael, his wife.

'Do you like Sèvres china?' Andrew now heard the slightly sharp tone of his Aunt Margaret. Princess Michael of Kent swiftly replaced the priceless vase. 'Just looking,' she replied gaily. 'Of course Michael and I would love to afford a service of Sèvres, but as you know we are not on the Civil List, so one will just have to live with the Denby,' she paused for a second, 'for now.' The ash of Margaret's Sobranie, in her tortoiseshell cigarette holder, trembled perilously and was about to topple down her Norman Hartnell gown, when at the last moment she flicked it into the Sèvres vase as if it was just a humble ashtray. In the same movement she turned on her heels.

Charles had now buttonholed his own wife, who was trying her best not to hurt his feelings and laugh out loud. Her merry eyes twinkled as Charles stared deeply into them. 'Really, Di,' Charles protested. 'You know, by just looking at one's iris one can tell just about everything about the digestive tract...' Good grief, thought Andrew, his elder brother was the only man in the kingdom who could stare into those gorgeous blue eyes and see only a kidney malfunction.

'Honestly, Mummy!' Andrew heard the Queen gently chide his grandmother. 'Just because there was no racing today.' The Queen Mother, bereft of her consuming hobby because the snow had closed all the race tracks in Britain, had just tried to wager the Queen a modest £5 that the full inch of ash on the end of Margaret's cigarette was about to fall upon the balding head of the seated Duke of Gloucester.

'Alright, Lilibet,' said the Queen Mother, 'just fifty pence, then.'

'No, mother!'

The ash fell unnoticed on the Duke's head. 'A dead cert if ever I saw one,' said the Queen Mother wistfully.

Charles appeared. 'I say, Mummy, let's just have a dekko at your eyes.'

'Certainly not, Charles,' said the monarch. 'Oh dear, look, no one is talking to Proggy and Brigitte.'

The Queen made towards the Gloucesters while Charles turned his attention to the Queen Mother.

'Granny,' he said, 'let's have a look at your eyes. I am interested in a thing called iridology which means that I can diagnose how you are feeling by looking at your eyes — wonderful, isn't it?'

'I am sure it is, dear,' said the Queen Mother sweetly, 'but I know exactly how I am feeling.'

At that moment her attention was caught by the curious behaviour of Socks, the corgi, who was circling an unsuspecting Prince Michael of Kent.

'I will give you five to one on,' she whispered, 'that Socks is going to lift his leg.'

'Granny!' said Charles, shocked.

'Alright, I'll make it ten to one.'

Charles watched with appalled fascination as Socks

gingerly approached Prince Michael and sniffed his patent leather pumps. Socks speculatively eyed his black barathea trousers. At that moment Prince William scooted out from a forest of legs and lunged for Socks's docked tail. There was another agonized canine yelp.

'William!' announced the Queen in her most decisive and regal of tones. 'Time for bed. And time for grown-ups to repair to table.'

As the Queen led the family procession to the dining-room Andrew lingered awhile by his station at the window. From high up on the battlements came three short and one long flash of a powerful torch. It was the signal he had been waiting for.

With a grin of satisfaction, he turned to follow his family. It had been a minutely-planned, commando-style operation, but the morse code from the battlements beamed the announcement he had been anxiously hoping for all evening. Stage two of Operation Eagle had been completed, Ilaria had been smuggled within the castle walls.

Just desserts

Downstairs, in the basement, the kitchens were humming. Steam was rising from the vast vats of stock ready to be turned into one of Mrs McCue's special soups. The brigade of cooks bustled, stirred, mixed, chopped, filleted and tasted. The traditional family Boxing Day Dinner was in preparation. Hunched over a candle the butler, in starched shirt and tails, was decanting the last bottle of Château Margaux '77 — a bit young and raw for the finest palates, but the Windsors were straightforward and modest in their tastes. The footmen, in a last-minute flurry of preparation, were shining the silver salvers, polishing the gold-rimmed Wedgwood service, checking that their white gloves were spotless and buttoning their splendid crimson tunics.

The one static figure in this hubbub lounged by the door. It was Frisk. Although he had no place in the kitchen, the valet had heard reports of a new recruit. Frisk's eyes alighted upon a youth struggling awkwardly inside his brand new Royal issue uniform. The stiff, starched outfit signified the gauche young man was an under-footman, nearly the lowliest rung in the castle domestic service. The blond youth was cack-handedly attempting to affix the removed claret corks on to the cut-glass decanters. His hands were shaking because the butler had informed him that each decanter was worth considerably more than his annual salary. The stoppers rattled.

Frisk noticed the charming pink blush on the boy's downy cheek. At that moment a bell sounded, signalling action stations; the Royal family were taking their seats

for dinner. Without a command a well-drilled line of
footmen formed bearing silver soup tureens, ladles,
garnishes and all the other pomp and impedimenta
necessary for a Royal supper. They moved forward at a
measured and stately pace on the half-mile march down
chilly corridors to reach the dining-room.

Frisk pressed himself against the wall as the snaking
line of servants passed before him on their triumphal
march. However, the reason for Frisk's presence in the
kitchens had not gone unnoticed. Each footman as he
brushed by the valet felt impelled to aim a sotto voce
remark in his direction.

'What brings you to the lower decks?'

'Certainly not the cooking.'

'No, sweetie, it's the ingredients he's after.'

'Mmmm,' added the fourth footman, 'who could be
on the menu tonight?'

The fifth, however, a tall fellow with a hint of five
o'clock shadow on his chin, did not take such a bantering
tone. 'Watch it, Frisk,' he hissed. 'Hands off the lad.'

Frisk, knowing his time was limited, made his move.
He sauntered between the stainless steel counters and
casually stopped at the lowly station occupied by the
object of his interest. He looked admiringly as the youth
tentatively burnished the silver-topped port decanters.

'What polish,' murmured Frisk. 'I can see your talents,
dear boy, are shamelessly wasted in this dungeon.'

'Beg pardon, sir?' said the lad, with a hint of country
innocence in his slow, rounded cadence.

'From the West Country, eh, son?' smiled Frisk
paternally.

'That's right, sir,' replied the lad eagerly. 'From
Dorchester way.'

'Aha,' said Frisk, touching him lightly on the hand,
'Hardy country!'

'Beg pardon, sir?'

The gaggle of footmen returned with a clatter through
the swing doors; there was a sudden fresh infusion of
chaos and noise. As they frantically prepared for the next

salvo of food, Frisk's conversation was killed in the rapid cross-fire of chatter:

'Did you see who'd been at the sherry?'

'Pissed!'

'Her Maj is a bit down in the mouth tonight...'

'Mmm — Miss Piggy-face.'

'And did you hear Princess Pushy?'

'Bitch!'

'Got all the sparklers on tonight. Like the Blackpool illuminations.'

Suddenly a low, threatening voice close by Frisk's ear said: 'I warned you, pal.'

Frisk turned. It was Reg Banks. His broad, coarse face glistened with perspiration. His large, fleshy lips curled with venom. 'Naff off!'

'Oh dear, Reggie,' replied Frisk sweetly, 'wrong time of the month is it?'

'Chop chop,' interrupted the first footman, bearing a large salver with a voluminous cover. 'No time for tiffs.'

The line of footmen reformed, in readiness to present the second course — raised turkey and ham pies, cleverly disguised leftovers from Christmas Day — and as they passed the valet they winked broadly. Not so the last man in line.

'Degenerate scum,' snarled Banks, his pig-like face reddened with anger. 'If you're still here when I get back, you bleeding nance, I'll bash your face in!'

Frisk bowed low and after the departing line of servants. 'I'll be here, dear...'

Her Majesty was not accustomed to being kept waiting. The dessert was already ten minutes late. The irritated drumming of manicured Royal nails upon ancient mahogany could be heard throughout the grand, oak-panelled dining-room.

Philip, too, was furious, though his anger vented itself in a lecture to the hapless Duke of Gloucester on the imperative need for Third-World types to take the ruddy pill or jolly well exercise a bit of personal restraint for once.

Princess Margaret, with cavalier disregard for protocol, had filled the gap by fitting a Sobranie into her holder and puffing away regardless.

'Having an intercourse, Auntie?' said Andrew with a smirk.

The claret on top of the pints of real ale had affected his judgement. Till now Andrew had sat quietly without making one inappropriate remark. He had even listened respectfully as his mother had addressed the assembled company about her plans for the Derby. She had delivered a homily on the importance to her of this event. She implored them all to act as a team — for once — to aid her in achieving this elusive goal, and finally she exhorted them to clear their diaries for the first week in June so they should all be on parade in full muster on the big day.

In the absence of pudding Andrew turned to Margaret, who was always a good audience for his risqué jokes. 'Do you know the one about old Porchy and the French filly?' asked Andrew, referring to the legendary father of the Queen's racing manager. 'Porchy is over in gay Paree for the Prix de Diane at Chantilly and staying in the frightfully stuffy Hotel Bretagne. He's met this really tasty Comtesse, and the old dog makes a rendezvous for 12 o'clock that night. Their secret signal was that he would knock three times on her bedroom door. Well, as the bewitching hour approached the Comtesse lay in the sack ready for l'amour. On the stroke of midnight she heard three dull thuds at her door... But it wasn't the sound of knuckles at all. It wasn't even his silver-topped cane. The Comtesse was startled to discover, on opening the door, that Porchy had been knocking with his vieux plongeur.'

Andrew's laughter was abruptly cut short when he realized that the table was hushed and everyone was staring at him.

The Queen Mother, adept at defusing tricky

situations, had taken up a silver nut cracker and was
affecting to crush a walnut. 'I can never get these gadgets
to work,' she announced loudly to no one in particular.

From the far end of the table Philip barked testily,
'Where's the bloody pudding?'

The butler engaged in bringing the vintage port to the
table unconsciously stood to attention. 'Dessert is on its
way, Sir,' he said, filling the Duke's glass to the brim in an
effort to distract him.

At that moment the flunkies arrived bearing the long-
awaited pudding. 'What's this?' said the Queen sharply
as the dish was placed before her. 'This doesn't look like
sherry trifle to me.'

'Hell's death,' spluttered Philip.

'It's bloody tinned cling peaches,' gasped Edward.

'And Wall's ice-cream, too,' said Margaret in mock
horror.

'Sprinkled with hundreds and thousands,' said Diana.
'Yuk!'

'Explanation please,' roared Philip.

The butler stepped forward nervously. 'Alas, Sir, the
trifle has met with an unfortunate accident.'

'Unfortunate?' repeated Philip. 'Typical of the slap-
dash attitude rampant in this country today. Do we
know the fellow responsible for this balls-up?'

'Yes, Sir.'

'Well, may it be upon his head.'

'Have no fear, Your Royal Highness,' said the butler
softly, 'it is.'

Frisk had been true to his word. As Banks reentered the
kitchen, balancing his salver in one hand, he spied Frisk,
wrestling with the unwitting object of their affection.
'Oi,' shouted Banks.

Frisk and the boy turned with a look of startled
surprise.

'I warned you,' snarled Banks, advancing menacingly.
'Ah, the noble Banks post haste from beloved

monarch,' declaimed Frisk in his best Shakespearian manner. 'What news, Sirrah?'

'I'll 'ave you.'

Frisk puckered his mouth disdainfully. 'You should be so lucky.'

'I saw what your game was — scum-bag.'

''Twas but a trick of the light, Master Banks. I was demonstrating to this downed youth a secret of the valet's trade.'

'Oh yeah?' Banks raised the salver in his left hand. It contained a congealed mess of unfinished cold mashed potato.

'Indeed — I was showing our young friend how to defluff his tunic by the simple expedient of applying Sellotape ...'

'Well, defluff that!' snarled Banks as he slapped the soggy mashed potato into the startled valet's face.

A smile of triumph had hardly begun to illuminate the dark face of Banks when Frisk seized the nearest object to hand, a deep cut-glass bowl. Gently he placed it upon his adversary's head like a crown.

A sticky avalanche of cake, jelly and jam trickled and slid down Banks's scarlet uniform.

'Alas, poor Banks,' trilled Frisk, 'all the trifles of the world upon his shoulders.'

As soon as the untouched dessert was removed, Philip rose. 'Let me take this opportunity to remind you that one of The Firm is working even now, toiling under the hot Indian sun.' He raised his glass. 'To absent members!'

'But Anne hasn't *got* a member,' muttered Andrew sotto voce as everyone drank the toast.

Thereafter they were quick to retire to the drawing-room, the apple log fire and the traditional after-dinner pursuits much loved by the Windsors. They began with the family's favourite highly competitive game of charades. The Queen had immediately been spotted in her none-too-flattering portrayal of the Prime Minister.

Subsequently Princess Michael of Kent had failed to
convey, through her overacting and her increasingly
desperate gestures, that she was Catherine the Great.
The Queen, who had guessed Rasputin, was heard to
whisper: 'That's far too regal for the likes of us.'

The proceedings were in full swing when a castle
servant sidled up unnoticed to Prince Andrew and
whispered conspiratorially in his ear: 'The eagle has
landed'. Andrew allowed a discreet five minutes to elapse
before getting up and making quietly for the door.

His exit went entirely unremarked as the family were
engrossed in trying to guess what on earth could be the
explanation of the grunts and groans as the Queen
Mother attempted to impersonate Conan the Barbarian.
'The Pope,' hazarded Edward.

'No, no,' suggested the Queen. 'It's Henry VIII.'

'Oliver Reed,' drawled Princess Margaret, 'in that
homo scene from *Women in Love*.'

Softly Andrew slipped out and closed the door behind
him as he set off down the chilly corridors towards his
assignation with Ilaria Pucci, the starlet. Andrew knew
she couldn't act. But then, she would not be playing
charades.

Read all about it

The following morning's front page of the *Morning Enquirer* was, for both Prince Edward and Nick Spalding, cataclysmic.

Each, though belonging on such disparate rungs of the social ladder, was very nearly knocked off his respective perch.

'WORLD EXCLUSIVE — MYSTERY BLONDE IN CASTLE CAPER,' screamed the 140-point Bodini bold type, the banner headline of the *Daily Disclosure*'s outrageous and unscrupulous arch-rival, the *Morning Enquirer*.

A five-column picture showed, as far as one could judge from the slightly out-of-focus photograph, an attractive, demure-looking young girl clad in a silk scarf. The snap had clearly been taken on the run through the window of a car. The overall effect was to suggest that this innocent-looking creature, who appeared to be of genteel stock, was doing something furtive.

'This Yule Bird was the sizzling surprise Santa brought yesterday for the Queen's youngest son, the handsome Prince Edward,' began the story.

'We can reveal it's the first joyous bloom of young love for the innocent student prince.

'While other members of the Royal Family went on the traditional Boxing Day shoot in Windsor Great Park, Educated Eddie entertained this lovely lass to tea and crumpets. The top-secret tryst took place in the Prince's private apartments — behind closed doors.

'A royal aide, who caught a glimpse of the clandestine couple, told the *Enquirer*: "Edward could be in hot water for this. The Queen will be furious. But they look to be deeply in love. They spent hours alone togther."

'The mystery blonde drove to her assignation in a red C-reg Mini Metro and three hours later left Windsor Castle at great speed by a back entrance.

'Late last night a close friend of the Prince said: "I can't say who the girl is. But Edward is head-over-heels".'

Spalding's news editor, Ron Snitch, wanted an explanation. 'Well done, laddie,' Snitch said with a sneer, 'there could be a knighthood in this for you — writing about ferrets when there's a bloody bird on the effing nest.'

Spalding seized the offending paper and examined the by-line under the photograph. 'Rinaldo — I might have known,' said Spalding. 'That conniving paparazzo. The story's total bullshit.'

'I'll tell you what, laddie,' replied Snitch, 'it's still a bloody good tale. Now that Andrew's spliced, we've got to have some bonking stories about Eddie. And I want you to name this mystery girl. Really dig the dirt.'

'No need, old boy,' boomed Spalding. 'That's Georgina Wallingford-Giles. She works in the Prince of Wales's office.'

'And in Prince Edward's bed it seems,' interrupted Snitch. 'Now get on the blower.'

Edward was in a similar predicament. His father also wanted an explanation. Prince Philip had burst into his room, while he was still in bed, brandishing the *Morning Enquirer*.

'Well done, Edward, my boy,' said his father in his most sarcastic manner. 'Explanation, please.'

Edward read the story, appalled. 'It's utterly untrue, Papa,' pleaded Edward indignantly. 'That's just Georgina.'

'I know that,' said Philip impatiently. 'But the point is — was she in your room last night?'

Edward — who could not countenance lying to his father — saw his way clear. 'No, Father, I swear that Georgina has never been in my bedroom. Not last night — not ever.'

'Fair enough — I accept your word, my boy,' said Philip, turning to leave.

A white garment caught his eye. He stopped and bent down to pick it up from underneath the tallboy. Edward observed this with horror: how was he going to explain that this frilly feminine article did not belong to Miss Wallingford-Giles, daughter of Brigadier, the Hon. Christopher Wallingford-Giles of Burwash, Sussex, but to an undistinguished and ambitious Italian film actress, daughter of a Neapolitan cigarette smuggler?

No. Who would ever believe — let alone the Duke of Edinburgh — that on retiring to his room, after the family parlour games of the previous evening, he had found a naked young woman sitting up in his bed? Her luxuriant raven hair tumbled sensuously over her naked breasts, and the only clothing she wore was a neatly tied pink ribbon round her neck. The gorgeous Ilaria Pucci gave him a dazzling and inviting smile.

'Oh no!' exclaimed Edward, horrified. '*Who are you?*'

'Your Chreesmis present,' smiled Ilaria sweetly, opening her arms.

'My what?' exploded Edward.

'Your present from Andrew,' replied Ilaria calmly. 'Happy Chreesmis!'

'Harborough!' yelled Edward at the top of his lungs.

Within seconds his detective had burst into the room, his service revolver drawn. Harborough summed up the situation at a glance: another of Andrew's pranks. He'd have to smuggle this trollop out pronto.

'Right, girl — move it!'

Oh God no, Edward groaned to himself, his father would never swallow such a story.

Prince Philip pocketed the brassiere, and without a backward glance at his blushing son, walked out.

'Georgina? Hello love! Nick here... Yes, yes, Spalding. Sorry to disturb your hols. Ah, you've seen the *Enquirer*... now wait a minute, don't hang up, darling, I

think it's disgraceful, too. Absolutely treasonable... I
agree, there's no depths to which they won't sink... yes,
I quite understand the Brigadier's point of view. So let's
put the record straight, love. Of course, Georgie —
starting with the blonde hair, I know you're brunette.
Now, love, what were you doing at the Castle?... Just
delivering work papers for Charles... oh, hang on, let
me get this down — and some chocolates for Diana.
How's that spelt?... C-H-A-R-B... Great! Now,
Georgie, did you meet young Edward? — Only in the
corridor. And he smacked your bum! Ho! Ho! Ho!
Splendid! No, I won't quote you... and you told him to
naff off? Terrific, that's my girl... of course it must be
embarrassing for your mother... and your fiancé. Don't
worry, we'll set the record straight. Chin up, love. Ciao!'

Spalding, having sent Leroy the office messenger
down to El Vino for a bottle of his usual Saint Emilion,
addressed himself to his ancient Remington.

'Budding Lothario Prince Edward, I can exclusively
reveal, is suffering the pangs of unrequited love for
vivacious brunette Georgina Wallingford-Giles, 26, a
Buckingham Palace secretary,' he typed furiously.

'The Prince is lovesick, and the Royal Family are deeply
concerned for his well-being. The normally cheerful
Prince has lost weight recently, and is looking gaunt and
troubled.

'The reason, I can disclose,' Spalding took a
contemplative swig of his claret, 'is that the young
Prince's cheeky advances have been spurned. Friends of
Miss Wallingford-Giles said yesterday: "Eddie got off on
the wrong foot by treating Georgie like a scullery-maid.
His style of wooing was to goose her, in a most ungallant
fashion."

'Contrary to ill-informed reports that the couple are
deeply in love, Miss Wallingford-Giles, known as "Wally"
to her friends, is engaged to Capt. Timothy Hackstall-
Smith, 29, of the 5th Royal Inniskilling Dragoon Guards.

'This love saga came to a dramatic climax in the
corridors of Windsor Castle on Boxing Day when Miss

Wallingford-Giles informed the Prince, in the bluntest of terms, that his feelings were not reciprocated.

'The Prince is said to be inconsolable. He did not appear on the traditional pheasant shoot.'

Suddenly a new thought struck him. He chuckled. Spalding drained his glass and with a flourish typed the final line: 'Prince Edward, a member of the Royal Family tells me, is stepping into Prince Andrew's old bachelor shoes — he's becoming the new Royal Romeo.'

Snitch appraised the story. 'Not bad, laddie,' he said grudgingly. 'But is it true?'

'True?' echoed Spalding. 'Better than that, old boy. It's undeniable.'

EPISODE TWO: SPRING

Whisky aid

The merciless midday African sun thrummed down on Spalding's unprotected head. While the rest of the Royal party had taken the advice of the Foreign Office and donned tropical hats, Spalding's sparse pate was already showing signs of first degree burns. Princess Anne and the official party were three hundred yards ahead up the arid, rubble-strewn mountain path, appearing through the shimmering heat haze to be no bigger than the swarm of insistent flies that buzzed round his portly, perspiring figure. The flies, who had been deprived of water for so long, were being attracted from the parched desert to the unique oasis of Spalding's drenched candy-striped shirt.

'Porco Madonna!' he swore. 'The things I do for England.'

By now the Princess had reached the tiny white-washed village of Dijbani, to which she and a phalanx of welfare officials were being escorted by Bob Geldof, the Irish rock singer turned charity superstar, who was showing her the new sewerage system paid for by a celebrity Kissathon.

Spalding stumbled. His swollen feet throbbed painfully inside his hand-made Italian shoes, the distinctive gold buckle of which was dulled by a thick layer of red African dust. The thin leather soles were perfect for the smooth pavements of Mayfair, but were already wearing through on the flinty road to Dijbani. His aching feet scorched, and every so often Jerry, his attendant photographer, was astonished to observe the distressed writer make a little bunny hop.

'A pox upon this pestilent country,' cried Spalding, sinking to the ground. A pair of sunbathing scorpions scuttled down a crevice in the parched earth.

Jerry stopped and turned. The photographer was more appropriately dressed for this mission, though his Yves Saint Laurent safari suit was curiously complemented by a knotted handkerchief upon his head.

He retraced his steps and held out a silver flask to his dehydrated colleague. Spalding accepted it gratefully and poured the liquid greedily between his cracked lips. He lurched forward with a convulsive fit of coughing.

'Christ, that's better . . .'

'Thought that would revive you, matey.'

'Just tell me something, Jerry — what the hell are we doing in this Godforsaken wilderness?'

'Simple, Nick. We are here to witness a miracle on behalf of the great British public. We have come to this wilderness to testify to the transformation of Princess Nasty into Princess Nice.'

Ahead, the Royal party had already reached the village. Jerry's first-aid helped Spalding to strike out again towards the hill-top hamlet, which with flagging fleet and a few more rabbit hops, they finally reached as the official party stood outside the head man's wattle hut.

Despite the best plans of the Palace to have an orderly queue of locals to greet the visiting dignitary, an expectant gaggle of ill-fed village children clustered around the Princess, in the hope that this strange visitor from a far land had brought them desperately-needed sustenance. The Princess continued smiling.

'And what precisely have you done here?' asked the Princess.

'What we've built here,' began Geldof, wiping the sweat from his face with his sleeve, 'are a whole series of . . .'

'Human waste disposal units,' interjected a charity official quickly, anxious to protect the Princess from the graphic description which he sensed was about to come from the forthright Irishman. 'A much needed sanitary facility, Ma'am.'

'Fookin' right!' said Geldof. 'But what these fookers really need is food.'

'You're right, Mr Geldof. We shall see to it,' said Anne, retreating before the insistent forefinger of the rock star, which was once again being prodded painfully against her already slightly bruised chest. The previous evening in the Umbana Hilton the long-suffering Princess had had to undergo a thirty-minute diatribe from Mr Geldof, punctuated by insistent stabbings of his admonishing digit.

Jerry couldn't believe his luck. What a snap! A commoner — an Irishman — daring not just to touch the Royal personage, but to launch what amounted to an assault.

Anne backed away into the head man's hut, followed by the relentlessly accusing finger.

'Grevious Bodily Harm,' mused the sweltering royal correspondent, already mentally preparing his story.

Now the Royal party had disappeared into the chief's hut, the throng of undernourished children pressed round the two bewildered newspapermen. Emaciated arms reached out beseechingly.

Spalding regarded them with alarm. 'What do these wallahs want?'

'Food!' said Jerry.

'And water, I suppose,' added Spalding.

'Hang on,' said Jerry, pulling out the silver flask from

his top pocket. 'I think we can help the poor blighters.'

He held out the flask and it was quickly seized by the nearest child.

'Christ, Jerry,' gasped Spalding, 'that's the Glenfiddich!'

But before he could intervene the child had thrown his head back and drained the contents. Immediately a dry gurgle issued from his throat; he keeled over, quite dead.

Springtime blues

The private walled gardens of Kensington Palace reverberated with the exuberant childish laughter of young Prince Harry while his mother, free for a moment of her public restrictions, whirled him round and round. The piercing squeals of the toddler Prince mingled with the soft fluted chuckles of encouragement from the glowing and wholesome young English rose. Her carefree mood matched the soft gentle April sunlight and her complexion looked as delicate as the dew on the leaves of the flowering grape-hyacinth.

From her drawing-room window Princess Margaret looked down on this happy scene. Her lips twitched with irritation and to calm herself she inhaled the smoke from her Sobranie held, as always, by her tortoiseshell holder. Deliberately, she managed for a moment to expunge this happy scene by snorting a cloud of smoke upon the polished window pane. In the background the low hum of the London traffic from Kensington High Street infiltrated the gloomy room where she stood alone, surveying with an edgy and uneasy mood the burst of spring in the gardens before her. As another joyful peal of laughter came from below she reached for the eighteenth-century embroidered bell-pull to summon a footman from the bowels of the building. At times she wondered why she had been consigned to the 'Aunt Heap' as Prince Charles had termed the red-brick Wren palace. She really felt the old place was being over-utilized, what with her nephew and his noisy family, the problematic Kents, and even the inoffensive Gloucesters and their tribe. This modern living was far too cramped. This egalitarian business could be taken a jot too far.

The footman entered.

'What do you want?' asked Margaret imperiously

'You rang, Ma'am.'

'Of course I did,' she said irritably, and turned back to the window to gather her thoughts. What on earth had she summoned him for? It was still too early for her mid-morning whisky. A scream of pure delight came from the gardens as Diana and her youngest son played ring-a-ring-a-roses.

'Whoopsie, whoopsie... We all fall down,' sang the future Queen of England.

Margaret looked with ill-concealed distaste as the third-in-line to the throne collapsed to the ground, shrieking with delight and kicking his little legs in the air.

'Do they know the meaning of that song?' murmured Margaret sourly.

The footman shifted his feet in embarrassment.

'I don't suppose they do,' sighed Margaret. 'It's all about the pox and falling down dead.'

Rapidly she scribbed a note and placed it upon the footman's silver salver with instructions that it should be conveyed post-haste to the Princess of Wales.

The note, Margaret could now see, peeping from behind the generous folds of the curtains, had reached its destination. Diana looked up briefly. She called out sharply: 'Come on, Harry darling, Auntie Margaret has got a headache.'

Margaret felt a pang of regret as once again silence enveloped her. Why, as solitude became increasingly painful for her, did she still push people away?

The private garden of Kensington Palace was coming into colour. The milky-white magnolia was about to blossom, the yellow stems of forsythia, the little primula and the delicate cherry blossom waved in the gentle breeze, while viburnum wafted its sweet scent across the lawns.

From around the corner of a box-hedge appeared a slender, well-dressed figure in pencil-slim designer jeans tucked into green wellington boots, and fine tweed jacket

with a jaunty matching hat. The strikingly handsome
man looked like a model who had escaped from the pages
of *Harpers & Queen*. He was the gardener.

Margaret gazed admiringly at the elegant fellow as he
gracefully bent to drink in the heady aroma of a cluster of
bosom-white narcissi.

How Wildean, thought Margaret, as dear, dear Roddy
gently plucked a single stem and placed it lovingly in his
buttonhole.

She drew gently on her cigarette holder, and closed
her eyes as she recalled her favourite lines from the
divine Oscar.

> 'It is sweet to dance to violins
> When love and life are fair;
> To dance to flutes, to dance to lutes
> Is delicate and rare ...'

Roddy was delicate and rare. That was why even
though what could be, was not to be, and Roddy had
married another, with her reluctant blessing, she was
glad that this had proved no impediment to employing
him to toil in her vineyard. It was Roddy who had for so
long kept alive in her the flames of impetuous youth.
Many another woman's spirit would have been crushed
by such disappointments as she had suffered all those
years ago: not being allowed to marry the subject of her
choice, and then being cruelly abandoned by her
damnably fickle husband for a younger woman.

It was the sensitive Roddy who had released her from
the cursed constraints of being royal, who had freed her
from those suffocating responsibilities of her position,
and allowed her to escape — for ever so brief a time —
into the carefree pleasures of anonymity. Those blessed
summer days spent digging cabbages and cauliflowers ...
oh, the unfettered joy of ordinariness!

Roddy's little hippy commune in the Somerset glades
had provided a blissful refuge — hideously uncomfortable, true, but it was the very rigours and inconveniences
which had been for her the unexpected treat. Oh the

sensual pleasure of washing up! The fun of making beds.

Those days were gone.

It had been a liberating escapade, like Marie-Antoinette's truant jaunts away from the stultifying formality of the court at Versailles to play at being a milkmaid. But reality would not allow such interludes to last for ever; for both, their pastoral idylls were forced to an unsentimental end. Marie-Antoinette lost her head. Margaret merely lost her heart.

Sadly she watched the retreating figure of the horticulturalist as he sauntered towards the potting sheds. He did not glance up once at her window. With a heavy heart, Margaret turned away and surveyed the oppressive room, whose cold, unwelcoming shadows were emphasized by the brilliant sunshine outside.

Margaret made an impulsive decision. She picked up her chrome-plated phone and instructed the palace operator to connect her with Lord Rubberton.

'Rubbers!' she cried. 'London's so drab at this time of year, don't you find? We're bored.'

'Oh, we can't have that, Ma'am,' replied Lord Rubberton uncertainly.

Though he owned a Jacobean stately pile in Northamptonshire and seventeen thousand acres of prime sporting estate in the Scottish Grampians, his main role in life was as a court jester and entertainments organizer to the capricious Princess.

'We find the social scene here so dreary. I don't suppose there's any chance of gathering together a little troupe to make a triplet to Mustique next Tuesday?' she asked, knowing full well that this idea of departing to the Caribbean at such short notice was by no means a request. It was a command.

'How amusing, Ma'am,' replied Lord Rubberton, successfully disguising the annoyance he felt at having to cancel a week's splendid salmon fishing in Scotland.

'So that's settled then,' said Margaret gaily. 'Oh, and do round up some swells, Rubbers.'

Lord Rubberton spent the next six hours, at not inconsiderable expense, on his new cordless telephone. Much endeavour went into tracing Patrick Lichfield, the Queen's cousin; after 28 calls, across six continents, he finally tracked him down to the Mojave Desert of Arizona where the Earl was photographing naked women for a tractor manufacturer's calendar. Carl Dwork, the controversial British modern ballet soloist, was not at the Sydney Opera House, nor the Kennedy Arts Center in Washington; he was taking tea with his elderly mother — Mrs Marge Wood — in Basingstoke. Mick Jagger had checked out of the Georges V in Paris, was not at Langan's, and Jerry didn't know where the hell he was; Mick was, in fact, in conference with his stockbroker in the City of London. Sir Peregrine Royston-Black, the notorious gambling baronet, was not at the Palace Hotel in Gstaad, the New York Yacht Club, the Clermont in Berkeley Square, or even at Madame Claude's in Paris; Perry was eventually pinned down at a cheap and sordid opium den in the teeming souk of Tangier. Finally, Hugo Hamilton, the debonair matinee idol, was caught between acts while performing to an adoring audience of middle-aged housewives at Penzance in a touring version of Noël Coward's *Private Lives*.

Hugo, like the others, accepted with alacrity.

As Hugo entered left, for Act II, he was humming his favourite Coward song:

> 'Poor little rich girl
> You're a bewitched girl,
> Better beware!'

Taking the stage

'Brilliant! Quite perfect. I loved every breathing moment. It was quite, quite ... I was moved.'

'Really?'

'One was completely won over. That performance had total conviction.'

'You're not just saying that?'

'Hand on heart. Sincerity, integrity, inner truth. I believed in you utterly.'

'Gosh, do you mean to say ...'

'One hundred percent, darling ... er, Ma'am.'

Diana giggled nervously. Her peaches and cream complexion was suffused with a delightful girlish blush. As happened more and more infrequently, and only in moments when she was unsure of herself, the Princess inclined her head to the side in that coquettish way which had so captivated the heart of millions on the occasion of her formal engagement photographs.

Sir Richard Attenborough stopped pacing and froze in a contorted pose, hands outstretched wide, eyes bulging and mouth open. He remained, still as a statue, in this somewhat curious posture, which was beginning to alarm Diana.

'Oh dear, gosh, Dickie, have I done something awful?'

'Bless you, no, dear heart. You've just created something divine, ducky ... er, Ma'am.'

'Dickie, do call me Diana — in this room, at least.'

Sir Richard beamed and glanced up at the rose pastel walls of the formal Kensington Palace reception-room. He visibly swelled with pride. Despite the Oscar he had won for *Gandhi*, despite the enormous commercial success of *A Chorus Line*, this was the zenith of his glittering career in show business; here he was, teaching the future Queen of England to be queenly.

'Freeze, hold it right there, Diana,' said Sir Dickie, immediately exercising his newly-granted right of *lèse-majesté*. 'Your head...'

'What? Is it my hair?'

'No, Diana, darling. It's the angle. That charming way you incline your head. What a lovely bit of business! It suggests such touching innocence. You must use that.'

'You think it's effective, Dickie?'

'Devastating, ducky.'

'Do you think it's better inclined to the left or the right?' said Diana, trying out the variations in the David Hicks mirror. 'I think my left profile is a weeny bit more effective, don't you, Dickie?'

'Both charming, both charming — but don't overdo it. As Larry says, when you find a twenty-carat diamond, don't flash it about like a doxy. Preserve its rarity value. Remember, ducky, always keep your public wanting more.'

Diana had been upset when, the previous week, after launching a new nuclear submarine in Barrow-in-Furness, she had been criticized by several of the newspapers. The *Daily Mail's* female commentator had remarked upon a lingering schoolgirl gaucheness, the *Daily Disclosure* had rather unkindly reported the fact that she had mispronounced the name of the ship, *HMS Ramillies*, while *The Times* had disloyally suggested that she lacked 'a certain intellectual gravitas'. Diana had instantly resolved to improve her poise, work upon her diction and generally polish up her act. There was only one man for the job: the unashamedly theatrical Sir Richard.

The director was now demonstrating how to enter a room.

'Passing through a portal,' lectured Sir Dickie, 'may seem frightfully banal. But believe you me, Diana dear, it is an art.'

'Eh?'

'Seriously, Ma'am, your entrance is your statement. You live or die by this.'

'It sounds horribly difficult.'

Sir Richard threw back his head and roared. 'No, no,' he exclaimed. 'It's really so simple. You see, it's magic time.'

'Terrif. I adore magic.'

'Goodee. I knew you'd understand. The trick is — you are the magician. You are pulling your performance out of a hat.'

'Like a bunny?'

'Exactly! It's all an illusion,' said Dickie.

Diana was totally absorbed. She followed entranced, like a child at a Punch and Judy show, as Sir Richard passed on the lore of his craft, conjuring up a dazzling virtuoso performance; he sailed in graciously, like a ship of state, smiled serenely, waved placidly, shook hands unhurriedly, surveyed all with Olympian composure, deported himself throughout as if born above the rank of other men and carried such poise as if it had been bequeathed to him by centuries of breeding.

'Brill!' Diana burst into spontaneous applause.

'See, my child,' said Sir Richard sweetly, still caught up in his performance, 'I AM the Queen.'

Diana, under his painstaking guidance, rehearsed all morning.

'My God, you've got it!' exclaimed Attenborough, close to tears with the excitement of it all. 'Fabulous. Absolutely and totally . . .'

Diana waited expectantly.

Attenborough's lip twitched. 'Totally . . .'

'Totally what, Dickie?'

'Totally . . .' Attenborough wiped away a tear. 'Totally wondrous, darling.'

Diana glowed under this shower of praise from the illustrious director who had coaxed great performances from the likes of Robert Redford, Sean Connery, Sir John Gielgud, Olivier himself.

Thrilled, Diana murmured: 'It is quite a mellow experience.'

Overcome by the response of his superbly pedigreed pupil, Sir Dickie clapped his hands excitedly. 'Let's go for the big one, baby — improvise!'

Slowly Diana rose from the Albrizzi sofa. She drew herself to her full five foot eight and a half, and for a moment she closed her eyes to compose herself.

Then, as she began a measured walk down the soft grey Wilton carpet, she gave him one clue: 'Westminster Abbey.'

'*Délicieuse*,' whispered Attenborough, hugging himself with glee.

Her walk was infinitely slow, dignified and imperial. Her carriage was proud, her chin held high and her eyes were fixed upon a distant point. She looked neither to left nor right. Her progress was stately, with the impressive certainty of the inevitable.

The performance was one of total conviction. She was there. All Diana heard in her head was 'Zadok the Priest', Handel's majestic coronation anthem.

The music ceased. There was an awed silence. Diana stopped, marking time for the page boys to drape her organza-laced train. Then gracefully she turned to sit upon the straight-backed black dining-chair that was her throne.

'Cut!' cried Sir Dickie ecstatically. 'Oh, Ma'am, angel, wondrous creature . . .' He wrung his hands, unable any longer to contain his emotion. 'That's the one. Print it! A thousand copies!' The tears flowed freely. 'Bravo!' he croaked.

There was a cough from the doorway. Dickie and Diana looked round.

Charles stood there uncertainly, looking baffled.

'Oh,' he said with a start, realizing they had at last noticed his presence. 'Darling, Nanny was wondering if William could go and play boaties on the Round Pond.'

'Not now, Charles. I'm busy.'

Without another word the Prince of Wales withdrew.

As he closed the door carefully behind him, Charles wondered what had become of that innocent child he had married.

Horses for courses

'Your Majesty, Her Majesty, Your Majesty,' said the Buckingham Palace switchboard operator as she connected the Queen with her mother.

'Mummy?'

'Lilibet?'

'Yes, Mummy.'

'I had a little flutter at the three-thirty at Cheltenham.'

'Whisky King won by three lengths.'

'I know, dear. At twenty-five to one.'

'Gosh.'

'Yes. A nice little earner.'

The conversation on equine matters continued for some while. But this knowledgeable exchange could not have been overheard by just anyone getting a crossed line, nor by curious and impertinent operators, let alone malignant foreign powers. For the Queen's telephone systems were scrambled: this security device ensured that the Queen's humble ramblings about this and that entered a mysterious box of tricks which mixed all words into an incomprehensible minestrone.

Finally, the Queen said: 'I don't suppose you'd care to join me for dinner tonight?'

'But it's six o'clock, Lilibet. This is jolly short notice.'

'Sorry, Mummy. But we haven't seen you for ages. Shall we say half past seven?'

And thus it was that within seven minutes of leaving Clarence House the Queen Mother found herself ascending the famous marble staircase at Buckingham Palace. Her progress was slow and she was only a quarter of the way up when at the top of the stairs there appeared the vigorous figure of her son-in-law in white tie and tails. Prince Philip came bounding down two steps at a time, and in his hurry failed to notice the elderly lady who had stopped next to a Rubens in order to catch her breath.

As Philip raced past her the Queen Mother pressed herself against the wall. She shouted after the flapping tail coat. 'Off to save the white rhino again?'

'No,' boomed Philip, without breaking stride. 'Grand Order of Water Rats.'

'Saving them as well, are we?'

But the Queen Mother's testy remark was lost on the Duke of Edinburgh, who had already leapt into the back of the waiting Rolls. By the time she reached the inner sanctum of her daughter's private apartments, the Queen Mother was not in the best of moods.

'Oh, I don't care for that dress, Lilibet,' she said.

'What's the matter with it, Mummy?'

'Too frumpy. Are we putting on weight?'

'Don't be a nag, Mum.'

The Queen Mother plumped herself down in a comfortable Parker Knoll armchair which had seen better days. Elizabeth handed her mother a stiff reviver in the form of a four-fingered Famous Grouse whisky.

'And have you had that little chat with Margaret?'

'Not yet, Mummy.'

'I assume we are dining à deux tonight?'

'Yes, unfortunately Philip had an important engagement.'

'Like most nights,' muttered the Queen Mother into her whisky.

'Seriously, Mummy.'

'Of course, dear.' The Queen Mother smiled sweetly. 'Raising money for rats.'

Their conversation was interrupted by the arrival of two of the Queen's footmen bearing the Royal dinner. They placed the trays on side tables beside the seated monarch and her mother. Simultaneously, with military precision, the footman lifted the silver covers to reveal

Heinz tomato soup, and for the second course a Scotch egg and baked beans.

'Yummy,' exclaimed the Queen Mother.

'You've forgotten something,' said the Queen gently.

Instantly one footman produced a bottle of HP Sauce, while the other conjured up the Lee and Perrins. The footmen bowed and departed.

'Can you pass the remote control thing, Mummy,' said the Queen. 'Time for "Dallas".'

As mother and daughter settled down to their television dinners, six little foxy faces appeared from round curtains, from under sofas and from behind the mahogany inlaid radiogram. The royal corgis had got a waft of din-dins. In the light blue glare of the television they arrayed themselves in an expectant semi-circle before Her Majesty.

But for once the dogs were not the centre of attention. The Queen was totally absorbed in the drama of the Ewings on screen. They were transported to Southfork, the Ewings' ranch, where in this episode the admirable Miss Ellie was once again battling to keep her fractious family from tearing each other apart.

'Families can be so awkward,' remarked the Queen Mother.

'Mmmm,' said the Queen, forking a crescent of Scotch egg into her mouth. 'Miss Ellie's got her hands full. Poor woman. I do so admire her.'

The scene cut to the bullying JR threatening to commit his wife to a sanatorium, while she was rolling around on the floor surrounded by empty vodka bottles.

'Sue Ellen's tipsy,' said the Queen Mother.

'Mmmm,' agreed the Queen. 'Absolutely stinking.'

'Doesn't her drinking remind you of . . .'

'Mummy!'

They watched the rest of the episode in rapt silence, and then, as the Nine o'clock News came on, the Queen rendered the newscaster mute by activating her remote control.

'I feel I almost know that family,' she remarked.

'Yes,' agreed the Queen Mother, 'so like real life.'

'And so addictive,' added the Queen.

'But I think I prefer "Dynasty",' said the Queen Mother. 'Doesn't that wicked Alexis remind you of our own...'

'*Mummy!*'

The Queen rose, and refilled her mother's glass. 'There's something I'd like to talk to you about,' she said. 'It's been worrying me.'

'Don't fret, dear,' replied the Queen Mother. 'Marriage is not a bed of roses.'

The Queen laughed. 'Oh no, Mummy! It's about Golden Orb.'

'Ah,' exclaimed the Queen Mother, 'now you're talking.'

The two were never happier than when discussing bloodstock. The Queen swiftly explained her dilemma: with Golden Orb proving to be her most outstanding chance of ever winning the Derby, the purchase by Sheik Mahoud al Mahoud of the magnificent Kentucky three-year-old, Desert Prince, loomed as a terrible threat to her ambition. Only that morning her racing manager, Lord Porchester, had a further bulletin of bad news from America: the grey was proving to be even more promising than the first glowing reports had indicated. Some informed bookies had even made Desert Prince the favourite for the great English classic.

'If I don't win the Derby Stakes this year,' announced the Queen petulantly, 'I shall jack it all in!'

'Not *abdicate*,' gasped the Queen Mother in horror.

'No, I shall retire from horse racing, Mother.'

'Oh,' said the Queen Mother, relieved. 'We can't have that, Lilibet.'

'But what am I going to do about Desert Prince?'

'Well, dear,' smiled the Queen Mother with a wicked glint, 'you'll just have to nobble him.'

The old lady looked at her watch. 'Gracious me, Lilibet, it's midnight. Time I was in bed.' She rose stiffly from her chair. 'Still no sign of that husband of yours.'

'Honestly, Mummy! Philip works frightfully hard. Do you know that the day after tomorrow he's off to Swaziland?'

The Queen Mother put on her turquoise hat. 'Saving the white rhino again, no doubt...'

Nature studies

The courtyard of Jesus, the Cambridge College founded in 1496 by Alcock, the Bishop of Ely, rang with the loud and hearty laughter of vigorous young men and the softer, trilling tones of the undergraduate girls, whose hemlines shortened by the day as the temperature rose. It was a gentle, balmy spring afternoon, and just above the windows of his room, in the ancient, rusting guttering, Prince Edward could hear the shrill twittering of nesting swallows. The sky above was a sparkling light blue, the first clear day of the year.

But it was what was going on below that interested Edward: the undergraduates in the billiard-lawned courtyard were gathered in groups of twos and threes. Even the groups of three or more tended soon to break up into smaller units of two, he noticed. It was a curious phenomenon. He wondered what it meant. On closer inspection these social groupings, or couples, proved to be composed of units from either sex. To Edward, their laughter seemed unnaturally loud. There was an uneasy, perhaps slightly aggressive edge to it.

Every so often the swallows would emerge from the guttering and swoop with a dizzying, dangerous dive, skimming low along the close-cropped lawns, and then suddenly soar in a graceful curving arch over the red brick fifteenth-century college walls and away into the blue distance on some mysterious, instinct-impelled errand.

All along the lovely banks of the river Cam the weeping willows were coming into bud. The very air itself seemed freshly uncorked and intoxicating.

In contrast, with the window closed, Edward's small

room was stuffy and cluttered; indeed it resembled nothing so much as the untidy, archetypal university male student's lodging — which, of course, was exactly what it was. The narrow single bed in the corner had clearly been hastily made, for the covering was lumpy and crumpled and a patchwork quilt had been thrown over the whole lot in an evident attempt to disguise the mess, while on top in a haphazard heap had been tossed a curious mix of rugger boots, a tennis racket, track suit and a pair of roller skates.

The only decoration on the whitewashed walls were two large posters: of Dolly Parton and Barbra Streisand, his favourite singers. In contrast to the disorder of the rest of the room, his plain and workmanlike desk was clean and tidy, devoid of any sign of activity; the only object on its leather-topped surface was an enlarged framed photograph of his mother in headscarf and wellies.

'Gosh, I'm bored,' sighed Edward wistfully as he stared down at the surging life in the courtyard below. He wished he could join those carefree students who for the afternoon had abandoned all studies and were simply luxuriating in the joy of their own unfettered youth. But there was something that held the young Prince back. It wasn't just his shyness, it was ...

He knew that never again would he have such an opportunity to forget his background. Later in life, with the accumulation of unasked-for responsibilites, he would be trapped in his role; even his closest friends would be ever mindful of him, not as a person, but as part of an institution. Good grief! All those officials and functionaries, whom it would be his fate to move among, would become foolishly tongue-tied and over-awed, as if he were the Dalai Lama or some living god, rather than the pleasant, average, third son of a family who had done exceedingly well for themselves.

Forever after he would be kept from normal human contact by this barrier of strange beliefs, which had the stamp of centuries as their guarantor of validity. Forever

after he would be treated like some kind of alien. Yet
even here at Cambridge, among the disrespectful
democracy of youth, there was still that invisible barrier
which kept him at arm's length from his fellow students.

Edward sighed deeply for the umpteenth time that
afternoon.

He turned away from the window, and the inviting
vernal scene outside, to see what his detective was up to.
Sergeant Alan Harborough was seated in a dilapidated,
frayed armchair, with an angle-poise lamp shining over
his shoulder, deeply engrossed in a book.

'Lovely afternoon,' said Edward loudly.

The sergeant looked up and blinked. For a moment he
looked startled. It was clear he had been miles away.

'Sorry, Sir. Beg your pardon?'

'Becoming a bit of a bookworm, aren't we, Harborough?'
said the Prince jocularly.

'Ah, well, Sir, the pressures of our studies are quite
onerous this term.'

'Quite so, Sergeant.'

'Especially if we want to do well, Sir. To shine a bit in
our exams, eh?'

'One doesn't want to overdo it, though, does one?'

'Don't worry about my eyes, Sir. Perfect twenty-
twenty vision. At my last reassessment course, I passed
out as the best shot in the Metropolitan police.' The
sergeant laughed, an infectious, friendly laugh, which
turned his ears quite pink. 'Hot-shot Harborough they
called me, Sir!'

'I don't mean that, Sergeant,' Edward's brow
furrowed, making him look almost middle-aged, as it
always did when he was misunderstood. 'I mean, we
mustn't make a spectacle of ourselves.'

'How so, Sir?'

'Bearing in mind what my pater said. Mustn't come
bottom... or top. Drawing attention to oneself is
vulgar.'

As Edward stood there facing him, with a leanness
that was almost self-sacrificing, and his hands firmly

behind his back as if on parade, Sergeant Harborough thought how much he sometimes looked and acted like his autocratic father, and yet at other times, with an almost Jekyll and Hyde abruptness, Edward could bear an almost uncanny resemblance to his mother, especially in the soft, almost female freshness of his complexion. His gentle, retiring nature was really more at home pottering round a farmyard, with a couple of labradors at his feet, than thrust into the more macho role of leader of men and public figure. Sometimes the tough and experienced sergeant felt a great sorrow for his callow charge, and he experienced an urge to put a fatherly arm round his shoulder and give the lonely Prince some warm words of comfort and encouragement. But protocol forever kept him at arm's length.

Instead, the sergeant laid down his book, careful to mark his page. 'Take a look at this, Sir,' he said, proffering a piece of foolscap paper. 'I've made a start.'

'The Colour of History,' read Edward.

'Rather a good title, don't you think, Sir? Alluring, yet faintly provocative.'

'But what does it mean, Harborough?'

'For our next essay, Sir, I thought we might tackle a subject which some people might regard as somewhat controversial.'

'We don't want to get involved in any constitutional brouhaha, Sergeant. You know what the press are like. Those vultures would go scavenging through my dustbins to find something the slightest off-centre.'

'This will be an entirely objective analysis, I assure you, Sir. Weighing the pros and cons evenly. We shall not take sides.' He laughed again, his ears reddening. 'Rather like the monarchy, if you don't mind me saying so.'

'But what's it about, Harborough?'

'The presence of black folk in Britain, Sir. The historical background. Did you know that some authorities assert that the Vikings introduced blackamoors to these shores as early as the 8th century? Brought 'em back from North Africa as slaves.'

'Steady on, Sergeant. This sounds like inflammatory stuff to me.'

'What is more, Sir, there was quite a significant black community in Norfolk in the 10th century.'

'Well, I've never seen any at Sandringham,' said Edward.

'And according to the volume I am perusing at the present moment,' continued the sergeant, 'namely, *The Disunited Kingdom: the anatomy of a forgotten history* by Professor Mauritius Mainwaring...'

'Alright, alright,' said Edward hurriedly. 'I'm sure you'll do a splendid job, Sergeant. Carry on.'

'Thank you, Sir.'

'There is another, more immediate problem.'

'Sir?'

Edward sighed. 'The fact is, Harborough... I feel I'm missing out somehow.'

'Not got anything on tonight, Sir?'

Edward checked his Mickey Mouse watch. 'A bit of rugby practice at six. We've got our last match of the season this Saturday. You're not an oval ball man, are you, Harborough?'

'Snooker's my game, Sir.'

'Not really a character-building sort of game though, is it?'

'I fail to follow your drift, Sir.'

'Well, you know, they do say that the Battle of Waterloo was won on the playing fields of Eton.'

'Quite so, Sir. But some also say that the battle for the industrialization of England was also lost on the playing fields of Eton.'

'You've lost me, Harborough. Of course there are no factories at Eton!'

'No, Sir,' said the sergeant with a polite laugh. 'I think what was meant was that the public school ethos was fine for training young men to go out and run an empire. But it doesn't really create captains of industry or...'

'Oh, honestly, Harborough,' interrupted Edward. 'Sometimes you sound like a bloody Bolshie or something.'

'Sorry, Sir.'

'Fact is, Harbers, I've got a rather personal question to ask you.'

'At your service, Sir.'

'It's about... girls, actually.'

'Fire away, Sir.'

'Well, the fact is, I met a rather nice one while picking up my socks and shirts from the college laundromat. Her name's Letitia. Third year social anthropology.'

'A comely name, if I may so observe.'

'Yes, Sergeant.' Edward paused, flexing his jaw worriedly. 'But what do I do next?'

'You must make your move, Sir.'

'That's all very well, Harborough. But, in my position, it could be rather embarrassing. I mean, what if she doesn't want to...'

'Want to, Sir?' chuckled Harborough. 'I think you will find with your position, as you term it, this will not be an insurmountable problem.'

'How can you be so sure, Alan?'

Harborough, aware that the rare use of his Christian name signalled a call for paternal advice, rose from his chair and beckoned Edward to the window.

'Observe the plucky swallow, Sir. There is not much in life that we cannot learn from this noble and simple little fellow.'

Edward followed the line of his detective's instructing finger.

'After the long flight from Africa the swallow will pick his mate. This is a curious and fascinating process, not unlike that followed by homo sapiens himself. Mr and Mrs Swallow find each other by a number of identifying factors — it being up to Mr Swallow to make all the running. What we find is that the most socially advantaged bird gets the pick of the flock. And who, in anthropomorphic terms, is this lucky fellow? It's Edward Swallow!'

'I see,' said Edward, the possibilities dawning upon him. 'So, as far as Letitia is concerned, I just... swoop?'

Court Circular

Tuesday, April 14th, was another working day for the Windsors. Her Majesty the Queen presented long-service awards at Buckingham Palace to members of the St James's Institute of Voluntary Nursing for Elderly and Disabled Civil Servants. Later that morning Her Majesty received His Excellency Señor Sandillo Marquez Y Jesus Portillo, the new ambassador to the Court of St James from Colombia. In the afternoon Her Majesty was at Lambourne, Berkshire, to open a heated indoor swimming pool for injured race horses.

The Duke of Edinburgh was abroad in Borneo as President of the World Wildlife Fund to further his campaign to save the black-ringed lemur.

HRH, the Prince of Wales, attended a luncheon in the City of Sheffield for the Society of Locomotive Engineers and Firemen. That afternoon the Prince opened an exhibition at the headquarters of the Institute of Heating and Ventilation Engineers. That evening he presided over the annual cocktail party of the Institute of Cost Management Accountants, before attending a performance of Donizetti's *Lucia di Lammermoor* at Covent Garden in his role as Patron of Royal Opera House.

HRH, the Princess of Wales, visited a refuge for battered wives in Chiswick in the morning, and that afternoon opened a fully automated Twiglet factory. The Princess was unable to accompany the Prince of Wales to the opera that night due to a headache.

HRH, the Princess Anne, spent the morning inspecting an open prison in Glasgow for first-time young offenders. In the afternoon the Princess attended the Scottish Reel Dancing Championships at Pitlochry.

Princess Michael of Kent had a private engagement. She opened a Mr Beefy along the M25, the first in a new chain of cheap hamburger take-away shops.

That night the Queen was to be found relaxing in her apartment at Buckingham Palace, taking an Amontillado sherry with Prince Andrew and her daughter-in-law Sarah, while she bathed her aching feet in a newly-acquired plastic personal foot jacuzzi.

'Gosh,' said Sarah sympathetically, 'I'd no idea. Being Royal is frightfully hard work, isn't it?'

'Hard, my dear?' said the Queen gently. '*That* is what we are paid for.'

Playmates at the Palace

'He didn't! Oh no, Carrots, kippers on the manifold!'

'Yah. And what's more, Hamster, rubber johnnies over the exhaust.'

'What a hoot!'

'Yah. And when they drove-off the rj blew up and shot off like a rocket — bbllzzzzzzzzzz...'

'Oh stop it, Carrots,' cried Diana, shrieking with laughter. 'My tummy hurts.'

'And you ought to have seen Lady Dowsett's face!'

'Critical!'

'Yah, shrieksville. And you should have seen Mungo, Hamster, he was on absolute top form. He shinned up a guy rope, with a bottle of champoo in hand, toasted the Queen from the top, and then tobogganed down the marquee on his botty and landed in the goldfish pond.'

'Oh no!'

'Oh yes. And guess what Mungo was clutching in his hairy mitt when he emerged triumphant?'

'Tell me! Tell me!'

'The bottle of Bollinger!'

The two girls collapsed back with a final fit of helpless giggles. Diana wiped away the tears of laughter.

'Oh, Carrots, what a scream.'

It had been another gruelling week for the Princess of Wales. Her schedule as usual had been rather frantic: her engagements had included the opening of a leisure centre in Leicester, a fact-finding mission to the north-east traffic division of the Metropolitan Police, a tour round the Llandudno DIY and Gardening Centre, and had culminated in a harrowing visit to an East London drugs rehabilitation clinic.

Diana regarded her old friend fondly. 'Good to have you aboard, Carrots,' she said.

Sarah had certainly livened things up of late. They were reclining on the pink and beige striped Albrizzi sofa, in stockinged feet, both with one leg tucked up comfortably underneath them. Her effervescent mood matched the optimistic lemony-yellow Dudley Poplak walls. It had been yonks since such carefree girlish laughter had echoed round the Princess's modern, designer drawing-room.

Diana felt she had every reason to be pleased with herself; it had been quite a coup, she mused, shoe-horning her childhood chum into the firm. She was desperately fond of Andrew, indeed she could play pranks with her hearty brother-in-law that she could never share with the older and more serious Charles. Andrew, it is true, had taken it a bit too far on occasion — like the time he'd goosed her in public. And with the lad consorting with females of the laxest possible morals, it had been imperative to get him matched. Thus by advancing Sarah's cause, she had ensured herself a playmate in the palace.

This was the first time the footmen at Kensington Palace had heard these peals of girlish laughter ricochet round the opulent marble corridors and tapestry-clad walls. It was a refreshing change from the hushed asides and discreet murmurings of the old courtiers.

Had it been up to them, without secretaries and equerries to remind them of appointments, the girls would have gone on chattering and gossiping all day. They found in each other an endless source of amusement.

'And did you hear about Annabel?'

Diana's eyes widened. 'No! What?'

'You mean... you don't know about Peregrine?'

'I thought Annabel was stepping out with Marcus.'

'God no, Hamster. Ancient history. That pathetic item was yonks ago.'

'But I never get any news about our lot these days.'

'Well...' Sarah lowered her voice conspiratorially, 'Annabel's been a naughty girl.'

'Tell, tell!'

'Some people think Bel's got anorexia.'

'Poor girl.'

'No, no, Hamster. The brutal fact is that Bel has been shagged to a thin whisker.'

Diana put her hand over her mouth. 'Not coiting?'

'Yah. Imagine bonking Peregrine. All those shag spots...'

'Errgh!'

The Princesses screamed with helpless laughter.

Their hilarity was abruptly interrupted by a sharp knocking on the floor from below. The insistent rapping halted their laughter. The two girls stared at each other in amazement.

'The witch!' exclaimed Diana.

'But how on earth did she manage that?' whispered Sarah. 'The ceilings are eighteen feet high!'

'Probably summoned the butler...'

'And climbed on his shoulders...'

'Imagine — a Princess banging on the ceiling with her broomstick.'

'The witch!'

They gave out a shout of laughter, which both attempted to stifle, without success.

A floor below, the forthright Princess Michael of Kent was getting over her irritation. Indeed she had almost regained that regal composure which she deployed so effectively in front of servants and the public.

'Thank you, Adams,' she said with a dismissive gesture. 'And you may take that broom with you. I am sure we will not be requiring it again.'

Princess Marie-Christine Anne Agnes Hedwig Ida von Reibnitz — born in Karlsbad, Bohemia — who stood six foot in her bare stockings, looked particularly imposing today in her Arnaldo Caraciolo creation in fuchsia pink,

with wing-like padded shoulders, like an American
football player. No wonder some of the family called her
'Our Val' after the blonde, powerfully-built Valkyries of
Norse mythology.

The phone rang.

It was her private secretary, who was entrusted with
finding worthwhile engagements where a regal presence
was required. The Princess and her husband, Prince
Michael of Kent, were not on the Civil List, so were
always eager to accept a free meal with plenty of
publicity, for they did not receive a penny from the
government.

'The opening of a nightclub? I don't think the Queen
would wear that. Oh... that much for charity, and
expenses? Mmmmm. Perhaps we could consider it.'

A curious dull banging at the window interrupted her
thoughts.

'Is it a respectable venue? Actually on the river? Oh, I
think we could see our way to...'

The banging on the window became more insistent.
'Hang on...'

Princess Michael turned to see, knocking against the
antique window pane, dangling on a hook from a fishing
line, an old, withered, mud-encrusted army boot.

She slammed down the telephone, colour rising to her
cheeks once more. 'Those ridiculous girls. Children!'

By the time Prince Charles got home from his private
evening engagement with the Hakomi Group, Diana
was already curled up in their seventeenth-century
French four-poster bed in her cream silk Janet Reger
nightgown. She was reading *Pandora's Box: a study of the
influence of soap opera upon the teenage mind — role model or role
confusion?*

In the gentle magenta glow cast by the bedside lamp,
the antique lace drapes enclosing the four-poster took on
a fairy-tale hue. Prince Charles, as ever, was caught
unawares, quite taken aback, as if seeing his wife for the
first time, enchanted by her impossible perfection. With

her golden locks spread upon the ivory-coloured linen pillow, Charles could not help but think of Sleeping Beauty.

The Prince, carried away by the magic of the moment and the faintest aroma of rose-petal pot-pourri on her table, perched like a beseeching suitor upon the edge of the bed.

'When the heart is right,' he whispered, 'for and against are forgotten.'

Diana snapped her book shut. 'You're talking riddles again, Charles. No wonder your father thinks you're a bit batty.'

'Oh,' said Charles, woken from his reverie. 'I thought that was rather beautiful. These are the words of Chuang Tsu.'

Diana rolled her eyes upwards towards the embroidered canopy.

'No, really, darling, it's terribly interesting,' continued Charles. 'Hakomi is a mind and body therapy.'

'Sounds like a Japanese microwave manufacturer to me,' replied Diana impatiently.

Charles shook his head earnestly. 'It's all about mindfulness. Unity. Non-violence. Organicity,' he said, having picked up all these phrases at the Hakomi Therapy Workshop at the Kensington home of the Countess of Midlothian. 'Absolutely fascinating business. It delves into the whole area of mind and body holism.'

'Quite honestly, Charles, I think microwaves have more to offer mankind.'

'Well, darling, I suppose it is a sort of spiritual microwave. Sort of jiggling around the molecules of the mind, and providing warm nourishment for the soul,' he said, searching through the pocket of his dinner jacket till he found a small pamphlet. 'Let me read this to you, darling.'

Diana stifled a yawn and closed her eyes.

Charles held the leaflet close to him, as he read out the Hakomi Method philosophy.

'Using present-centred, mindful awareness to shed light on these organizing beliefs and the childhood events that shaped them, we re-evaluate those parts of our belief system which limit us, developing and incorporating alternative choices and more satisfying options. By going slowly and gently, being non-violent and protecting the spirit, an atmosphere of safety evolves, where defences can be examined and willingly yielded, rather than confronted and overpowered.'

Diana opened her eyes. 'In other words, as I've always thought, you're hung up on your nanny.'

'Now listen to this bit,' said Charles, continuing to read. 'We access and utilize special states of consciousness (ie, "mindfulness" and "the child") probing gently beneath our everyday patterns of habit and automatic response, to those richly non-verbal levels where basic beliefs organize and direct our quality of experience...'

'And that, dear,' interrupted Diana, 'is why you're still stuck in the nursery.'

'Nonsense, Diana.'

'OK, bread and butter pudding?'

'Yes, well, alright, I admit I still have a partiality for bread and butter pudding.'

'Exactly! And tell me this — what's your favourite room in Buckingham Palace?'

Trapped, Charles stammered, 'Um, er, ah...'

'You see!' exclaimed Diana triumphantly. 'The nursery!'

'Well, I suppose in a sense, that's what we are trying to work through,' said Charles in a conciliatory tone. 'You see, Hakomi is a Hopi Indian word meaning "How do you stand in relation to these many realms?" Which is their way of saying "Who are you?"'

Diana stared at her husband in irritated disbelief. It was late, and there was a pressing subject which Diana wished to raise. She came to the point.

'Enough of that, Charles. The fact is that I've had some trouble today with 'Er in the size eight shoes.'

'Oh lawd,' murmured Charles. 'No more bad vibes.'

'Not bad,' said Diana. 'It's becoming a Jacobean hassle. One can't make a squeak without 'Er Downstairs kicking up a fuss.'

'I know our Czechoslovakian cousin can be tricky, darling, but one must try to be understanding. Remember what Tsu said — "When the heart's right, for and against are forgotten".'

'I see,' said Diana, suddenly flaring. 'Whose side are you on?'

'It's not a matter of sides...'

'Oh no?' cried Diana angrily. 'I want to know — who are you for and who are you against?'

'When your heart is,' Charles began to quote.

'Stop it,' yelled Diana furiously. 'Come off the fence, Your Highness!'

There was a sharp banging on the floor below.

'Oh crikey, now we've done it,' mumbled Charles, with a worried expression. 'I suppose I'd better go down and placate that woman.'

As he made for the door Diana fired another salvo at the departing figure.

'Oh, and one last thing, Your Royal Highness,' she said with a wicked giggle, 'if you don't have a showdown with Battleship Reibnitz tonight, you can expect to find the door of the Bedchamber closed on your return.'

Charles, relieved that his wife's humour had returned, chuckled to himself, though as he set out down the dimly-lit corridor he was surprised to hear a metallic click behind him as the door of the inner sanctum was firmly bolted.

Charles never did have his meeting with Princess Michael. The reason was terribly simple. He got lost.

An hour later the Prince of Wales was still forlornly wandering around the reconstructed Wren palace, now darkened and hushed, with only the old street-lamps from the adjacent Millionaire's Row to cast a dim, eerie light on his midnight wanderings. The fact was that the

Prince did not know the geography of his own palace. He
had already paced several miles of dark corridor. An
Englishman's home is his castle, mused Charles ruefully,
but when one has a castle, one does not have a home.

Built in 1605, in the then village of Kensington, the
palace had been acquired by William of Orange. Sir
Christopher Wren had aggrandized the red-brick
building to its present pleasing and harmonious
proportions. But it was decidedly sizeable. And now
Charles was hopelessly lost. He simply couldn't find his
way to the Kents' apartment.

Half an hour previously Charles had missed his one
opportunity of being pointed in the right direction. He
had been wandering down yet another portrait-hung
corridor, outside the Gloucesters' rooms, when he came
across a shadowy, recumbent figure slumped on a chair.
There was the gentle, regular sound of a man in deep,
contented sleep. But as Charles tried to tip-toe pass the
duty policeman, the slumbering figure woke with a start.

'Who goes there?'

'Shhh,' whispered Charles. 'Only me.'

The sergeant snapped to attention, struggling to
button up his uniform.

'Everything alright, Sir?'

'Splendid,' replied Charles automatically.

Suddenly he felt absurdly unregal. Here he was in his
own home, hopelessly lost, meandering the corridors
after midnight in a dinner jacket and a pair of
monogrammed slippers.

'Absolutely splendid,' repeated Charles, with no
conviction whatsoever. 'How are your charges, tonight,
Sergeant? All well? All tucked up?'

'Yes, Sir. Lights out at nine thirty, Sir.'

'Excellent. Back to sleep, Sergeant. Must be on my
way.'

Charles, with due authority, and without the faintest
idea of where he was going, turned left. Behind, he heard
a diplomatic cough.

'Scuse me, Sir,' called the sergeant.

'It's alright, Sergeant,' replied Charles testily, 'I know where I'm going.'

He opened the door in front of him. Instantly the darkened room erupted with the alarmingly loud barking, howling and yapping of assorted labradors, dobermann pinschers and dachshunds. He had entered the Kensington Palace dog room. Appalled, Charles quickly closed the door and rapidly retraced his steps past the astonished sergeant.

Charles glanced at his watch; it was one o'clock. Grief. The Kents would be asleep by now anyway. Mission unaccomplished, he resolved to brave the certainty of his wife's displeasure and headed back to his own room. However, when he arrived there, the door was firmly closed and unyielding to his muted knock.

Not daring to awaken anyone, Charles retreated.

'Hell's bells,' he muttered angrily, as he set out for his Aunt Margaret's apartment.

At her door, he paused. He could hear the sleazy trumpet of Miles Davis and the sound of muffled voices and clinking glasses.

'Shizer!'

Finally giving way to despair and exhaustion Charles sought the refuge of the Cupola Room. Once it had been the main reception hall of the palace. Now, open to the public by day, it was a mere mausoleum. Wearily Charles sank into a George III giltwood bergère. Oy vey!

Charles woke from an uncomfortable and troubled sleep. He was still slumped in the Georgian armchair. He felt stiff in every joint, and his old polo injury was nagging him. A grey, tentative dawn was beginning to break over Kensington Park Gardens. He realized he had been woken by the half-hearted chatter of birds, which could not yet be called a full dawn chorus. In the ethereal half-light he could make out the elegant outlines of Hawkmoor's Orangery. He felt strange, bodiless, quite detached.

Suddenly, he sensed that he was not alone in the room.
He felt as if — as always — someone was watching him,
observing him. He turned round. Arrayed along the
walls stood a sentinel line of shadowy figures dressed in
their court finery. They were the costumed models of his
royal predecessors. Charles shivered. Sometimes he felt
like one of those overdressed dummies, a museum piece,
something to be gawped at; and doubtless one day many
of his own collection of forty-four military uniforms
would take their place in historical exhibitions... and
what had he, the twenty-first English Prince of Wales,
Baron Renfrew, Duke of Cornwall and Lord of the Isles,
what had he ever done?

The fact was that he had never really been allowed to
do anything. Oh yes, he'd been encouraged to pilot
aeroplanes, jump out of the damn things, captain ships,
dive to the bottom of the ocean, ski, play polo, and
indulge in all those hairy-chested pursuits so admired by
his father. But what had he ever, actually, achieved?
Well, in another five hours he was due to open yet
another monument to capitalism, to meet the self-
important captains of industry, and to exchange
meaningless platitudes with their lickspittle wage-slaves.

God, any man in this country of similar age, education,
experience and intelligence would have risen to senior
positions of power in their chosen fields by this time.
And where was he? Still waiting in the wings.

He looked up at the ornately decorated ceiling. A
public fantasy, that's what he was. An object around
which people wove their dreams and hopes and
expectations. He was just a passive partner in this
curious process: he was born to this; it was God's will, he
supposed.

All the same, when you thought about it, there was
really nothing for a Prince of Wales to do, but wait, and
wait, and for how long? Quite likely, another twenty-
five years. Huh. He'd be well into his sixties. And what
sort of country would it be by then, and what chance
would he have to change anything for the good? He'd

never minded the idea of being a figurehead: but he'd wanted to project a new and vigorously modern image for his beloved Britain. But instead it looked as if they'd have an arthritic old grandfather at the helm.

Above, the ingeniously-designed cupola formed a *trompe-l'oeil*; the dome appeared to stretch timelessly towards the sky, distant, intangible, phantasmagorical, like his future.

The view from on high

Two miles east and two hours later the sun had risen above the tree tops of Buckingham Palace Gardens, affording Ryder St Bartholomew a privileged view of its secret forty acres. St Bartholomew adjusted the focus of his powerful Zeigard hunting telescope that stood on its tripod by the large window permanently trained on that protected haven.

At the far end of the garden there was a sudden flurry of wildfowl on the lake. St Bartholomew increased the magnification: now he could see the mallard, pintails and Canada geese taking off from the lake in alarm. What had disturbed them? Ah. From behind the exotic shrubbery at the water's edge, led by a liveried footman, came an orderly, bustling line of six barrel-like little dogs.

St Bartholomew checked his watch: it was 09.30 hours precisely. Bang on time.

The view from the twenty-third floor of the Park Lane Hilton served his purpose to perfection. Although its panoramic window afforded one of the most breath-taking views of the city, his field of interest was very narrow: it was centred on those forty pampered acres below him. Despite the bright spring day, the curtains were drawn, and only the fat snout of his Zeigard lens poked out ominously through the drapes.

He had lived here for the past two months, but the darkened room revealed nothing. There was no personal indication or clues as to the background, business or character of the 6-foot 3-inch, well-set figure in the tailored mohair Huntsman suit. Chambermaids and waiters had been expressly forbidden to enter the private suite, the most expensive the hotel had to offer. Only Mr

St Bartholomew's personal assistants were permitted access, and they came and went mysteriously at all hours of the day and night.

St Bartholomew panned the telescope, sweeping past the Waterloo Vase and the armless nineteenth-century Aphrodite, and out of a side entrance he saw, stepping smartly, a squad of royal gardeners.

It was 09.40. Like clockwork.

There was a rap on the door, three quick knocks followed by two slow; it was a pre-arranged code. The door opened, but St Bartholomew remained hunched over the telescope, intent on his quarry.

'Everything alright?' said the voice behind him.

'Bloody right,' drawled St Bartholomew. 'Their schedule's as tight as a Pom's arse.'

Life in a vacuum

One hour later, and 35 miles due west, the red Wessex helicopter of the Queen's flight alighted on the tarmac forecourt of the new Weston Home Appliance and Electrical Goods factory. Right on schedule. The Prince of Wales had spent the twenty-minute flight from the gardens of Kensington Palace in a state of inner turmoil. Not once had Diana glanced at him. She had spent the entire journey peering down in unnatural interest at the grey suburbs below. Charles, exhausted after his uncomfortable night, longed to lean across and utter the emollient words which would end this ridiculous hostility. But the roar of the Rolls Royce engines made any such gesture impossible. And no sooner were they out of the aircraft than the Royal couple were surrounded by the official welcoming party. Once again they were separated and the property of other people.

'Where are we?' whispered Charles to his equerry, Sir Robert Lander, as the line of alarmingly large dignitaries loomed before him. 'It's been a rough night.'

'Weston Home Appliances, Sir.'

'Not trusses and corsets again,' groaned Charles.

'No, Sir. Vacuums.'

Already the first pudgy hand was extending towards him.

'Welcome to Weston's, Highness,' said the chief executive nervously.

'Your Royal Highness,' whispered Sir Robert discreetly in his ear.

'So,' said Charles, looking up at the hideous new concrete, glass and plastic factory. 'We're Hoovering for Britain, eh?'

'Oh no, Your Royal Highness,' said the chief executive aghast. 'That's our rivals. This is Weston's UK PLC, Your Royal Highness.'

'Aha,' said Charles with a characteristic contortion of his mouth. 'So we're Westoning for Britain, eh!'

Covering his nervousness, the chief executive laughed overheartily. Hearing this merriment from the direction of the Royal entourage, the rest of the long line of executives began to heave with sycophantic laughter, too, though not one of them had heard the joke.

Following the rigid dictates of protocol, Diana was three paces behind, rather like a good daughter of Islam. Hearing this explosion of laughter she turned to the managing director.

'What was that?'

'A rather good joke, Ma'am,' replied the managing director, grateful for something to say. 'Cracked by the Prince, actually.'

'I missed it. Tell me again.'

'Oh, um, er, er... have you seen our new recyclo-turf?'

Diana's professionalism, despite her lingering ill-humour with her husband, came to the fore; she displayed an intense interest in the durability, practicability and cost-effectiveness of what she really considered to be the most unutterably vile fake grass. She listened in apparently rapt silence as the managing director, prompted by his butterflies, gave an eloquent and lyrical hymn of praise to the qualities of recyclo-turf.

'And it doesn't even need watering,' observed Diana when he had finished. She was astonished to see him dissolve in a fit of uncontrollable laughter, which in turn rippled back down the line of executives.

Charles, still three paces ahead, turned to the chief executive. 'What's the joke?'

'One cracked by the Princess,' said the chief executive, between gasps of giggles. 'A rather good one, actually, Your Royal Highness.'

'Oh, I missed it,' said Charles, wishing he could have heard it from her own lips. 'Do tell.'

'Oh, er, um ... rather interesting what you're walking on, actually. Dog resistant recyclo-turf, Your Royal Highness.'

Sir Robert Lander, ever watchful for the transgressions of protocol, stepped forward again. Into the confused businessman's ear he whispered the following invaluable advice: 'You are permitted to use "Sir" from now on.'

'Thank you, Sir,' said the flustered executive.

'Not to me,' hissed Sir Robert impatiently. 'The Prince of Wales.'

By now they were at the entrance to the factory floor. The Royal party were greeted by a familiar smell. Fresh paint.

Charles felt in the pocket of his double-breasted pin-striped suit and found the tiny phial of homeopathic pills. After years of visiting schools, hospitals, factories, ships, airports — indeed, entire towns — which had been given a new coat of paint just for his benefit, the Prince had developed a rather discomforting allergy. It brought on an embarrassing fit of sneezing. Charles discreetly manoeuvred the pill into his mouth.

So thorough was this tarting-up process for royal visits that Charles had once been under the impression that the entire world — outside his family's own residences — was perpetually and forever freshly painted. It was only recently, making surprise private forays into inner city areas, that he had discovered the existence of a curious manifestation of local feeling: graffiti. Always on public visits such signs of life had been expunged.

Already Charles was in front of yet one more piece of incomprehensible machinery that pressed, clamped and wheezed before spitting out another element of the vacuum cleaner. Above the din Charles shouted to the machine minder: 'Enjoy your job?'

'Very well, thank you, Sir,' shouted back the deafened worker.

'Jolly good,' exclaimed Charles, moving on.

He now stood before a group of women attaching rubber bands around the vacuum bags.

'How long have you worked here?' asked Charles.

The girls giggled.

'Three weeks,' said one.

'That's right,' said another. 'Three weeks.'

'And you?' Charles asked the third.

She looked back at the distinguished visitor, puzzled. 'Three weeks,' she said. 'That's how long the factory's been open.'

'Jolly good,' said Charles, as the Royal party moved along the assembly line. He glanced back, trying to catch his wife's eye. But she was being instructed on the problems of blocked bags.

'Our new product, the SY45LT, has a two pound per square inch suction capacity to facilitate the greater disposal of unwanted matter from modern day shagpile carpet,' droned the Weston's assistant technical designer. 'We now have an operative capacity demonstration. Terry will crumble a named-brand digestive biscuit upon three types of domestic carpeting. First sample, being deep pile, the second medium pile, and the third — if you will excuse me, Ma'am — quite frankly, bald . . .'

Diana sneaked a look over towards her husband. But Charles, now having reached the end of the line, was forced to admire the finished product.

'Jolly interesting,' said Charles, distractedly. 'It sucks here, does it?'

He caught his wife's eyes. Was that the hint of a smile?

'Proud of your work, are you?' said Charles, addressing the assembled sales force, all of whom were sporting shiny polyester suits and uniformly drastic haircuts for this special occasion.

The head salesman cleared his throat, stepped forward, and delivered the speech he had been practising on his wife and children for days.

'We build a hundred and twenty-one machines a day which on a pro rata basis means a weekly output of seven hundred and twenty-six a week which constitutes two point six seven per cent of the home market but when you consider the Middle East market with particular reference to the Omanis, who as a people are particularly keen on domestic hygiene, our product has achieved a market dominance...'

Charles's attention drifted to the woman, tall, slender, and now so self-possessed, who was attracting more attention and excitement in his wake. Workers had left their post to catch a glimpse of her. Fondly he thought, I never attract that kind of devotion. He was proud of his wife. She was so totally a star.

Momentarily their glances met. Charles took in, afresh, those startlingly untroubled azure blue eyes, the glowing dewy complexion, the luxuriant blonde hair and above all the fresh natural radiance of her smile. Diana, as ever, made his heart beat just a little faster.

'Which, on an annual basis, means we are moving to the consumer in excess of thirty-five thousand units per annum which in turnover constitutes a not unhealthy total, if I might blow our trumpet in your ear, Sir of...'

'A great service to mankind,' said Charles.

'Yes, indeed, Sir,' said the salesman, utterly perplexed.

Twiddling round the signet ring on his little finger of his left hand, Charles continued: 'What you are helping to do is to alleviate mankind from base necessity — or should I say womankind...'

The party, confused, chortled.

'It's freed people from the trivial diurnal treadmill of banal chores, in a sense liberating them for the higher, indeed transcendental, aim of enlightenment and self-knowledge.'

The sales force stared at their future king, wide-eyed. Swiftly Sir Robert Lander moved in.

'Our schedule, Sir...'

'Ah, yes,' said Charles, 'the tyranny of our time-table. We must continue this fascinating conversation at another time.'

By now Diana and her entourage had also reached the

end of the assembly line. The Royal visitors were ushered on to a podium in the corner of the warehouse.

'Wasn't that an absolutely fascinating tour?' whispered Charles to Diana, with a half-smile upon his lips. Had she forgiven him?

Diana looked at him full in the face. 'Yes, darling,' she whispered back. 'So worthwhile.'

Thank goodness. Forgiven!

All they had to endure before being alone again was a speech from the chairman and, according to the written time-table prepared for Charles by his dutiful equerry, an 'unexpected' presentation.

'Unaccustomed as I am to addressing such distinguished, and charming, personages...' began the portly chairman in those measured and pompous tones that indicated to Charles the infallible signs of a verbose man whose well-worn clichés and self-satisfied platitudes would run a full ten minutes over schedule.

Charles sneaked a sly, sideways glance at the Princess of Wales.

'... and it is my great and inestimable pleasure on this happy and honoured occasion to welcome for the blessing of this exciting, and dare I say, vital contribution to British national industrial resurgence...'

Diana smiled wickedly back.

'... and so in conclusion — and I apologize for taking up these precious minutes of your valuable time — it gives me tremendous pleasure to announce a small surprise. Please accept with our humble gratitude the most advanced model off our production line...'

Diana surreptitiously slid her hand under the tail of Charles's jacket.

'... the Deluxe slim-line Weston Astro-Turbo Carpet Bug.'

Diana's gentle caress became a saucy tweak.

Suddenly, everyone froze!

The repeated rapid-fire whine even stopped the chairman in mid-platitude. There was mayhem on the platform as detectives scrambled to action stations to head off a possible assassination attempt. The secret servicemen swung their guns towards this threatening sound. The chairman was spreadeagled on the floor, his head covered. Dignitaries ducked.

Charles, moving swiftly with great presence of mind, shielded his wife with his own body.

All this frenzy, however, proved to be unnecessary. For when the six armed bodyguards had leapt upon the man, dressed in a Weston boilersuit, the offending weapon proved to be no more lethal than a Nikon 180mm automatic-drive camera.

The wildly gesticulating man was carted off, shouting: 'Carlo, aiuto! Help! Sono solo Rinaldo.'

'Don't worry, m'dear,' said Charles, hugging his shaking wife. 'It's only that bloody paparazzo.'

'I do hope they won't hurt him, though,' she said, looking up admiringly at her brave, resolute husband.

'Don't worry about that, darling. Our Mr Rinaldo always lands on his feet. I think you'll find those photographs are quite valuable.'

'Oh,' said Diana, 'why's that, darling?'

'Because it's good publicity for their firm,' Charles paused and smiled thoughtfully, before adding sotto voce — 'and, I suppose, for ours, too.'

Ryder in the dark

In the darkened suite on the twenty-third floor of the Park Lane Hilton, Ryder St Bartholomew got straight down to business with the Hon Henry Fairlie, layabout son of a Shropshire baronet, whom he had employed to inveigle his way into English society.

'Well, son, did that sheila bite?'

'Yes, Barty. Good news, old bean,' said the Hon Henry, trotting out the language of the public school, circa 1930. 'Absolutely splendid news in that direction, old boy.'

'Spit it out, son,' said Barty, who had not built up his multi-million pound Australian conglomerate by wasting time with pleasantries.

The Hon Henry, disconcerted by the gloom and unable to see the face of his boss across the room, switched on the light. St Bartholomew, who in his native Sydney had never been photographed in the daylight, had a quite preternaturally pale face. The mouth was fleshy and cruel and a sardonic smile seemed to play across it. But that was an illusion; it was perpetually stuck in that expression due to a small scar across the right hand side of his lips.

'Turn off that bleeding light, Fairlie,' snapped Bartholomew, showing that electric anger so well known to his employees — which had led to rumours he had once killed a man, over a business deal in Singapore, in his mysterious early days.

The Hon Henry obeyed with alacrity. Henry, whose family had been ennobled on the battlefield of Agincourt, was unused to work; indeed he was the first generation of Fairlies to attempt it.

'Well, my son,' said Barty with a return of that genial

good humour which could come back as suddenly as it disappeared, 'lay the good news on me.'

'I've got her. Princess Michael has agreed to do the opening — for £3,000.'

'Jeez — good work. Two grand cheaper than we hoped,' said St Bartholomew excitedly. 'That great big beautiful blonde. Jeez, I love 'er.'

Henry smiled. It had been a good day's work, for in fact Princess Michael of Kent had agreed to be guest of honour at the unveiling of Barty's £2-million floating casino, The Busted Flush, for £2,500. Henry had pocketed the difference. He was learning fast.

'Too bad we couldn't get Andrew,' said Henry.

'No worries. I've got a little chequette in the safe, sitting there like a ticking time-bomb. It's just a matter of knowing when to detonate it.' St Bartholomew rubbed his meaty stevedore's hands together in gleeful anticipation. 'It's a real beaut — made out to a certain dubious dame by the name of Ilaria Pucci and signed with the most handsome flourish, by His Royal Bloody Highness.'

'God,' said Henry nervously. 'That's dynamite. What are you going to do with it?'

'Don't you worry your aristocratic head about that, son.'

Through the gloom Henry saw his scarred mouth twitch, whether in a grimace or a smile he could not tell.

'I've got big plans, boy. The big one...'

Moonlight on the Stones

All that morning the Wiltshire police had been busy devising a plan to divert traffic from the A303. The Ancient Monuments people had been instructed to close Stonehenge to the public for that day. They, like the county police, were given no reason. A team of county council workers were drafted in to clear the neolithic site of litter, to paint the waste bins and attempt to erase some of the graffiti on those mysterious monoliths. Staff from the Parks and Recreational Department were given the task of tending to the grass within that magic stone circle. And over a hillock nearby, deployed across the Salisbury Plain, was a platoon of the Royal Green Jackets in full battle-dress, backed up by armoured personnel carriers. They too did not know the reason for this military manoeuvre: the order had come from on high.

Quite simply, Prince Andrew, blissfully unaware of the dark threat hanging over him, had dreamed up a spontaneous treat for his adored wife.

A picnic. At Stonehenge. Under the moonlight!

Damn romantic, he thought. The girl would appreciate that.

He had casually mentioned this notion in passing to his aide-de-camp, Major Clutterbuck, of the Blues and Royals, asking him to arrange a hamper from Fortnum and Masons. The Prince, with his delightful naivety, had been unaware of the military-style campaign of preparation which went into such chivalrous gestures.

'Look, Clutters, don't want to cause any bother,' he had said. 'I'll borrow the chopper and fly the Princess there myself. It'll just be the two of us.' Andrew winked. 'A moonlight dinner à deux. The wife's a romantic. You know, women.'

101

Thus it was, as the reddening sun dipped over the Wiltshire hills, the Prince's Sea King helicopter hovered over the now immaculate Stonehenge, and made a professionally sweet landing on the nearby freshly-mown grass.

'How lucky to have this all to ourselves, darling!' exclaimed Sarah in delight, as the soft twilight played upon those ancient granite slabs that had seen so much over the centuries.

With a gallant flourish Andrew laid down the Black Watch Tartan rug, and spread out before his delighted Princess's eyes the delectable feast from the carefully prepared hamper: terrine de fois gras, a dozen truffles from the foothills of Piedmont, a saddle of hare flown down from Balmoral, an exotic variety of salads, a box of Pont l'Evêque cheese, and an earthenware pot of rich-veined Stilton, a tarte aux frambroises, with a bottle of Château Gruaud Larose and a chilled bottle of Pouilly Fuisse. Finally Andrew produced from the wicker basket an icy-cold bottle of Bollinger champagne.

'Darling, how clever!' gasped Sarah in amazement. 'How did you do it?'

'It was nothing, my heart,' replied Andrew modestly, taking her hand gently and there planting the most delicate of kisses.

'A feast fit for a king,' said Sarah.

'Steady on, old girl,' said Andrew. 'Heaven forbid.'

As the young couple lingered over this sumptuous banquet, lit by the soft caresses of the rising moon, Sarah gradually became conscious of the presence of at least half a dozen shadowy secret servicemen lurking silently behind the great stones. Not wishing to destroy the magic of this idyllic moment, she forebore to mention such a mundane detail. Yet, once this unforgettable repast was over and they were again airborne, she couldn't help noticing the headlights of thousands of cars tail-backed over the straight roads of the plain.

'Thank heavens we flew, darling,' she remarked. 'There's a horrendous traffic jam down there.'

'That's odd,' replied Andrew, banking his helicopter sharply to the right. 'Over on the port side there appears to be a bloody great army manoeuvre. Look, there's even a troop of tanks.' He paused thoughtfully. 'Wonder what the hell can be going on?'

A sniff of scandal

Princess Michael's green Jaguar purred through London's early evening traffic. It picked up speed down Park Lane, where to the left Princess Michael spotted a line of men in dinner-jackets and women in ball gowns and tiaras entering the Dorchester Hotel. Momentarily she wondered whether she should instead have accepted the invitation to the 'Fashion for Africa' charity evening. They flashed past the exclusive Les Ambassadeurs Club, sped down Constitution Hill, and there on the right was Buckingham Palace itself, with the Royal standard fluttering in the evening breeze. The lights in the Royal apartments were on, she noticed. Another evening at home. They headed down Bird Cage Walk, past Winston Churchill's squat, belligerent statue, and now, with the Houses of Parliament and Big Ben in sight, Princess Michael instructed: 'Turn the lights on, John.'

The chauffeur, baffled, switched on the headlights' full beam.

'No, not the headlights, dolt,' she said with the slight Austro-Hungarian inflection which she had adopted in recent years. 'The internal lights.'

Princess Michael, Marie-Christine Anne Agnes Hedgwig Ida von Reibnitz, was a woman who liked to be noticed. The courtesy lights inside the Jaguar displayed the Princess like a jewel in a glass case. She wore an electric royal blue taffeta gown, with a plunging neckline, allowing the Windsor heirloom diamond and sapphire necklace to show off to its best advantage against her discreet tan on that extraordinarily elegant neck, which was so long that it had been known to accommodate eight rows of pearls. Her blonded tresses were swept up imperiously, revealing the full extent of her haughty and intelligent brow. She inclined her head graciously, both to the left and right, to acknowledge the curious stares of passing Japanese tourists.

The Jaguar pulled up opposite the Westminster Pier, where a claret-coloured canopy with gold lettering announced: THE BUSTED FLUSH, *Riverboat Casino*.

The small crowd which had been attracted by the crush of press photographers at the entrance gave a ragged cheer as the Princess emerged. There to greet her, at the steps of the red-carpeted gangplank, was the egregious Honourable Fairlie. On the bridge of the expensively-restored Mississippi paddle-boat, Ryder St Bartholomew, dressed as a river captain, spied the Princess's arrival with a thin, sardonic smile of pleasure. He had spent £135,000 on this goddam party. It was well-spent, but he was going to squeeze it for every last drop of blood, royal or not. He pulled the steam whistle, the signal for the sixteen trumpeters on the foredeck to herald his glittering guest of honour.

Below decks the party was already swinging. Not for a decade had London seen such a star-studded, lavish extravaganza. Real jungle creeper hung from the timbered ceiling, tropical butterflies alighted on the guests' heads, and above the excited babble could be heard the lulling whirr of humming-birds and the shrill cries of parakeets.

'Jesus, Jerry, this fountain's actually real champagne,' exclaimed the delighted Nick Spalding.

'Yeah, but have you seen Fiona Fullerton,' gasped Jerry, overawed. 'She's dressed only in a lion skin, and she's got a live cheetah on a lead.'

For the dozen top newspaper writers and gossip columnists, who, like Nick Spalding, had been invited to this bizarre event, the guest list was a gold mine. Somewhere in that heaving crush was Linda Evans, who had flown in from the set of *Dynasty*, while Dirk Bogarde had made one of his brief forays from his South of France retreat. Omar Sharif was already ensconced at the chemin de fer table.

Spalding, his notebook open, reeled off his tally: 'So far I've got one duke, three earls, a pair of viscounts, a smattering of baronets, a brace of politicians, and God knows how many thespians.'

But Jerry had already disappeared into the crowd, his Nikon held high above his head, flash firing away at a new arrival: Princess Stephanie of Monaco.

Spalding began to ease his large frame through the mass, trawling for information as he went.

'Evening, Your Grace. Riding to hounds again this year? Not retiring at seventy, eh? Capital . . . Gervaise! going to do the decent thing and marry that gorgeous creature? She's gone off with Roman? I didn't know that. And you're now knocking on Angelica's door? Capital! Hiya, Keith. Stones going to hit the road again? No? Imagine —' Spalding laughed hugely, 'Mick a house-husband!'

A blonde waitress, blacked-up and dressed in the torn and scanty rags of a plantation slave, refilled his coconut with a potent, rum-based liquid which was already beginning to make Spalding boom a little louder.

In the corner, being photographed against the bars of a cage, inside which was a disturbed and restless lion, he noticed the three top gossip column paparazzi, Messrs Davidson, Grisbrook and Young, snapping away at a girl whose sole claim to fame was that once, many years ago now, she had spent the evening with Prince Charles.

Suddenly the stalking reporter came face to face with the Prince's valet, who also appeared to have let the coconut concoction go to his head. Spalding grabbed his elbow.

'Frisky!' he peered closer at the valet's fancy dress. 'Who the hell have you come as?'

'Can't you guess, dear?' said Robin Frisk, doing a tidy pirouette. 'I'm Rhett Butler!'

'And I suppose this is Scarlett O'Hara,' replied

Spalding, noting Frisk's young, fresh-faced companion.

'Cheeky!' laughed Frisk. 'He's just a young lad, fresh from Dorset and new to royal service. I'm showing him the ropes. Come along, young fellow, you don't want to be seen talking to gentlemen of the press.'

Spalding elbowed his way past the unlikely trio of Bjorn Borg, the former footballer George Best and the 1960's society hairdresser Rex. No story there. Passé figures.

Suddenly, from the stern of the boat, there was a loud commotion and a piercing cry of: 'Man overboard!'

Spalding ran to see if it was anyone important. He joined the figures at the rail peering into the murky waters of the Thames.

'What happened?' inquired Spalding.

'The bastard made a grab at me knockers,' said Lorna Willie, the well-known nude calendar model, 'so I groined him.'

On the end of a boat hook emerged Lord Stronge, the moral reform campaigner.

'You going to write about this?' asked Lorna eagerly.

'No, my dear, I think I'll leave this one for *The Times*.'

By now the paddle-boat was churning past Tower Bridge. Up on the command deck he espied the VIP group being entertained by their host, the mysterious Ryder St Bartholomew. He noticed the soap-opera star Linda Evans bore a striking resemblance to Marie-Christine, with her huge shoulder-pads and high-piled hair. Spalding made a note.

'You know why, back in 'stralia, they call that man Dracula?' said a soft female voice behind him. It was Koala, the lovely former confidante of Prince Charles who, since his marriage, had been frozen out of the Royal circle by a suspicious Princess Diana.

'No, Koala,' grinned Spalding, 'but you are obviously going to tell me.'

'They say if he exposed himself to daylight he'd melt like an ice-cream on Bondi.'

Spalding chuckled. 'Can't write that — it's libellous.'

'Everything about that dingbat is libellous, pet. Dangerous man. I wouldn't cross him. He's got kangaroos in the top paddock. Cuckoo! Bats — out to lunch.'

'How did this dark horse make all his money, then?'

'In Sydney they call him the Kangaroo King. He turns bouncing marsupials into cans of doggie's dinner. He also owns half of Kowloon.' Koala looked over her shoulder: 'Seen that scar across his face?' She dropped her voice. 'They say that he got involved with the Triads.' She nodded towards the bridge: 'And now look who he's hobnobbing with.'

'Yes, another Aussie made good,' muttered Spalding. 'I wonder if he'll lose his accent, like Marie-Christine.'

'Can't say the girl hasn't done well since those humble days when she was seamstress in little old Melbourne.'

'Something puzzles me,' said Spalding. 'Why is this Bartholomew type spending all this loot to buy his way into English society? What the hell is that man after?'

'Ah, ha, find that,' laughed the departing Koala, as she made her way back towards the party, 'and you will have a sensational story.'

At the far end of the promenade deck Spalding was delighted to spot two colleagues. As he made his way towards them he passed a lifeboat swaying rhythmically on its davits. Standing on tip-toe he drew back the corner of the tarpaulin. He shrugged and replaced it quickly.

'We won't allow you to drown, Spalders,' cried Nigel Dempster, the renowned *Daily Mail* diarist. 'Here, have some of the bushwhacker's champagne.'

'D'you know what I just saw?' said Spalding, his coconut held out for a splash of Moet et Chandon. 'The inglorious sight of a baronet's daughter having a leg over in the lifeboat.'

'Not Samantha Motcombe again?' Dempster roared with wicked laughter. 'Who's the poor victim?'

'Dunno,' shrugged Spalding. 'I only saw his bum.'

'God what an awful evening,' groaned Peter Tory, the witty columnist, sounding like Eeyore and looking more than ever like a cashiered cavalry officer. 'Frankly I wish I was at my local, The Contended Parson.'

'You're right, Tory,' agreed Dempster, who was enjoying the occasion enormously. 'I've just seen someone doing something absolutely disgraceful to a monkey.'

Two hours later, having paddled down the river as far as Greenwich, *The Busted Flush* had turned back and was passing the lights of Limehouse on the right. By now St Bartholomew's lavish hospitality had taken hold, leading to some extremely louche behaviour on the strobe-lit disco floor. Great care was taken to keep Princess Michael away from there, and from the appalling sight of Reg Thwaite, the notorious gangland boss, who was outrageously entwined with the now-topless Lady Davina Constable.

As she was directed towards a quieter spot, Princess Michael had to step over a pair of Gucci shoes poking out from beneath a table.

'Who's that?' inquired Marie-Christine.

'That, Ma'am,' said an aide dismissively, 'is William Hickey.'

On his ceaseless search for a story, Spalding, whose coconut had sprung a leak, came across the wild-eyed figure of Henry Fairlie, who was calmly stroking a growling and irritated panther.

The beast's minder, fearing an attack, tugged at its leash. 'I would be careful if I was you, sir. Sharka hasn't eaten for a few days.'

'Nice, pussy,' said Henry languidly as he nuzzled the snarling panther.

'Come on, old boy,' said Spalding, grabbing him by the collar of his dinner-jacket. 'I fear the jungle juice has got to you.'

'Not a drop of that stuff has passed my lips.' Henry staggered to his feet unsteadily. 'What's passed my nose, is another matter.'

Spalding looked at the dissolute Fairlie with disgust.

He was one of those young aristos-about-town who acted as tipsters to newspapers, shopping their friends for pocket-money.

'My dear man of letters, come with me to the heads and there we will partake of snow.'

'Heads? Snow . . . ?'

'To the lavs for a soupçon of coke.'

In the gents, Spalding was astonished to witness an array of famous people with straws up their noses. There were two lords, an MP, the appalling television quiz-master Quentin Twining, and that year's face, Farika.

'What's your pleasure?' offered Henry. 'Amyl, ecstasy, crack — or I can offer you the coke at retail price.'

'Where's it coming from?'

'Barty, of course. The business we've done tonight should pay for the party.'

Spalding, realizing that he had at last unearthed a scandal, scuttled off in desperate search of his photographer.

'Jerry, I've got our story: *"Princess Michael in Drugs Orgy Cruise"*. Get your Nikon down to the gents — they are shoving thousands of pounds worth of stuff up their nostrils. I'm going to get a quote from you-know-who. This is the big one, baby.'

Extracting a statement from the Princess proved to be a difficult task. Out on deck, with the floodlit dome of St Paul's looming into view, Marie-Christine was being monopolized by the man from *The Times*. He was asking her about her views on fashion and her lifestyle.

'In my mind, I live in the eighteenth century,' she was saying, picking her words carefully, all too aware of the audience that would read them. 'You see, I see my whole life as a cultivation of taste. You ask me what is the objective of my life? I would say — leaving apart my husband and my children -- it is to improve the quality of my life, intellectually, culturally and in the vey I ectually choose to live . . .'

Spalding interrupted. 'Excuse me, Ma'am. Do you

have any views on drug-taking?' The *Times* man glared at Spalding, furious at this uncouth intrusion into the tête à tête it had taken him so long to achieve.

But the Princess did have views, and was eager to share them. She would have been appalled had she known what was going on below decks — indeed, if she had had the slightest inkling she would not have stepped aboard in the first place.

'It's evil —' she began. Before she could elaborate, out from the shadows stepped the imposing figure of Ryder St Bartholomew. He was still wearing tinted glasses despite the darkness of the May night.

'Move along, matey,' St Bartholomew smiled. It was a chilling, murderous smile.

Spalding backed away. He found a quiet corner and with half an hour to go before his deadline began to scribble furiously:

'The Princess of Kent was guest of honour at the opening of London's luxury floating casino, The Busted Flush, where I witnessed amazing scenes of abandoned drug-taking by showbiz stars, leading politicians and members of the aristocracy.

'When I tried to interview the Princess I was threatened by her host, the mysterious Australian entrepreneur Ryder St Bartholomew, known as the Kangaroo King, who paid for the £200,000 party.

'The Princess appeared upset and disturbed and claimed she lived in the 18th century . . .'

On the other side of the dance floor, Frisk, the royal valet, was bopping uninhibitedly with his young protégé from the Palace when one of the waiters, blacked up as a plantation slave, pushed violently against him. Frisk swung round angrily. He stared, baffled for a moment, into the charcoaled face; he recognized those piggy eyes.

'Oi,' said a familiar voice. 'I warned you . . .'

'Banks!'

The royal footman, the valet's rival for the affections

of the young Dorset lad, was moonlighting for the evening. Banks grapsed Frisk by the lapels of his velvet dinner jacket, and shook him violently.

'You bleeding nance...'

'You bent ape,' shrieked Frisk, thrashing his arms wildly in an attempt to free himself from Banks's powerful grasp.

The two royal retainers fell to the floor in a heaving, yelping mêlée. The semi-naked Banks and the once immaculately tailored Frisk rolled over and over around the illuminated dance floor. A crowd formed around them, cheering the two jealous gladiators on to further feats of violence. But the crowd suddenly fell silent when a knife appeared in Banks's hand. A woman screamed. Banks lunged, Frisk parried, blood flowed, ambulances were called, and as the paddle-steamer docked, like rats leaving a sinking ship, a dozen reporters raced ashore to catch their deadlines.

The next morning all the daily newspapers carried on their front pages the sensational story of the fight between Prince Charles's valet, dressed as Rhett Butler, and a Palace footman, dressed as a near-naked slave.

The headline in the *Daily Disclosure*, instead of 'Drugs Orgy Cruise', read: 'ROYAL VALET IN GAY CAT FIGHT — FUR FLIES!'

Royal justice is swift and arbitrary. By mid-day Banks and Frisk had been summarily dismissed. The House of Windsor does not tolerate such public embarrassment; from its servants, at least.

EPISODE THREE: SUMMER

Foreign affairs

The hedgerows were burgeoning; cowslips blossomed and wild daisies bloomed. The oak and ash were in full leaf. From the fields on either side came the alluring fragrance of freshly-mown grass, and as the official Rover turned the corner into an even narrower country lane a less fragrant aroma of pastoral life assailed the fastidious nose of Her Britannic Majesty's Foreign Secretary.

The blazing late May day heralded the arrival of a longed-for hot summer. But the Minister was in a foul mood. As they turned into the driveway of Sandringham, after a three-hour journey from Whitehall, he wished that archaic Cabinet protocol did not require him to deliver his information in person, rather than on the telephone.

It was a surprisingly long driveway as Sandringham, the Queen's private Norfolk residence, was set in twenty thousand acres. The house finally came into view; though enormous, with two hundred and seventy

rooms, it was not the most beautiful of sights. A real old
Victorian hodge-podge, with a mock Jacobean exterior, it
had been bought by Queen Victoria for her roué son
Edward in the vain hope it would lure him away from the
fleshpots of London.

The Minister realized Her Majesty would not be
amused by what he had to impart. He appreciated that
summer was a busy time for the Royal Family. There
was polo for Charles, Badminton for Anne, Wimbledon
for Diana, Cowes and carriage-driving for Philip, and the
Derby and Royal Ascot for the Queen.

As the Minister's black Rover drew up outside the
main door, a brace of fat pheasant cocks waddled
leisurely across the immaculate greensward. Their
iridescent colours flashed in the clear light. They won't
be so cocksure come winter, thought the Minister, when
the Royal Purdeys blaze.

The Queen's estate manager led the increasingly
miffed Minister, who by now was beginning to sweat
uncomfortably in his city clothes, to the royal stud where
Her Majesty was to be found in horse-shoe patterned
headscarf, sensible tweeds and green wellington boots.
The Queen felt it only courteous to show her Minister
the full extent of her magnificent stables after his long
and arduous drive from London. The Minister was not a
lover of the horse; he was more at home slouched on the
Front Bench in the House of Commons or enjoying a
good bottle of claret in the Carlton Club — never more
so than now that the Norfolk mud was creeping up his
trouser leg. They spent an hour going round the yard as
Her Majesty slapped rumps, admired fetlocks and
discussed form.

She showed him the stalls which had lodged Edward
VII's two Derby winners, Persimmon and Diamond
Jubilee. She also, appearing greatly moved, showed him
the hallowed spot where a shaggy Shetland pony called
Peggy had been laid to rest. Peggy, the Queen explained,
had been a present from her father at the age of three,
and had led to her lifelong passion for these fine

creatures. You could say, the Queen confided to the apparently agog Minister, that this had been one's first step in one's dedicated quest to win the Derby.

The tour round the pungent farmyard with the pleasant and practical middle-aged lady, Head of State and Defender of the Faith, had been one of the most severe tests of the Minister's political acumen. But as he sank back into the cool, leather-seated comfort of his Rover, he reflected that at least he had achieved what he came for.

She could hardly have refused. Even so, he had quite a job persuading her to take on this state visit, especially at such short notice. They had enacted that ritual which Majesties and their Ministers were apt to go through. It navigated that tricky passage between constitutional necessities and regal egos. The Queen had only relented when he'd explained that at stake was an order worth £3 billion for a military hardware package of Harrier jump jets, Chieftain tanks, rocket launchers and assorted police riot gear.

There was one aspect of their conversation which still puzzled the Minister. The startled expression of Her Majesty when he had mentioned the name of the visiting desert sheik: Mahoud al Mahoud.

A manicured paradise

As usual, a week in her Caribbean island holiday home had worked its magic on Princess Margaret. Those long, idle poolside days under the tropical sun had eased away the lines of tension and disappointment; she now had a deep rich tan, which took years away from her face, and restored that impish, free-spirited Margaret they had all once known. Her uninhibited laughter set the informal tone for this exclusive little coterie from London. In her daring fluorescent one-piece swim suit the starchy protocol of court life seemed like a distant memory.

It was a steamy, fetid evening, made only bearable by the faintest of off-sea breezes. In the glow of the full moon the long crescent of white sand shimmered, and the white peaks of the rhythmically breaking waves could be seen against the dark ocean. The faces of her six companions were illuminated by the blazing barbecue fire, while behind them was a row of hissing hurricane lamps, swaying gently in the zephyr. In the background was the never-ceasing chirping of cicadas.

At the edge of the beach, behind the first line of palm fronds, Princess Margaret noticed hundreds of tiny flickering dots.

'How romantic,' she exclaimed. 'Fireflies.'

Lord Rubberton, the master of ceremonies who had organized this evening's beach party, did not disillusion her. In fact those flickering dots were the protective wall of burning mosquito coils, carefully staked out to prevent any buzzing inconvenience to Her Royal Highness, let alone a loss of blue blood.

'Ah, blissful, what a paradise,' sighed Margaret. 'All we need now is music. What a pity Mick couldn't make it.'

'Yes, Ma'am,' agreed Rubberton, whose blistered face was liberally daubed with calamine lotion. 'Alas, at the last minute Jerry put her foot down.'

'How pathetic,' remarked Margaret, reloading her cigarette holder with another Sobranie.

There was a flash of white, intense light, like a sudden bolt of tropical lightning. The startled company looked up to see, flowering above the Olympus, the familiar bouffant locks of the Earl of Lichfield — known to Princess Margaret's children as Captain Plastic.

'I hope you're not going to flog off that snap, Patrick' said Margaret, hitching her swimsuit higher over the bounteous bosom. 'You know the Queen was jolly fed up at you selling those portraits from Charles's wedding.'

'But they were so spontaneous, PM,' protested Lichfield.

'That may be,' replied Margaret. 'But we all looked like chumps. Our sister was livid.'

Out of the darkness appeared a wandering group of minstrels strolling down the beach. To the accompaniment of guitars and maracas they sang a carefree calypso.

'Oh, perfection,' cried Margaret, clapping her hands. 'What an unexpected treat. How unaffected native life is.'

Again the faithful Lord Rubberton did not disabuse her of this pleasant notion. These calypso-players had been paid twenty dollars apiece to appear casually at half past ten, on the dot, to serenade the Princess.

'Life here is free and easy, you see, without the cares of civilization,' Margaret was explaining. 'There is a multitude of fish in the sea, coconuts abound, and the good earth is so fertile that a toothpick cast aside would take root and flower.' Margaret extended her empty glass, to no one in particular, and the squatting group moved as one. Hugo Hamilton, who was desperate to make up for his catastrophic faux pas of the previous evening, got their first; he trimphantly bore the glass away to be replenished with another slug of Mustique Mugger, the dangerously alcoholic cocktail which the sybaritic Rubberton had devised to make the balmy nights sing.

Out of the circle of light, discreetly hovering, were the hand-picked team who kept the revellers supplied with food and drink, directed by the resourceful Toussaint d'Orleans, the handsome black barman, the only soul to whom Lord Rubberton had entrusted the recipe of his secret cocktail.

'Rousseau, don't you agree, Carl, hit the conundrum right on the head. Your noble savage is so much more at one, so much more together.'

Carl Dwork, the spiky-haired ballet dancer whose irreverence delighted Princess Margaret, whooped with laughter. 'From what I hear, Ma'am, they're at it all the time.'

Sir Peregrine Royston-Black, who up to now had been largely silent due to the effects of the hookah he had enjoyed earlier in his room, spoke up. 'Nothing compared with the practices of the primitive Sumbuburra from the jungles of South East Asia, who are quite astonishingly prolific. Several times a day is quite normal for a post-adolescent tribesman. Funny thing though,' continued Perry,' the old Sumbi have a curious form of beautification. Unlike the Kikuyu, who extend their necks, and the Sagaree who elongate their lips, the Sumbu stretch much-abused Mr Mouse. Strap-me-vitals, the longest one I ever saw—.'

'Perry, dear,' interrupted Princess Margaret sharply, 'one is in grave danger of being boring . . .'

The Princess, who liked to consider herself one of the gang, expected liberties to be taken, but only so far. She liked to forget that she was Royal; but she didn't like others to do so.

It was past midnight, and many Mustique Muggers later the group had dispersed. Only Hugo Hamilton remained amid the debris of the party. Sir Royston-Black had led off the impressionable Carl Dwork to Baz's Bar in pursuit of unmentionable pleasures. Lord Rubberton, proving the strength of his concoction, had passed out. Patrick Lichfield had gone to bed soon after the departure of the Princess who, much to everyone's astonishment, had taken home with her Toussaint d'Orleans. She had announced in an airy voice: 'Come, my noble savage.'

'Noble?' repeated the jealous Hugo out of earshot. 'All he did was sing those Carib ditties passably.'

Now, alone with the still-hissing hurricane lamps throwing light upon an empty beach, Hugo looked up morosely at the star-splattered sky. He felt his cheeks burning at the memory of the previous night.

What an ass he had made of himself. With all his theatrical experience and connoisseurship of women, he had behaved like a fumbling teenager? But then, how does one make a pass at a Princess? He had so utterly misinterpreted PM's invitation to dine at home à deux. She was looking enchanting, and with her fresh tan was temptingly alluring. And then she suggested they take their liqueurs out on the verandah. In the Noël Coward plays, of which Hugo was the leading exponent, this was always the prelude to an elegant and witty seduction scene. As soon as he was seated in the rocking-chair opposite the Princess he began to ponder the sheer practical difficulty of making an advance upon a personage of Royal Blood. The more possibilities that came to mind the more desperate he became. In his torment, the more he began to rock as he rejected each possibility.

Oh God, the horror, he thought, as he recalled his ultimate solution to the exquisite dilemma. Despite the cooling breeze off the ocean his cheeks burned fiercely with shame.

As his rocking had become more frenetic he had hit upon what seemed like a brilliant notion; he would rock himself to such a point of momentum that he would shoot across the verandah and into the eager embrace of HRH. And with a breathless whisper of 'My Princess', their lips would meet.

With a little whimper Hugo turned his face to the sand. That horrendous moment, which could never be retrieved, when he catapulted himself into that abyss — when, with a flailing of arms and an ungainly tangle of legs, he crashed into the satin lap of the Queen's sister. The Princess shrieked in alarm.

The tears of hot humiliation flowed down Hugo's cheeks at that ghastly memory of his inglorious retreat with stammered apologies and excuses. Both had passed the appalling incident off as an unfortunate mistake, blamed totally on the innocent rattan rocking-chair.

As dawn broke over the still Caribbean, Hugo had no more tears to weep. Wearily he rose and dusted off the sand from his now Mustique-Mugger-stained white ducks and silk cravat. He *must* go and apologize.

A few minutes later, having rehearsed his mea culpa speech, he arrived outside Les Jolies Eaux. But the sounds he heard from within made him dejectedly pass on.

To the accompaniment of a piano, a dark baritone voice and a husky soprano sang the Billie Holliday blues standard:

> 'If I get the notion to jump into the ocean
> 'Tain't nobody's business if I do . . .
> If I chose to stay up late on Sunday and
>   sleep all day Monday,
> 'Tain't nobody's business if I do . . .'

The plop factor

In preparation for an official visit by Princess Anne to their well-fortified Armagh barracks, the Regimental Sergeant Major of the 17/21st Royal Avon Fusiliers was pacing out those last vital steps. Every yard of this secret, security-conscious visit had been measured, rehearsed and timed.

The MLU hut had been towed into position in the corner of the field where later that afternoon the Princess was due to observe the dismantling of artillery field guns and the construction of a Bailey bridge. But certain measures, aside from the stringent security precautions, had to be taken. The MLU hut had been requisitioned for the use of the Princess, should the need arise. The 17/21st prided themseves on planning for every eventuality.

Inside the MLU, armed with three pounds of Walls pork sausages, was Corporal Eddie Taylor who had been detailed to carry out this mundane but vital dress-rehearsal. Corporal Taylor was standing in for the Princess.

Outside he heard the RSM's bark: 'Ready, Corporal. Sausages away!'

The corporal swiftly executed the order.

'Audible!' shouted the RSM, pacing out the distance. 'Thirteen, fourteen, fifteen ... repeat!'

The corporal, now bored with this routine procedure, again obeyed.

'Audible! Sixteen, seventeen, eighteen ... repeat!'

The corporal released another Walls banger at the prescribed height of precisely 0.47 metres.

'Inaudible!' yelled the RSM, 'Range, eighteen yards. Stand down, Corporal.'

The sergeant major now began marking out security lines beyond which no soldier could step should Princess Anne avail herself of this facility, while, his mission in the freshly-painted Mobile Latrine Unit completed, Corporal Taylor relaxed. He sat on the karzi and rolled himself a cigarette. Into the pan the unsuspecting corporal tossed a lighted match. The sergeant major was instantly thrown to the ground by a powerful explosion. Before his eyes the MLU disintegrated.

Moments later, out of the smoking debris, staggered a singed and stunned Corporal Taylor. What the Princess's stand-in had not known was that the latrine had been filled with decorator's white spirit.

By Royal Appointment

The next morning the Queen was taking her breakfast above the shop, as she called Buckingham Palace, at eight thirty sharp, as she did every morning. She had polished off her Quaker Oats (By Royal Appointment), her coddled eggs and bacon, and was now eating little soldiers of toast, spread liberally with Cooper's Marmalade (By Royal Appointment). She had already studied *The Sporting Life*, and now turned to *The Times* to read about the abysmal performance of her government.

'Listen to this, dear,' she said, from behind the broadsheet. 'Do you see what that unpleasant little Home Secretary has gone and done? He told the House yesterday that hanging may have to be reintroduced.' She paused for a reaction from her husband.

Hearing no reply, Her Majesty put down the paper. There was no one there. Apart from a pair of surprised footmen, she was quite alone. Good heavens, where was Philip? She flicked through to page 18 of *The Times*, and consulted the Court Circular: the Duke of Edinburgh, she learnt, was in the Faroe Islands, discussing the future of the whale.

Down at Highgrove, their Gloucestershire home, the Prince and Princess of Wales were still in their dressing-gowns, and with them at the breakfast table were their two sons, the Princes William and Henry. Charles was complaining to his sympathetic wife about the resistance he had met from the Privy Council concerning his imminent private visit to Nepal. He had been particularly upset by the Prime Minister's suggestion that he should instead go to Oman to help the arms export drive. Charles, spooning in a mouthful of flaky nut muesli, informed the delighted Diana that in the end he had won the day by pulling rank.

'You see, dear, I just feel the need to get right away and do a bit of trekking,' he said, taking a sip of dandelion coffee. 'Mmm, rather good. Should be By Appointment, really.'

A few miles down the road at Gatcombe Park, the Princess Anne, Mrs Mark Phillips, and her husband had already finished their hearty country breakfast of sausages and eggs. Anne was furiously thumbing through all nine national daily newspapers for any reference to herself and her visit the previous day to the 17/21st Royal Avon Fusiliers in Northern Ireland. There was none.

'Bloody heck!'

Captain Phillips looked up from the pages of *Horse and Hound*. 'What are they saying about you now, my precious?' he asked.

'Nothing. That's what's so damnably disgraceful. There I was risking my neck in Ulster, where one squaddie was even blown up, and look at the coverage that butter-wouldn't-melt-in-her-mouth Diana gets for opening a jelly bean factory.' Princess Anne swept the papers off the table angrily. 'She's even made the front page of *The Times* and *The Telegraph*!'

Paradise postponed

Back in Mustique three dull days had passed since the courtiers had caught sight of Princess Margaret — the sole reason for their being there. She was occupied, it seemed, with the island's most talented barman and amateur baritone, Toussaint d'Orleans. He now seemed to be a permanent house guest at Les Jolies Eaux. After the second day Lord Lichfield made his apologies and took a flight back to London where he pleaded assignments were stacking up. Carl Dwork, the toast of the Royal Ballet, whose purpose had been to provide the Princess with a competent dancing partner, was next to crack. He booked a flight back home on the following evening.

This left a confused trio. Lord Rubberton, though he did not dare voice his darkest fears, was a very worried man. Would the establishment blame him? Would society point a finger at him and lay the responsibility for this dreadful state of affairs at the door of his Eaton Square house? He'd spent two sleepless nights imagining the Queen summoning him to account for her sister's bizarre fate. He had seriously considered calling the Foreign Office to seek their advice, but had flunked it, fearing the Privy Council would be alerted and call him to book for bringing such dishonour upon the name of England.

Sir Perry Royston-Black, who had experienced most things in life ('Even folk dancing and incest') had been imported to the island for his ability as a raconteur about the darker side of life. He had run through everybody the island had to offer and now filled those dull days by the pool-side, a bottle of arak in hand, entertaining his two downcast companions with the amusing story of his depraved life. He was explaining why he never married.

'Marriage so easily leads to murder,' Perry said grandly. 'I am reminded of my distant kinsman from the eleventh century, a certain Count Gulielmas, who took an entirely reasonable relish in observing his wife being rogered by his pet ape. But, alas, all good things must come to an end. One night when the count had the temerity to mount the countess the besotted ape, seized by a fit of jealousy, attacked my innocent relation and murdered him.'

Hugo Hamilton was inconsolable. He sulked. For three days he did not lift his head from the thick volume of *The Noël Coward Diaries*.

'Listen to this, beleaguered friends,' said Hugo finally breaking the silence with sepulchral tones. 'The Master makes an interesting annotation for January 15, 1955, on the occasion of a visit by PM to Jamaica.' He read: ' "Apparently it had been laid down that on no account is she to dance with any coloured person".'

Now the unmentionable subject had been raised Lord Rubberton exclaimed: 'Extraordinary, isn't it? Peter, Billy, Tony and that Llewellyn boy. Why, oh why does she choose such unsuitable chaps?'

'Toussaint?' said Perry. 'Capital fellow. Damn sight more amusing than Norman.' But even Sir Royston-Black when pressed had to admit that for the good of the Windsors the present situation was perhaps a bit dicey.

Finally the trio came to a decision to neutralize what Lord Rubberton increasingly saw as a humiliating national scandal.

'Fair enough,' said Perry languidly. 'We snuff him out. As a matter of fact I have as a present from the cannibalistic Watami of Sarawak, a potent draught of . . .'

'Steady on, Perry,' cried Lord Rubberton, aghast. 'After all, the fellow is a decent enough cove — for a local.' Instead, as a decent sort of British compromise, they decided to buy the bounder off.

Each came up with an offer which they felt Toussaint

d'Orleans could not refuse. Lord Rubberton, stating the most generous of terms, offered him the post of white hunter at his theme safari park in Scotland, Mr d'Orleans declined.

Sir Peregrine Royston-Black, over a Singapore Sling at Baz's Bar, suggested he might like to accompany him as his man on his not-unamusing world travels. 'I think you might find it quite educative and not unprofitable.' Mr d'Orleans, with enormous charm, declined.

Hugo Hamilton, after pondering at length which of the many strings he could pull, rejected them all — because they meant the fellow going to London and that was what they wanted to avoid at all costs. As penance for his awful blunder, Hugo finally decided to plough the not inconsiderable profits from his last touring production into a beach bar. To his astonishment Toussaint was unimpressed with the prospect held out by Hugo of a vast neon sign announcing 'D'Orleans Place'.

All three had failed.

Then, to their despair, came a sudden summons from Princess Margaret: we leave for London tonight.

As they boarded the plane the trio were delighted to see she was alone. As they looked back down at the island, shrouded in the roseate mantle of a Caribbean sunset, everyone kept their thoughts to themselves. Finally Margaret, who had been looking dreamily out of the starboard porthole, sighed: 'Oh, noble spirit.'

Fearful of what was to come, her three companions strained to catch her words.

'What a fine free spirit, so knowledgeable, so wise, so totally at peace. Such a beautiful singer . . .'

'Splendid fellow,' said Lord Rubberton, 'You are quite right, Ma'am, these primitives are such happy folk.'

'Primitive, Rubbers?' said Margaret, surprised. 'Toussie had been a Manhattan lawyer. He's a drop-out y'know.'

It was not until they changed planes in New York and were half way over the Atlantic that Hugo's irritation boiled over. Having offered a small fortune to the ungrateful blackamoor Hugo felt it was his right to inquire: 'And what, if we may ask, Ma'am, was one doing all the while?'

'Ahh,' smiled Margaret fondly, 'why, we spent the entire three days singing Schubert *Lieder*.'

A horseman riding by

Gatcombe Park, the Gloucestershire residence of Captain and Mrs Mark Phillips, had been bought by the Queen in 1976 for the newly marrieds, partly in order to give her son-in-law a new career. Being married to a Princess made his army career difficult so he settled down to being a farmer and a horseman.

As a former Olympic Gold Medallist the clean-cut Captain Phillips had managed to find commercial sponsorship for his equestrian pursuits — for which he had been roundly castigated, as also for his habit, when in the company of horsey friends, of beating up bars and hotel bedrooms in an excess of high spirits.

Anne, in recent years, appeared to have distanced herself from this lifestyle, and took on an incredibly busy workload of official engagements as well as frequent trips abroad for the Save the Children Fund.

The one thing they still had in common was their love of horses and every year they admitted to Gatcombe, as working pupils, a number of young international hopefuls. This year's intake stood round nervously in the stable yard. They included two girl riders from Canada, a shy lad from New Zealand, a young local prospect and a startlingly confident youth from Forsythe, Montana.

'Hal Bean,' he greeted the Phillipses, hand extended. 'Hi Prince, hi Princess. Mighty pleased to meet y'all.'

'Nice to meet you, Mr Bean,' said Princess Anne. 'And by the way, the correct form of address, if you don't mind, is Ma'am.'

'Right, Mam,' said the exuberant Hal, unabashed.

'And my husband is not a prince.'

'Oh, so sorry to hear that,' replied Hal.

'You will call him Captain Phillips until such time as you get to know him better and then you may possibly be able to call him Mark.'

The group of shy young riders laughed nervously.

'Time, I think, to show you lot your quarters,' said Captain Phillips, leading them off to their rooms, which were above the stables.

'Hey, Mam, can I see the horses first?' said Hal.

'Oh alright then, quickly,' said the Princess who quietly admired the naturalness of the lean, loping American, although she was doing her best not to show it. She hated sycophancy.

'Oh! This is great,' he whooped as he raced across the stable yard where the Gatcombe mounts were stalled. He stopped before a handsome eighteen hand bay.

'Jee-zus, wow, too much.' He was through the gate and with an agile leap he was bestride the bay gelding. Before Princess Anne had time to utter a word of warning Hal had urged the horse out into the yard and the two of them took off at a gallop. Hal sat low, rising and falling easily on the horse's back, and with one fluid movement the two of them jumped the high farmyard stone wall. Princess Anne gasped in admiration.

The next two weeks were happy ones for Anne. She threw herself into the task of training the new team of prospects with an enthusiasm and vigour which astonished the Gatcombe staff. The princess seemed to thrive on this challenge, and she was up all hours with them, rising early to help muck out the stables, and joining in at night with the young folks' sing-songs and horseplay. There was no question who was the star of the new intake. Hal Bean was a superb, natural horseman. Despite his unorthodox, somewhat uncouth cowboy riding style and his utterly undisciplined and exuberant excesses, she had to admit that she had never seen such an obvious Olympic prospect. Hal had all the requirements: strength, vigour, nerve, confidence,

control and that indefinable, unteachable affinity with
the animal which made rider and horse as one.

Because of his unquenchable eagerness to learn, and
his extraordinary stamina, Anne had taken a special
interest in his coaching, and after the others had retired
exhausted for the day, she gave him an extra hour's
tuition in the paddock. Hal was mustard keen to work till
light failed. Such a willing horse, thought Anne. What a
splendid sight.

That evening, as usual, Anne was giving extra
schooling to her star pupil. She was trying to instil in this
raw, bumptious young man the finer points of dressage,
and he was becoming restless.

'Oh gee, Mam, let's go for a goddam canter,' shouted
Hal impetuously. 'Let's shoot the breeze a bit!'

'Don't be silly, Hal. My horse isn't saddled.'

She was standing in the centre of the paddock, and Hal
came trotting towards her on his huge bay, Alacrity. As
he came by, he impetuously leant down and swept her
off her feet and into the saddle.

'Hal! Just what do you think you're doing?'

He laughed. 'Just a little ol' trick I learnt from John
Wayne.'

'Put me down at once,' she said heatedly.

But already Hal had spurred the bay into a canter and
they took the paddock gate with a bold leap.

'Hal, slow down. Mind the horse!' exclaimed Anne.
'Poor Alacrity. There's two of us.'

'OK, Mam, you're the driver. Where to now?'

'Well,' said Anne, quite taken aback by the boy's cheek.
'No further than Partridge Copse and back. This is
absurd.'

They trotted at an easy pace through the gathering
dusk. In the distance, from the wood, they could hear the
soft coo of the ringed doves. They rode for a moment in
silence.

A thought had been worrying Hal. 'Mam, you mind if I
ask you something? Why do the grooms call your
husband "Fog"?'

The Princess exploded with laughter, so loud that two startled pheasants squawked and whirred out of the hedgerow in alarm.

'Did I say something funny, Mam?'

'No, no, Hal. Just ignore it.'

How could she possibly explain to this callow foreigner that this nickname was supposed to imply that Captain Phillips was 'thick and wet'?

The intrigued Hal was not to be put off. In his short stay he had begun to realize quite how rich, powerful and goddam historic these folks were: so much more real than the TV pictures of the British Royal Family presiding over Walt Disney-type ceremonials that occasionally reached Forsythe, Montana.

'Look, I've just gotta ask this, Mam — how d'ya get to be royal?'

'Are you serious, Hal?'

'Sure.'

'Well . . .' Anne paused. She'd never had to answer that question before. 'One's, er, born to it, really, I suppose. It goes a long way back.'

'Like, how far?'

'Egbert of Wessex. AD 829.'

'Neat.'

'Actually, we're also related to George Washington.'

'Really? That's something.'

Anne, aware that her words were having quite an effect on the young man perched behind her, added: 'It might amuse you to know that it's said we are also related to Charlemagne, Genghis Khan, El Cid, Shakespeare and Count Dracula.'

'Holy cow!' Hal fell silent.

His instructor was something quite outside his experience, something he couldn't quite put into words, but which suddenly he found quite daunting.

For the first time since Anne had known him, Hal was subdued and uncharacteristically quiet on the ride back to the stables. As they dismounted, Anne said: 'You seem tired, Hal. Would you care to join Mark and me for a drink before dinner?'

This was quite a privilege, not yet afforded to any of the other trainees.

'You're very kind, Princess,' Hal said quietly. 'But you're right — I am kinda tuckered. I think I'll turn in early tonight.'

A call of nature

In the noisy, disordered newsroom of the *Daily Disclosure* Nick Spalding was on the second folio of a tedious and uninspired feature for the women's page, with a working title of 'Life aboard Britannia', about which he knew nothing. The phone rang. It was a tipster. One of his best; a mole on the staff at Gatcombe Park. And the titbit imparted from a pay-phone booth caused Spalding to rip that dreary page out of his old Remington and toss it into his waste bin with a whoop of glee.

He bustled over to the newsdesk, where Ron Snitch was shouting down a telephone: 'Keep on that doorstep till ye drop, laddie.' He slammed down the receiver and turned to Spalding. 'And what do you want, you overpaid, champagne-swilling scribbler?' he snarled.

'Your elegant signature on this chitty,' said Spalding insouciantly, 'allowing me to draw the sum of six hundred pounds from cashiers — romance is in the air in Gloucestershire!' Spalding laid out the facts.

Snitch beamed. 'On your bike, laddie.'

Spalding collected his money from cashiers, his Zeiss binoculars from his drawer, Jerry from the White Hart pub (known to Fleet Street regulars as The Stab in the Back), and within ninety minutes was parked by the roadside, peeping over the stone wall of Gatcombe Park, undertaking surveillance.

Spalding handed his binoculars to Jerry. 'There's the paddock over there,' said the royal reporter, as happy as a hound on the scent. 'My nark tells me they meet every evening for lessons.'

'So what's the age difference?' asked the photographer.

'About sixteen years.'

'Blimey — toy boy situation.'

Spalding spread out an Ordnance Survey map upon the roof of his office Ford. They studied the layout of the seven hundred and fifty-acre Gatcombe Park.

'This is the path they took last night,' said Spalding tracing the route from the paddock which Anne and Hal had taken on their unorthodox ride. His stubby fingers came to rest on a small patch of woodland marked Partridge Copse.

'That's our objective, Jerry. Get on your yomping clothes, old boy. We've got some undercover work to do.'

Twenty minutes later they were crawling through the undergrowth.

Both had changed into their camouflage kit. Spalding was wearing a baggy green and brown one-piece boiler-suit while Jerry was clad in battle fatigues with Polisario Guerilla markings. They were inching forward on their bellies through the high bracken, fern, thistle and stinging nettles.

Jerry was festooned with equipment. He had four cameras in all — two Nikons, a Leica and in his pocket a little automatic-focus Olympus Trip for close quarter snatch photographs. His lenses ranged from an 85mm right up to a huge 1,200mm long-tom which could pick up the whites of their eyes at a thousand feet, and in the right conditions, a pimple. In addition he had several wide-angle lenses, including a fish-eye for the odd arty shot, as well as the indispensable flash gun. Strapped to his back was a tripod, a spade, and a collapsible ladder. In the hot April afternoon Jerry was already soaked with sweat.

'Adder country,' muttered Jerry uneasily.

'Don't worry, old boy,' whispered Spalding from in front where he presented his photographer with the unwholesome sight of his large camouflaged posterior. 'I have got the antidote in my Gladstone bag.'

Indeed he had. The resourceful Spalding — who over the years on behalf of the *Daily Disclosure* had spent many

uncomfortable hours outside palaces, up trees, sub-
merged in rivers, concealed in hedges and on perilous
roofs listening down chimney-pots — knew how to
prepare himself for any eventuality. He was as likely to
have to follow the Royal Family to either ends of the
earth. In his battered old Gladstone bag Spalding had
everything a gentleman could possibly need in adverse
circumstances.

His leather portmanteau contained such necessities as
a first aid kit, mosquito repellent, Debrett's *Peerage*, a
Swiss Army penknife, sun-tan oil, a bottle of Eau
Sauvage, a tape-recorder, a pad of Queen's Velvet paper,
a roll of toilet tissue, his telephone contacts book, a
change of underwear, thermal underwear, *The Royal
Handbook*, food, drink and a collapsible fishing rod.

After hours of strenuous crawling on elbows and
knees the two newsmen reached Partridge Copse and
took up their positions. While Spalding disappeared into
a thicket Jerry found himself a vantage point twenty feet
up an ash tree, which gave him a clear field of vision of
the path that his quarry were expected to ride down.

There was a burst of static on Jerry's walkie-talkie.

'Hello . . . hello. Come in, Fox Two,' said Spalding.

'Receiving you, Fox One,' replied Jerry into the
mouthpiece. 'This perch is dead uncomfortable. Hope
bandits appear pronto. Over and out.'

'OK, Roger. Now observing radio silence, Fox Two.
Over and out.'

After a painful hour on the branch a flash in the fading
sunlight caught Jerry's eye. It couldn't be his own
equipment, for every silver surface had been blackened
with the care of a sniper preparing his rifle. There was
another flash. Jerry looked down and was appalled to see
his colleague tucking into a feast.

Already he had consumed a round of smoked salmon
sandwiches and half a small bottle of cool Chablis. Now
he appeared to be struggling to open something with a
knife.

The irritated Jerry focused his long-tom on the object.

It was an oyster. With mounting fury the photographer observed the prising open of the mollusc and through the magnified lens he witnessed it wriggle when Spalding squeezed a freshly cut lemon upon it.

'Come in, Fox One,' he hissed into his walkie-talkie.

'Roger, Fox Two,' replied Spalding excitedly. 'Bandits?'

'Not bandits, Fox One. A fat pig!'

'Roger, Fox Two,' said Spalding as he slipped another succulent oyster down his gullet. 'Kindly observe radio silence. I am now switching off my machine. Over and out.'

Having polished off the rest of the Chablis, Spalding settled down contentedly in the bracken to do some homework. He took out *The Royal Handbook* and began to read: 'Monarchy is show. The British Monarchy is one of the greatests shows on earth and among the longest running ...' Spalding felt a little twinge in his gut. '... An estimated fifteen million visitors who have come to Britain, spending £6,500 million within these shores. A fair proportion of them will have come to London to see the Queen ...'

This time from the depths of Spalding's pot came an unpleasant gurgling sound followed by an acute stab of pain.

'Bloody oyster,' cursed the reporter as he tore at the zips of his cumbersome boiler-suit. He pulled, tugged and ripped at the restricting garment There was another bayonet-like stab in his stomach, followed by an even louder retort. Spalding finally liberated himself from his clinging camouflage outfit just in time for the call of nature.

From his vantage position above Jerry suddenly espied a lone rider. He scrambled for his walkie-talkie.

'Come in, Fox One, come in.'

There was only silence. Spalding's machine was firmly turned off. The rider was now cantering towards them at alarming speed.

Panicking, Jerry croaked urgently, loud as he dared: 'Spalding!'

The portly court correspondent, caught unawares in his squatting position, jumped up in alarm. As his naked torso rose from the bracken he was astonished to find himself face-to-face with Princess Anne.

She in turn, from the lofty height of her horse, looked down with disbelief at this naked rotundity.

'Evening, Ma'am,' said Spalding with an involuntary bow.

'Flasher!' screamed the startled Princess. She activated her micro panic-button, immediately setting off sirens all over Gatcombe Park.

Spalding fled.

From his tree-top hide Jerry observed the surprising sight of his bulky, ghost-white colleague hot-footing it across the open field.

And the last that Princess Anne saw of this fleshy apparition, as it dived head-first over the estate wall, was a pair of fluorescent green socks.

Sugar Puffs and rolled oats

Radio One was playing in the background, and Sarah was ploughing into the second bowlful of her favourite cereal, Sugar Puffs. It was already half past ten, but the young couple were allowed much leeway. The bowl from which she ate, one of a set that had been a wedding present from the ex-patriate community in Buenos Aires, depicted the silhouettes of famous British battleships. Sarah was reading the *Daily Mail's* Diary while Andrew, uncharacteristically quiet even for that time of morning, had just finished his Scott's porridge oats.

'Buttons,' said Andrew tentatively, pouring himself a cup of coffee from the exquisite early American silver pot, vandalized by the engraved signature 'Ronnie & Nancy', 'do please kill your trannie. Can't stand that DJ.'

'Feeling fragile, Ferret?' queried Sarah acidly, helping herself to some toast from the matching modern silver racks, a gift from the grateful people of New Zealand.

'Yah. Some senior drinking went on last night.'

'Quite, Ferret. But one's rather irritated that Calthorpe thought it was so amusing to relieve himself on the yucca. Just look at it.'

Andrew laughed at the memory. 'Oh come on, Buttons — you know what those boys from the Army Air Squadron are like. Bit mad.'

Sarah was not prepared to forgive the Prince that easily. As a sign of her displeasure she refused to look at him, and instead studied the place mat in front of her, part of a series of 'distinguished Governor-Generals of Australia', a present from New South Wales.

'It's time to jolly well grow up, Andrew. Honestly,

140

keeping company with people like that frightful Digby-Jones. It was just not on to play rugby with that lovely embroidered cushion.'

'It was a fun game,' objected Andrew 'My team won.'

'How do you think those nice people of Fiji would feel, knowing their present was in bits all over our hallway?'

'Put a sock in it, Buttons, there's a good fellow.'

'Marmalade, please,' said Sarah tartly.

Andrew picked up the silver filigree marmalade holder on wheels, a wedding present from the Grand Duchy of Luxembourg.

'Vroom, vroom,' he said, and whizzed it at high speed down the length of the table. In the middle it crashed into a silver sugar shaker, a present from the King of Belgium.

'Now was that responsible?' demanded Sarah.

A footman entered, bearing the mail. There was only one letter. It was for Andrew. The vellum envelope had been hand-delivered and was marked PRIVATE AND CONFIDENTIAL. He began to read it.

'Do you know what Diana told me yesterday?' said Sarah brightly, not wishing to be accused of nagging. 'That little monster William is having his portrait painted in KP. He was perched on a high stool, and the artist was trying to get the light right. He went to move William and stool together a few feet to the right, when Willie piped up, "Put me down! Just who do you think you are?" Hilarious, yah?'

The colour drained from Andrew's face.

'Anything the matter, Ferret?'

'No.'

Andrew stared numbly at the curiously precise italic script before him. Slowly he read the letter again. He couldn't believe this. He'd never heard of the man before. But now every word burnt like acid into his heart:

'I have in my possession, Your Royal Highness, a Coutts cheque made out in the sum of £1,500 to my business associate, Miss Ilaria Pucci. The disbursement of such a not inconsiderable emolument from a

*distinguished personage like yourself to someone of lesser social
standing, like Miss Pucci, could in certain circles be misinterpreted. I
am sure you would agree, Sir, that should such a disagreeable
conclusion be drawn the result would be catastrophic for yourself, your
family and the nation.'*

Andrew forced himself to read the final, chilling
sentence.

*'Should you wish, as I earnestly do, to avoid any scandal, you can
reach me at any time at the above address.*

'I have the honour, Sir, to remain your obedient servant.

                    Ryder St Bartholomew'

A bone of contention

The beams of refracted light from the diamond tiaras and priceless historical jewellery bedecking the Windsors had already impressed the Sheik at the pre-banquet reception, but as he entered the Buckingham Palace ballroom on the Queen's arm Mahoud al Mahoud gasped. The shimmering grandeur of the opulent room staggered even this oil-rich ruler from the desert. Gold and reds predominated: in the uniforms of the attendants, the carpet, the chairs, and spread over the magnificent horseshoe table itself. Even the Sheik had not seen so much gold all in one place at one time. The plates, the fruit bowls, the candlesticks and even the cutlery, all were solid gold.

The fine mahogany table, which seated one hundred and fifty, had taken three days to prepare. Under-butlers, supervised by the Palace Steward, had been busily creating this lavish spectacle; the lightest and deftest of these flunkies had stood in their stockinged feet on the exquisite patina of the table with a tape measure in order to achieve that awesome symmetry. Each cut-glass goblet was thirteen inches from the next, the gold candelabra were placed at precisely equidistant points round the table, while every gorgeous flower arrangement was as alike to the others as nature would permit.

The diminutive Sheik, magnificent in his flowing white robes and gold-tassled head-dress, was enchanted by the charm and attentiveness of his hostess, and above all by her flattering knowledge of his tiny but influential Gulf state. For an hour Her Majesty animatedly discussed the great progress of his desert peoples, who

only a generation ago had been wandering tribesmen
and fearless warriors. She showed enormous interest in
irrigation projects and the huge desalination plant that
was being constructed on the coast.

The two heads of state were seated at the apex of the
horseshoe; spread out on either side of them was an
impressive array of Royalty and some of the country's
most distinguished names. The Duke of Edinburgh, the
Prince and Princess of Wales, Princess Margaret and the
Queen Mother were all in attendance, as were the Duke
and Duchess of Gloucester, Princess Alexandra and her
husband, Angus Ogilvy. On the right was the Prime
Minister, on the left the Leader of the Opposition, and
sprinkled everywhere were the bemedalled and berib-
boned Generals, Admirals and Air Vice-Marshals. The
only two men in this entire company who were actually
discussing affairs of state were al Mahoud's Foreign
Minister, and his British counterpart, the pushy fellow
who had pressed the Queen at such short notice to host
this regal event.

The band of the Grenadier Guards had struck up a
slow march as the line of fifty footmen swept in bearing
the main course. The Queen gave an imperceptible
signal for it to be served.

The wine waiters, deprived of their normal duties in
deference to religious beliefs, were serving a choice of
Malvern Water (still or fizzy) and Del Monte orange
juice. Suddenly there was a commotion down the left
wing of the table. One of the gold buttons on a footman's
tunic had got caught up in the delicate shoulder strap of
the British Foreign Minister's ample wife. A tussle
ensued.

The sharp eye of the Sheik registered the embarrassed
tango between the footman and the Minister's wife as
they attempted, in vain, to extract themselves from their
unlikely union. The Queen, with the faintest smile,
continued discussing her husband's recent trip to Brunei
in aid of the rare golden-crested desert falcon.

As with all state banquets the Yeomen of the Guard

were placed strategically all around the room, pikes in hand, to guarantee the safety of Elizabeth II and her distinguished guests. As the main course was being eaten the Captain of the Guard, in plumed helmet, strode the length and breadth of the vast table. At the top of it the Queen and Mahoud al Mahoud were in deep conversation about the subject which, for both of them, was a consuming passion — horses. They debated in general terms the respective merits of English thoroughbreds versus Arab stallions. The Sheik, a wily diplomat himself, greatly admired the Queen's ability to discuss this subject in such knowledgeable detail without once mentioning the event uppermost in both their minds.

Then finally, as the Sheik was finishing his rack of lamb, the Queen casually remarked: 'I believe you have a horse entered in next week's Derby.'

The Sheik, picking up an almost cleaned bone from his plate, nodded before taking a last bite and, forgetting himself for a moment, chucked it over his shoulder.

Out from under the table scuttled the Queen's favourite corgi, the only one allowed to attend such grand occasions, and with one gulp Socks swallowed the bone.

The gentle buzz of conversation was halted by the burst of pitiful coughing from the distressed corgi. The sharp L-shaped bone had lodged firmly in the dog's throat. Socks collapsed.

Two footmen stepped smartly forward and bore up the gasping, wheezing Socks. Accompanied by the Captain of the Guard, they spirited him out of the hall. The royal vet was summoned post-haste.

Back at the banquet the sweet, Glace aux Noix, had been served, and the Queen with an extraordinary display of sang-froid had engaged the Sheik in an informed discussion of literacy rates among his nomadic population.

The Captain of the Guard returned and bent close to the ear of Her Majesty. The news was tragic: Socks had died, for Britain.

As the Sheik struggled hopelessly with his green walnut ice-cream, a dish he had not encountered in the desert, Elizabeth shot him a steely look of pure hatred.

But, professional as ever, Her Majesty simply carried on.

Om-Mane-Pedme-Hum

Early the next morning Charles took off from RAF Brize Norton on his private visit to Nepal in one of the new Queen's Flight British Aerospace 146 jets. So secret was this trip that the Prince took no entourage with him, save for his ever-present detective, Robert MacLeod.

For the two days he was in Kathmandu Charles stayed with the Eton-educated King Birenda, the only Hindu monarch in the world, in his delightfully exuberant palace, bedecked with colourful domes and huge rotating prayer-wheels. By day Charles wandered the over-flowing streets of Kathmandu. His detective had his work cut out to keep his charge in sight as they wandered down the famous Pig Alley: people and animals jostled down the narrow cobbled lane, mendicants supplicating for alms vied with flute-sellers, street urchins, beetle-nut vendors, hawkers of every description, bullock carts and wandering holy cows. From all sides came the exotic medley of a busy Eastern market.

Charles was attracted by the rhythmic hammering of metal emanating from a tiny, darkened workshop, lit only by the wood fire of a furnace. It was a cutler making kukris for the tourist trade. Despite the deft salesman-ship, and the offer of a bargain price, the Prince shook his head politely: he did not need another of those lethal curved Gurkha knives. After all, he was already Colonel-in-Chief of the 2nd King Edward VII's Gurkha Rifles.

In Freak Street, so-called because it was the end of the hippie trail, Charles was astonished to find a surprisingly large contingent of Western drop-outs, the leftovers of the 1960's Karma-Cola generation which had made the confused pilgrimage to the East in the idealistic but deluded hope of stumbling upon Nirvana. To his great joy Charles was able to meander unrecognized, even by these discarded children of the consumer society. It would be nice, he thought as he observed those ageing waifs, if when one is in a position to influence such things, rejects like this could come home and alter their own society from within.

Wordlessly, with pleading eyes, a crippled child held out a withered brown hand. Charles had no money, for like all Royals he simply never carried any.

'Lend us a fiver, MacLeod,' he said.

'It's rupees here, Sir,' said the detective, handing over a generous wad.

Before dawn on day three Charles, MacLeod and Sherpa Urkein Tashi set out in a Land Rover for the Thyangboche Monastery, high up in the Himalayas, nestling under the shadow of Mount Everest itself. Abandoning the Land Rover at 12,000 feet the trio, fortified by a gift of zum milk from the villagers, pressed on by foot towards the isolated monastery, which they reached at dusk the next day. The holy place, run by refugee Tibetan Buddhists, reverberated with the lulling chants of the monks' prayers and the magical boom of their eight-foot-long horns, which echoed back from the mountains like a ghostly chorus of spirits.

That night, after a frugal dinner of porridge and monastery-brewed beer, the head lama, in broken English, told the Prince of a fabled holy man who lived as a recluse in a cave, higher up even than the last inhabited hamlet. This fabled ascetic, said the lama, was the object of pilgrimage by only the most dedicated seekers: for the road was hard, the way unknown.

'Those who have the fortitude to find the path,' he added enigmatically, 'will find the way.'

To Charles, this was an irresistible challenge.

When the Prince told MacLeod of his plan to proceed alone, aside from Sherpa Urkein Tashi, the detective objected strongly.

'MacLeod, I shall be in good hands,' replied Charles

firmly. 'Anyway, I very much doubt if the Yeti will have much interest in abducting the future king of England.'

At first light the Prince and Urkein Tashi set forth. Not far behind, but undetected, was the tenacious MacLeod: the Prince's life had been entrusted to his charge, and he had no intention of letting him out of his sight.

That morning, as the sun grew warmer, the scent of daphne and wild magnolia filled the crisp mountain air. Primulas abounded, and above the occasional black kite soared on the warm thermals. There was no other sign of life as they climbed up the gradual incline. By midday the heat was debilitating, the path steeper, and their breathing more laboured. MacLeod was grateful when the two figures before him decided to take a rest.

But that afternoon proved a tougher assignment. As they climbed higher the vegetation petered out and the large boulders, behind which he had been hiding, became more infrequent. Finding a foothold on this dauntingly inhospitable mountainside also proved tricky. The detective slipped and slid as he struggled to keep up without revealing himself.

Soon they were in deep snow, which at times came up to their knees. Suddenly this gave way to a golden valley, the grassy floor of which was strewn with wild flowers and aromatic herbs. The going underfoot was soft and easy, the thick moss and lichen a welcome carpet for their aching feet. Strewn all round were clumps of exquisite orchids.

Concealing himself behind a boulder, the only cover available in this heavenly valley, MacLeod observed his Prince commence the difficult scramble up the steep face of the far side.

Every so often Sherpa Tashi would have to extend a helping hand to the slipping, stumbling figure. For an hour the detective watched his slow and dangerous ascent. Apart from the occasional crash and echo of stones dislodged by Charles's uncertain feet, the only sound was the soft hiss of the westerly wind through the

snow grass. At last the distant pair reached the crest, and
MacLeod could just make out the tiny figures heaving
themselves up over on to the plateau.

MacLeod followed. At times the detective thought he
would never reach the top. Finally, exhausted, he hauled
himself on to the welcome ledge.

Before him was the dark entrance of a cave. Nearby
was the recumbent form of the sleeping Sherpa, and at
the mouth of the cave was Charles's canvas knapsack.

Concealing himself in a crevice, MacLeod waited for
the Prince to emerge. But by the time dusk fell the weary
detective was already fast asleep.

MacLeod was woken early the next morning by the
sound of a voice. It was making a strange, low, rhythmic
humming. The detective was immediately alert.

At the entrance of the cave, seated in the lotus
position, was a robed figure, facing towards the sun.

The man was swathed in a rough-wool peasant's
garment of a dull earth brown. A cowl hid the stranger's
head.

Then MacLeod saw the familiar signet ring with the
Prince of Wales feathers. In astonishment he leaned
forward. But all he could hear was the incomprehensible
chant:

'Om-mane-pedme-hum, om-mane-pedme-hum, om-
mane-pedme-hum, om-mane-pedme-hum, om-mane-
pedme-hum . . .'

Young rolling stock

Prince Edward, emboldened by Sergeant Harborough's elucidation of the birds and the bees, phoned his mother at Buckingham Palace to ask if he could borrow the royal train. At first the Queen demurred.

'It's busy, dear,' said the Sovereign. 'One of our trains is taking your father to a wildlife conference in Porthcawl, while another is carrying poor Socks to Sandringham. The dear love is to be buried there tomorrow.'

'But it's only for a jaunt up to Pontefract in Yorkshire, Mummy. It's for a Duke of Edinburgh Award Scheme dinner.'

Hearing the disappointment in the voice of her youngest son, the Queen relented.

'Oh, alright, darling,' she said. 'Just so long as you open something while you're there.'

In fact, on the advice of Sergeant Harborough, Edward had chosen the royal train as a suitable vehicle for his first venture into the realm of amorous pursuits. When Edward had finally taken the swoop, the little swallow of his fancy had indeed (just as Harborough predicted) accepted his offer to share a nest — in this case, the royal train. Letitia Younger, a doctor's daughter from Bristol, had not hesitated when asked by the Prince if she would possibly, maybe, care to join him on an official engagement in the north of England.

The train at their service was not the newest of the royal rolling stock; however it had a gracious old-world charm, furnished as it was with original Edwardian wood panelling, converted brass gas lamps, rare prints of famous old engines, brown velvet curtains and, in the

elegant saloon, comfortable leather chairs and a
voluminous Victorian chaise-longue.

A Co-op supermarket duly opened and the speech
delivered at the dinner in Pontefract, the royal train set
off back on its homeward journey, pulling into a quiet
siding at Cudworth for the night. Edward, still following
Sergeant Harborough's instructions, settled his companion down on the chaise-longue with a crème de
menthe, and dismissed his staff for the night.

Letitia pulled back the velvet drapes and exclaimed
with delight as she saw the moon disappearing behind a
mountain. 'How romantic,' she sighed. 'Oh Eddie, how
clever of you to pick such a super spot.'

In fact, outside in the dark stood half a dozen silent
members of the South Yorkshire Constabulary, and
behind them the mountain was no more than a National
Coal Board slag heap. Beyond that was a vista of
steaming cooling towers, belching factories, the stark
outlines of pit-heads and row after depressing row of
uniform terraced housing.

An hour of uneasy meandering conversation ensued.
Prince Edward fidgeted and plied Letitia with crème de
menthe. After the sixth, the worldly social anthropology
student said: 'Oh, not another, Eddie. I think I'm a little
tipsy.'

Realizing it was up to her, Letitia Younger, to
introduce the Prince of the Realm to the ways of the
flesh, she put down her glass and took his hand.

'Oh Eddie,' she sighed, and firmly placed her lips upon
his.

After a few aborted fumblings when Edward had lost
his nerve — and way — she again took his hand and
placed it firmly on her breast.

Time passed. Her lips had become dry and sore. Letitia
now understood that it was left to her to take the
ultimate initiative. She detached her chapped lips and
whispered seductively: 'Come.'

Without waiting for a reply, she seized the shy Prince
by the hand and led him to her bedroom.

Three minutes later Edward exited. Eagerly he telephoned Sergeant Harborough.

'Alan? Geronimo!'

'Congratulations, Sir. How was it?'

'Everything went according to plan.' Edward hesitated. 'But, Alan, can I ask you something?'

'Of course, Sir.'

Edward cleared his throat. 'Is that all there is to it?'

'Ah, well. It's a bit like rugby, Sir. I suggest you keep on practising.'

Derby Day

Around Tattenham Corner came the first Rolls in the Royal procession; the glass-cabined limousine turned into the final straight of the Epsom racetrack. The Queen, in a cream silk and lace dress with matching hat, smiled radiantly and waved to the cheering crowds. The June sun reflected sharply off the crisp marquees from wherein came the sound of bubbling laughter and the regular pop of liberated champagne corks. What a glorious day for the Derby Stakes.

Next to her Majesty sat the upright Duke of Edinburgh in his black morning coat. Careful as ever not to upstage the Sovereign, whom the crowds were lined six deep against the rails to see, he occasionally simply touched the brim of his top hat to acknowledge the enthusiastic clapping and cries of 'Bravo'. Accompanying the Royal couple, in deference to his rank for this special day, was the Master of the Horse.

A fleet of six other Rolls Royces followed down the race course. In the second car was the doughty Queen Mother, wearing the inevitable powder blue outfit with matching floral hat, and the Princess of Wales in an eye-catching black and yellow two-piece and low slung netted black hat, adorned with the daring addition of a sweeping white swan's feather. They were accompanied by a grinning Prince Edward, looking enormously pleased with himself.

Next came the Queen's guest of honour, King Juan Carlos of Spain and his wife (described by the Queen Mother as 'Frederica's girl'), Princess Margaret and the Queen's racing manager, Lord Porchester. In the other black limos were Prince and Princess Michael of Kent,

Princess Alexandra, the Lord Steward of the Household, the Crown Equerry, a couple of foreign Ambassadors and an assortment of noble friends and Ladies-in-Waiting.

Her Majesty, though outwardly serene as she waved a gloved hand to her subjects, was not at all calm. Prince Philip knew what a bundle of nerves she was today. He knew how important it was to her. Still smiling to the applauding racegoers, he felt along the leather seat for his wife's right hand and squeezed it reassuringly. She was always excited on Derby Day, but this year was crucial. He knew how much her accumulated hopes were riding on the slender back of Golden Orb.

The going was perfect. The grass of the Epsom racetrack was a startling emerald green. The clear blue sky was dappled with wisps of cirrus cloud, and as far as the eye could see the Surrey Downs were peopled with an incredibly colourful throng.

The popular side of the course was seething with life: beer-swilling punters, shouting bookies, three-card tricksters, hot dog salesmen, fortune-tellers and gypsy girls selling lucky heather. Adjacent to the track were the parked rows of open-topped, double-decker buses, hired for the day by merry groups tucking into their bumper picnics.

On the grandstand side the more prosperous punters in their private boxes were wolfing down gulls' eggs, smoked salmon, lobster salads and dressed crab, all washed down with cases of the very best champagne. The first race had begun, but the real excitement was not till later.

In the Royal Box the Queen took Lord Porchester aside.

'Henry,' she said nervously, 'what do you think?'

'Well, Ma'am, it's up to Golden Orb now,' said her racing manager in that reassuring manner of his. 'We've done all we can. I can't tell you what a picture he looked on his early morning canter, very sharp. The fellow couldn't be in better fettle. He's straining to go.'

'I do hope so,' said the Queen, biting her lip.

'Incidentally, Ma'am, a good omen — I heard that young Wilkinson has wagered £500 on Golden Orb.'

'The groom?'

'Yes, Ma'am. Almost a month's wages.'

'Oh. How loyal.'

The Sovereign moved among her guests in the glass-fronted Royal Box. Although seemingly as attentive and charming as ever, she was distracted. Her mind was on other matters.

'There, there,' said the Queen Mother, patting her daughter on the arm. 'I know what you are worrying about.'

'Oh, Mummy,' said the Queen quietly, 'this is something I've longed for ever since you put me on Peggy.'

'Calm down, dear,' replied her mother. 'I've got a feeling in my old bones that this is your year.'

'I can imagine what you two are talking about,' said Princess Margaret, blowing her cigarette smoke into the air.

'Meg, I do wish you would stop smoking. You heard what the doctor told you,' said the Queen.

'Don't get snappy, dear. I know you are on edge. But I read your horoscope this morning.'

'Oh heavens. What did it say?'

'I've cut it out.' Margaret extracted the piece of torn newspaper from her handbag, and read: '"Taurus. Home and working life bring a clash of interest. But it should be possible to settle a money matter amicably late this afternoon..."'

'That sounds auspicious,' said the Queen Mother. 'Must mean the prize money.'

'Hang on,' said Margaret, 'it gets better ... "There are lively social meetings on offer tonight".'

'Celebrations!' exclaimed the Queen Mother.

'Amazing how apposite one's stars can be,' said Margaret. 'The final piece of advice for Taurus today is — "Resist the urge to shell out advice".'

A footman came round with a tray of champagne. The Queen took her third glass. Her mother caught her eye. 'Are you sure you should have another drink, Lilibet?' asked the Queen Mother gently. 'After all, you do have to reign all afternoon.'

On the opposite side of the red-carpeted, flower-bedecked box, Prince Philip buttonholed Diana.

'Why isn't that husband of yours here? It's his mother's big day.'

'He's abroad,' said Diana, sipping a Buck's Fizz.

'Again?' said Philip testily.

'Well, it's his first trip since our official visit to Canada,' said Diana. 'It's a private visit — he needed a break.'

'Still say he travels too much. Got a young family. Responsibilities at home.'

'Charles is the perfect husband,' said Diana loyally. 'I couldn't ask anything more of him.'

As the hour for the big race drew closer the Queen found it more and more difficult to concentrate on entertaining her guests. At last the time came to go down to the paddock. As she commenced the walk along the track, flanked by Philip and Lord Porchester, her nervousness finally surfaced. She could not restrain herself any longer.

'Henry.'

'Yes, Ma'am?'

'The other horse. How is it placed?'

'Three-to-one, Ma'am.'

'Ah. So we are still the favourites.'

'Indeed, Ma'am — by a nose.'

'I suppose that's because we are the housewives' choice,' said the Queen, alternately acknowledging the clapping crowds on either side.

'No, Ma'am, I think you'll find that the clever money is riding on us. It has to be said the other fellow is not used to English conditions . . .'

They reached the paddock. Already the sixteen entrants — among the finest horses in the world — were circling the arena, led by their stable lads.

As the Queen and her entourage took up their position
in the centre of the ring, her eyes followed the graceful
steps of Golden Orb wearing number seven. She was
thrilled to see how the handsome chestnut had been
brought on. The magnificent thoroughbred, its muscled
shoulders rippling under its silky coat, stepped lightly.
With her knowledgeable eye she could see at a glance
that her horse was at his peak.

At that moment the unemotional voice came over the
public address system: 'And now being led into the ring is
Number Five — Desert Prince. A superb Arab grey, bred
in the United States, ridden by Art Dowd, trained by
Colonel Mackenzie and owned by Sheik Mahoud al
Mahoud . . .'

After forcing herself to wait a few moments, the
Queen shot a surreptitious glance at the nervy, shying
grey stallion, which was pulling impatiently at its leash.
Confirming her worst fears, the Queen realized Desert
Prince was a superlative beast. She couldn't restrain her
admiration.

'He looks a picture, Henry.'

'Touch frisky for me, Ma'am,' said the racing manager
reassuringly. 'Don't forget the horse is probably a bit
nervous away from home.'

The horses were led towards their owners where they
stood in a huddle with their jockeys and trainers. The
grey was brought before the diminutive figure in
flowing white robes and the famous American champion
jockey, Art Dowd, dressed in his silks of yellow with
green hoops, who had a reputation for tough, uncom-
promising riding. The Sheik patted his restless steed.

'That's the little fellow who killed your dog,' said
Prince Philip.

'Yes, dear. That's the man,' the Queen said, nodding
across the paddock to the Sheik who returned the
acknowledgement with a salaam.

'Don't know why you are so polite to that bloody type,'
muttered Philip. 'Personally I'd run the fellow out of the
country.'

'Don't worry, dear, I've thought of that,' said the Queen with a gentle smile. 'But on reflection it wasn't quite on. Instead, one is hoping to teach him a lesson this afternoon.'

She turned her attention to Golden Orb and stroked him on the nose. 'It's up to you,' she whispered in his ear, giving the horse a final pat.

'He knows what he has to do, Ma'am,' said her jockey, Sammy Owen, looking splendid in the Royal racing colours of purple, black, crimson and braid topped off with a gold tassle on the cap.

'You know, Sammy, I think you are right,' said the Queen. Forgetting her horoscope for a moment, she added: 'Don't give him his head immediately and try to avoid the rails at the Tattenham turn.'

'Yes, Ma'am,' said the jockey patiently.

'Don't mind me, Sammy, I'm a bit nervous. I know you will do your best.'

The jockeys began to mount, and before being led back to the Royal Box the Queen called out: 'Good luck, you two. God bless.'

While the Queen polished her binoculars, the bookies were taking a flurry of last-minute bets, and even the most hardened socialites had put down their glasses of Bollinger and taken up their positions for the world's greatest horse race. There was an air of expectant excitement as the babble over the Downs quietened in anticipation.

Suddenly over the loud speakers came the announcement: 'They're under starter's orders!'

On the other side of the Downs sixteen pent-up horses were lining up. A hush fell over the crowd.

'They're off!'

In the distance the dark mass of horses moved away in a close, fast-moving bunch. Over the public address system came the excited voice of the course commentator.

'It's Second Slip leading from Harptree and Tallaheree, and then comes Rebellion followed by Easy Over. Then in a close bunch are Worth's Delight, Catherine Wheel, Chanteclair, Kentucky Dish and Oasis. The back marker is Athena...'

In the Royal Box the Queen sat expressionless.

'Now it's the sixty-six-to-one outsider Harptree from Second Slip, followed by Tallaheree and Rebellion. And here comes Desert Prince. Golden Orb is not yet showing, Garth's Gossip now making a run on the outside — the back marker is still Athena...'

The Queen lowered her binoculars and turned to Lord Porchester with a grimace and a shrug.

As the field approached Tattenham Corner the voice over the PA began to rise in excitement. 'Harptree's beginning to fade now, Second Slip still making the running with Garth's Gossip third and Desert Prince beginning to make ground. Desert Prince coming up strongly. As they make the turn it's Second Slip — Garth's Gossip — Desert Prince. Desert Prince coming up to second place now. Tallaheree — Rebellion — Oasis — Catherine Wheel and coming up on the inside close to the rails is the purple-black-crimson-and-gold of Her Majesty the Queen as Golden Orb makes a late bid...'

By now from the stands the horses could be seen clearly as they thundered into the final straight. The crowds began to shout encouragement.

As the ten front runners separated themselves from the field the Queen put down her binoculars, and leaned forward excitedly in her seat, failing to notice that in her enthusiasm she had knocked over a glass of champagne. The colours of the leading riders were now quite visible to the naked eye.

'Approaching the final furlong,' screamed the commentator, 'it's Desert Prince just in front from Garth's Gossip, Rebellion and continuing to make ground is Golden Orb...'

By now the sound of drumming hooves was audible in the grandstand as the straining horses, urged on by the flailing whips of their crouching jockeys, went for the winning line.

The Queen was on her feet, her fists clenched tight, shouting encouragement. Behind her, as one, the Family and courtiers rose to urge on the Royal hope.

'And it's Golden Orb making its bid on the inside, it's Golden Orb, it's Golden Orb from Garth's Gossip and Rebellion, now Golden Orb neck-and-neck with Desert Prince. With a hundred yards to go it's Golden Orb and the grey...'

As the two front runners came in front of the grandstand the crowd had risen to its feet. The commentary had reached a crescendo of hysteria and Her Majesty, inflamed with passion, completely forgetting her status, screamed as loud as she could: 'Come on, Golden Orb — *come on!*'

The two horses, their colours a blur of silk, were inseparable.

The commentator bellowed: 'They're neck-and-neck,

it's Golden Orb, Desert Prince, nothing in it and a slight
bump, good gracious, a little collision there . . .'

The noise from the crowd was deafening, drowning out
the Queen's yells as the horses devoured the final yards.

'There's hardly anything in it but as they cross the
finishing line it's Desert Prince from Golden Orb; Desert
Prince has it, to my mind. Desert Prince has it, Golden
Orb second. What a race!'

The Queen sank back, stunned.

She sat alone, silent and dejected for a few moments. Her
dream was shattered. In that last furlong it had looked as
if Golden Orb, having saved himself so well, would in
those closing strides bring home her crowning moment,
and then, and then . . .

'Bad luck, old girl,' said Philip, putting a hand on her
shoulder.

The Queen put her hand up to his, but remained silent.
She couldn't speak. She was too choked with emotion.

'Not that luck came into it,' added Philip. 'Far as I could
make out, the bloody Arab swerved into your nag. Clear
obstruction, if you ask me.'

The Queen looked up, her eyes filled with tears. 'You
think so dearest?'

'Damn right. You were baulked, old stick. I'd lodge an
objection.'

The Queen, mindful of her position, hesitated. Did she
dare?

An objection was lodged.

Within minutes the Public Address system was
announcing to an astonished crowd: 'There will be a
Stewards' Enquiry . . . Stewards' Enquiry . . .'

Down in the bunker-like rooms beneath the
grandstand, the distinguished group of Jockey Club
Stewards gathered, their faces betraying the gravity of
the momentous decision which they had been called
upon to take. It was a select group, chosen from among
the most blue-blooded sporting men in the land,

including a marquis, two earls and a baronet — all of whom knew the Queen personally.

'God's teeth, Freddie,' said one. 'Damn difficult decision, eh?'

'Bally hell, Buffy, a chap now knows what Solomon must have felt like.'

They regarded each other glumly.

'Damn and hell's bells! Why the Queen's horse?'

'Well, Buffy, the answer will be on the film. Must do our duty. Roll the video, clerk.'

The six wise men of the Jockey Club strained forward in a huddle as they watched the replay of the final stages of the race.

'There it is, Freddie — clear as daylight!'

'Damn right, Buffy, clear as the nose on your face.'

'No question about it, old man.'

'Unequivocal!'

Within moments the PA system crackled into life again. The crowd stilled. The tension in the Royal Box was unbearable.

The slow, measured, unemotional tones of the announcer blared out: 'Ladies and gentlemen, may we have your attention, please? The result of the objection raised in the last race has been decided by the Stewards.'

The Queen bit her lip. Her knuckles were white as she gripped Philip's hand tightly.

'The winner of this year's Royal Derby Stakes,' continued the phlegmatic announcer, 'is...'

The tension over the silent race-track was like the stilled moment before an electric storm.

'... *Golden Orb!*'

The Downs erupted with a roar of delight. Hats filled the air and the cheering in the Royal Box was deafening. The Queen beamed and beamed and beamed.

EPISODE FOUR: AUTUMN

The road to Chew Magna

For the Royal Family June and July had been busy, and they were all looking forward to their two-month-long break at Balmoral. But before they could board the Royal Yacht *Britannia* for the relaxing journey up to Scotland, there were still a few outstanding engagements to attend. The Queen was opening a new fast-breeder nuclear power station on the Kent coast, on the way to which she had to drive through a chanting line of demonstrators — one of whom was indelicate enough to bare his bottom, which had two painted downstrokes thus completing a good impression of a CND sign. Prince Philip had popped over to France, never his favourite country, to attend an ornithological symposium in Marseilles where he intended to bollock the delegates about their disgraceful habit of massacring migrating birds. Edward was The Firm's sole representative this year at Cowes Yachting Regatta, while Charles was helicoptering himself down to the West Country, destined, so his itinerary said, for the brand new, ultra-

modern, computerized Contented Chicken factory at
Chew Magna in Somerset.

The Prince of Wales was descending on Chew in the
red Wessex on behalf of his mother, to present the
founder of the booming Contented Chicken chain with a
Queen's Award for Industry. Reginald Swayne was one
of the success stories of rural England, having
transformed his father's modest smallholding into a
massive battery hen concern, which not only produced
eggs and fowl for the home market, but exported gullets
and giblets in vast quantities to France and chickens' feet
to China for God-knows-what. He was exactly the salt-
of-the-earth-type-made-good that the Prince admired so
much, was keen to meet and delighted to encourage with
such royal patronage.

As Charles began his crouched dash from the
helicopter, whose blades were still rotating, his carefully
laid hair flew in all directions, revealing an expanse of
white pate. Swayne's strong yeoman hand gripped
Charles's in a vigorous handshake, and his rubicund face
cracked into a broken-toothed smile:

'Welcome, Zir! Welcome to the Contented Chicken
Ranch.'

Charles attempted to straighten the wisps of his stray
hair.

'Sounds a bit like a brothel to me.'

Though not everyone heard the remark, the
welcoming committee broke into roars of hearty
laughter.

'Only feathered birds in there, Zir,' chuckled Swayne,
indicating the half dozen low-slung terraced plastic
sheds, with air vents sprouting from their grass green
roofs. The Prince caught the first whiff of fresh paint.

He went down the line shaking the usual anonymous
hands, swopping pleasantries about this and that, and
cracking one or two pre-prepared jokes.

It was a splendid late summer's day, and under the mild
August sunshine the surrounding countryside epitom-
ized to Charles all that was so right about the garden of

England. The factory nestled under the brow of the Mendip Hills, cattle and sheep grazed in the adjacent fields, that lush pasture which was responsible for the Cheddar, that noble cheese of old England. The song of thrush came from nearby hedgerows.

Charles filled his lungs with fresh air and smiled happily at his bucolic host. 'Mr Swayne, this day is truly ... blessed.'

But Charles had not been prepared for the sight inside the factory. The shed, one hundred yards long, contained row upon row of caged chickens, thousands upon thousands of them and at the same instant they all began squawking hysterically.

Swayne had to shout: 'Not used to humans, Zir. They're a bit ruffled.'

Charles stared down the uniform lines of barred cages, stunned at the sheer inhumanity of this spectacle.

'Them's eaters,' yelled Swayne above the cacophony. Taking the Prince by the arm he led him down the first row.

The cages were piled on top of each other, four storeys high, making use of every square foot and leaving hardly enough room for the birds themselves to turn around.

'We breed 'em for big breasts,' continued Swayne proudly. 'Your Contented Chicken flesh is as white as a virgin's wedding-dress. Consumers don't go for brown meat no more.'

Charles was appalled. Above the din he heard the catalogue of Swayne's success.

'We have six more sheds here, housing ninety-five thousand birds, which gives us one thousand, six hundred frozen items a day ...'

As they reached the end of the shed and the last row of stacked cages, which now reminded Charles irresistibly of Alcatraz, Swayne leaned forward and blew on the feathers of a totally freaked chicken, revealing a plump breast.

'Lovely pectorals,' said Swayne with a wink.

Out in the yard Charles closed his eyes and drew a

deep breath. The things I do for England, he thought.

'That was the raw product,' said Swayne. 'Your top-of-the-market-broiler. Now I should like to show you the pride of our little operation — our hi-tech processing laboratory and packaging plant.'

'Could I just ask you one thing, Mr Swayne?' said Charles hesitantly.

'Be my guest, Zir.'

'You call them contented chickens ...'

'That's right. Happy as sandboys.'

'Yes, but what proof do you have of their well-being?'

'Their taste. The chicken that don't die happy, to my mind, don't taste as good as them that do.'

'What about the quality of their life, Mr Swayne?'

'That be Grade One. They have ample sunlight, or the impression of it, constant water and as much food as they can eat — sounds like a holiday to most humans. 'Tis a brief life for our feathered friends but it's a happy one. 'Tis the only life they've known, see.'

Charles could see the similarity with Royalty.

He was now led to the processing plant where he was to receive an even greater shock. Inside it was cool and quiet, save for the gentle hum of automated machinery.

Charles blenched as Mr Swayne launched into a fresh commentary.

'Them fowls, what is attached to tha' pole by their legs, see, they comes down 'ere at a rate o'knots — proper Stirling Mosses, them — and their 'eads go into this basin full of water. And it's electrified, see.' Swayne permitted himself a smile. '*Zap*. Dead as a doornail.' He pulled a switch. 'Look, 'ere comes one now.'

Through the hatchway came a condemned chicken. Charles realized he was the first Royal for centuries to witness an execution.

The trussed fowl, head downwards, came whizzing along the wire with what appeared to the Prince to be a look of sheer horror on its face. Its disbelieving eyes disappeared under the water. Its wings gave one last involuntary flap, as if to take flight.

Charles gasped.

Swayne chortled. 'Have no fear, Sir. It's already with its Maker. Its soul has departed — an instant transition.'

'I believe we are always with our Maker,' replied the shaken Prince. 'Life is a transition.'

'if you care to have a look there you'll observe the head being sliced off. This is done by the 'ead remover...'

Charles shuddered. 'How horrible.'

'Not really, Sir,' said Swayne. 'In the old days when I begun this lark we used to wring the necks of them fowls with our own hands. This is much cleaner and quicker and altogether more humane. We used to get terrible chapped hands in them days.'

For the remainder of the process — the plucking, the degutting, the leg amputation, cleaning, dressing, wrapping and weighing — Charles was in a daze. Not a moment too soon they reached the end of this macabre assembly line. The Royal entourage stood expectantly around a curious apparatus with a shute emerging from it, waiting for the grand finale.

Swayne looked at his watch and counted: 'Five, four, three, two, one...' Out before them popped a neat package, shrink-wrapped in cellophane.

'That, Zir,' said Swayne, 'is the bird you saw but one hundred and thirty-five seconds ago as happy as Larry. Now he be a Contented Chicken.' Swayne picked up this neat packet.

'May I proudly present him to you, Zir?'

Charles passed the dead bird so quickly to his detective that the offending cadaver hardly rested in his hands. Then he heard the voice of Swayne saying: 'Lunch.'

Numbed, Charles followed him to the staff canteen, which had been transformed for his visit into a small restaurant smelling of fresh paint.

'We have a bit of a treat for you, Zir,' announced the jolly Swayne. 'A French delicacy — the nature of which I cannot yet reveal as it's a bit of a surprise, see. However, I am at liberty to reveal that it's garnished with truffles, foie gras, flavoured with cognac and madeira, and done to a turn in a pig's bladder.'

The waiter appeared bearing a steaming dish and ceremoniously placed it in front of the Prince of Wales.

'That, Zir,' crowed the triumphant Swayne, 'be Poularde Dauphinoise!'

Charles looked at his plate. He felt sick.

It was a Contented Chicken.

Rule, Britannia

The Royal Yacht *Britannia* lay anchored off-shore from the Isle of Wight, acting as it always did as guard ship for the Cowes Regatta. On the main mast the Royal Ensign fluttered proudly in the south-westerly breeze, while from the mizzen flew the Union Jack and at the stern the White Ensign. All around on the Solent, splendid in the evening sun, were the colourful sails and spinnakers of hundreds of different types of small craft, and from on shore came the dull boom of the Royal Yacht Squadron cannon signalling the end of another race.

The dark-blue-hulled *Britannia*, the largest private yacht in the world, was an elegant, old-fashioned tub, whose white superstructure was as impeccable and crisp as the ratings' uniforms, while inside it resembled a chintzy but grand country house. At the rear of the main deck stood the glittering stateroom — the drawing-room (with fireplace) which could hold 200 people, the dining-room, with its Hepplewhite chairs, which could seat 60 for a banquet, the sitting-room with its silver-grey fitted carpet overlaid with Persian rugs, plus assorted anterooms and other more cosy reception rooms. Below decks was the accommodation for the 277 naval crew, in addition to the 20 cabins for the household courtiers, plus another 40 for the domestic staff.

On the verandah deck, their elbows leaning against the rail, were two figures looking out across the water towards the little town, spruce and festive, festooned with bunting. On the wind came the faint sounds of a rowdy party and the snatch of a ragged male chorus. A gang of beefy young men, all dressed in bright orange waterproofs, spilled out of a hotel, reeling and waving their arms, one or two of them falling flat on the road.

'Must be those splendid Aussies,' remarked Prince Philip, delighted to be back from hateful France. 'Celebrating their victory in the channel race.'

Edward watched the departing rabble of weaving yachtsmen with a twitch of envy. But he didn't have time for such wishful thoughts: their guests would be arriving on board any moment. Behind them the twenty-six-man Royal Marine band played jaunty sea shanties by Vaughan Williams, and Edward would see that the royal barge had already cast off from the Royal Yacht Squadron jetty and was ploughing its way back through the ragged flotilla of dinghies with the first batch of that evening's guests.

As the launch drew alongside, and the guests began to clamber up the companionway, the band struck up a medley from *My Fair Lady* while the ratings piped the VIPs aboard.

'Right my boy, action stations,' said Philip. 'You're co-host tonight. don't be shy. Speak up. Remember who you are. Mix with the guests — and for God's sake don't drink too much.'

The Chief Petty Officer had begun to announce in stentorian tones the arriving guests. He bellowed: 'His Royal Highness, Prince Michael of Kent.'

'Come on,' said Philip.

'And Her Royal Highness, Princess Michael of Kent.'

'One's relations!' groaned Philip.

Edward's nervousness had been wrongly interpreted by his father. He wasn't concerned at having to play host in lieu of his mother, who seldom visited the regatta; in fact, his present state of jitters had been brought about by a surge of over-confidence.

After breaking his duck with the compliant Letitia, he had indeed taken Sergeant Harborough's advice and was practising hard. Over the past two months he had stepped out with eleven young ladies, the last of whom was none other than Rear-Vice Admiral Sir Johnny Cumming-Brice's daughter, the sensational Amelia, who had been tipped by the social editor of *The Tatler* as the top prospect of the season. Edward, who had met her twice now during Cowes week, was completely smitten. Unfortunately tonight, as young men are wont to do on occasion, he had double booked.

'Commander of the Royal Yacht Squadron...' the Chief Petty Officer was announcing. Edward stood at the top of the companionway, beside his father, welcoming the guests. He became increasingly anxious. How was he going to cope? He looked across at the lurking Sergeant Harborough, who winked discreetly back. Good old Alan. He would think of something.

The Chief Petty Officer was barking: 'Rear-Vice Admiral Sir John Cumming-Brice, and Miss Amelia Cumming-Brice.'

Amelia had a dark, sultry, almost Spanish colouring. Her features were fine and delicate, with the slightest retroussé nose, while soft wavy brunette hair tumbled over her bare shoulders; she was wearing the most gorgeous ankle-length pearl pink duchesse satin evening gown. Edward felt his mouth go dry. What colouring, what grace, what style, what humour and intelligence lay behind those sleepy mauve eyes. Amelia was the sum total of ... of what was that word Harborough had used the other day... of — of — complete pulchritude!

An hour later, as the party was hotting up, Edward at last contrived to get the lovely Amelia to himself. He had all but forgotten his nerves, such was the social grace and infectious laughter of this amazing creature. Suddenly Harborough hove-to. Out of the corner of his eye Edward could see him hovering.

'Excuse me, Amelia, don't go away.'

Edward approached the sergeant irritably.

'Can't you see I'm busy, Harborough?'

The sergeant leaned forward and whispered: 'She's arrived, Sir.'

'Who?'

'Her, Sir.' Harborough indicated with his head across the crowded room. Oh God! It was Letitia Younger. Crikey!

After the interlude in the railway siding the Prince had, in gratitude, invited the third-year social anthropology student to Cowes. But that was before he had met Amelia.

'What the heck are we going to do, Harborough?'

'Leave it to me, Sir.'

Harborough strode purposefully across the floor, a smile of welcome on is face.

'Good evening, Miss Younger. How nice you could come.'

'Hello, Harborough,' said Letitia, 'I am just going to say hello to Eddie . . .'

'You've never been aboard *Britannia*, have you?' said Harborough, taking Letitia firmly by the arm. 'Let me show you some of its treasures.'

He guided her into the dining-room and stood before the miniature oasis. 'It's the gift from the Sheik of Dubai. The palm trees are solid gold, so are the two little camels. And those coconuts,' said Harborough, tinkling the grape-sized gems, 'are themselves made of rubies.'

'Most interesting, but I'm quite anxious . . .'

'And over here is their white Minton china collection,' continued Harborough without pause. 'The rim, you'll notice, and Royal cypher are made of gold.'

'Thank you, Harborough, but . . .'

'Let me show you this — you'll want to tell your grandchildren about it.'

Harborough guided the reluctant Letitia down the elevator into the holds. Keeping up an uninterrupted commentary in order to prevent her from getting a word in, the detective droned on: '. . . and on board the matelots wear white plimsolls so the noise of their footsteps on deck is reduced to an inaudible pad, so as not to disturb you-know-who. And likewise on the upper decks orders are indicated by hand signals in order to avoid verbal disturbance . . .'

They had reached the door of a hold in the bowels of the ship. He opened it with a flourish. Letitia gasped.

'Thought that might impress you, miss.'

There stood the black Royal Rolls-Royce Phantom IV with a silver emblem of George and the dragon on the bonnet.

'Very impressive, Harborough, but now if you don't mind, please take me back to the party,' said Letitia.

Back in the buzzing drawing-room, desperate to keep the increasingly agitated student occupied, Harborough continued his relentless guided tour: '... not just for the exclusive use of the Royal Family because she doubles up as a naval hospital ship, and indeed when on NATO exercises *Britannia's* sophisticated satellite equipment makes her the perfect communications centre...'

'Blast your damned ship...'

'Yacht, actually,' corrected Harborough.

'Yacht, dinghy, submarine — I couldn't give a toss. I want to — *must* — meet Edward,' said the furious Letitia.

'Certainly, miss. Oh, by the way, may I introduce a most engaging local gentleman.' Harborough reached out for the arm of a tall, gawky man with two glasses of champagne in hand.

Mr Bonham swung round, accidentally splashing a glass of his champagne over the satinwood desk that had belonged to Queen Victoria.

'That's right,' the entire room heard Prince Philip bark, 'go on — ruin my bloody ship.'

As the flustered Mr Bonham attempted to make his apologies, Letitia hissed to Sergeant Harborough: 'Listen here — I have something very, very important to tell the Prince. I know you are keeping him from me. But I promise you this — if I can have one minute of his time I shall leave the boat.'

She looked directly at Harborough.

'Deal done,' said the Sergeant.

Edward managed to extract himself from the company of Rear-Vice Admiral Sir John Cumming-Brice, who was expounding his theory as to why Nelson need never actually have lost an eye, let alone his life.

Out on the darkened deck, by the companionway, Edward found Letitia. By now his fellow student was exceedingly angry.

'I can see you are terribly busy, Your Royal Highness, and I wouldn't dream of wasting your precious time,' she said sarcastically, her pent-up anger putting a quiver in her voice,' but there was just one thing that I felt honour-bound to tell you.'

She started her descent of the companionway, turned and announced quietly: 'I'm pregnant.'

Britannia Rules the Waves

The next morning *Britannia* weighed anchor to start the long Western Isles cruise, much looked forward to by the Windsors, because it signified the beginning of their long autumn break.

First the yacht had to sail for nearby Southampton to take on some essentials — chocolates, dog biscuits, books (*The Times Crossword Book*, a collection of Jackie Collins's novels, some Gerald Durrells, *The Tibetan Book of the Dead*); fishing tackle, shotguns, films (*Seven Brides for Seven Brothers, National Velvet*); videos (*The Two Ronnies, Miami Vice*), sea-sick pills, Carmen rollers, and piles of records (Perry Como, the Beach Boys, Barry Manilow, Duran Duran, Mozart's *Marriage of Figaro*) — not to mention the Queen and the Princess of Wales.

The *Britannia* steamed onwards past Weymouth and Plymouth, and as it rounded the southernmost point of England, Land's End, a squall hit them full on. The Royal Yacht, despite having stabilizers, was notoriously unstable.

The Queen resorted to her Kwells in time. Not so Diana. Philip, on the other hand, was in his element, standing out on the bridge deck, hands behind his back, his face pointed into the driving, briny wind. The *Britannia* pitched and heaved.

'What fun,' said Philip. A rating was sick. 'Bloody hell, boy — can't you keep it down?' said the former naval officer, who as Philip Mountbatten RN had been First Lieutenant on *HMS Whelp* in the war.

For dinner, at the huge mahogany table laid for ten, sat only Philip and Edward.

'Now what's for nosh?' boomed Philip. 'Hungry, m'boy?'

From the far end of the table Edward nodded weakly. Philip picked up the menu.

'Excellent! Oeufs poches aux moules, followed by steak Tartare...'

Edward fled.

Philip grabbed at a ship's decanter which was about to slide off the polished table as it pitched and rolled alarmingly. Spread around the room, braced against the walls and holding on to any fixture they could, were half a dozen pallid footmen. The Duke took the opportunity to read Jackie Collins's latest saucy paperback, in which he was so absorbed that he failed to notice the heroic efforts of his footmen to serve him.

The flunkies had to time their lurch towards the table between the rolls of the bucking ship as precisely as the beat of a metronome. If not, they — and the dish they were serving — would have been catapulted across the room, with catastrophic consequences.

Even the Bombe Surprise was delivered successfully to the Duke, who was left in peace to devour both the sickly sweet and raunchy novel with a hearty appetite.

By the next morning the storm had abated, enabling the yacht to heave-to off Fishguard to collect Prince Charles, who had been giving a speech in tortuous Welsh to the Dyfed Farmers' Association. His theme had been: 'Organic Fertilizers Versus Profits — Can We Love Ourselves if we don't Love our Soil?'

However, the calmness of the Irish Sea was not reflected in Diana's mood. When at last they were alone together in their cabin, Charles found that his wife was in a state of some agitation. As the *Britannia* slid by Aberystwyth, Caernarvon, Liverpool and Blackpool, Diana's fears could not be quieted:

'Ever since you got back from Nepal you have been so detached, distracted. I feel I can't get through to you. We were so close, darling, and now... well, I know you say that you love me but your head is always in the clouds.

You're in a perpetual dream — even your father says so. Yes, yes I understand that, I quite appreciate that you have to find something to do and find your way but there's me, Charles, and William and Harry and Nanny to consider. We want to be included, you know — but you seem to have cut us out. I feel that you are thinking of something else. Is there another woman?... Well, you say not, but what can I make of your behaviour, then... Alright, well, someone *has* said something actually. Oh Charles..." She burst into tears.

Charles put his arm around his distraught wife and the whole saga came pouring out. She had been shopping in Kensington for some tweedy outfits for the Braemar Games and a couple of country jumpers for him. She had purposely gone into a boutique called 'Koala Bears' to stem the gossip about the liaison he was supposed to have had with the owner, a glamorous Australian socialite.

Diana had found that by freezing Koala out she had only fuelled the rumours. That beastly reporter Spalding took every opportunity to refer to this so-called special relationship. In the end curiosity had got the better of Diana — and now she regretted it. Koala had proved to be exactly the kind of woman that intimidated Diana: naturally blonde, tanned, outspoken, intelligent, witty, enormously confident and clearly secure in her own sexuality. Furthermore, Koala had dealt with this unannounced visit with considerable élan, and had even dissuaded Diana from purchasing an Urquhart tartan jumper and the crew-neck Shetland. Instead, the brazen woman had sold her that charcoal-grey cashmere and the blue Guernsey fishing sweater — both of which had proved such a great hit with him.

'She obviously knows you backwards,' sobbed Diana.

'It's simply not true, it's so unfair,' pleaded Charles. 'Koala's a nice enough chap, but she has her faults. Far too loud, for a start. I'd never climb up a tree with that marsupial.'

Charles had hoped his little joke would lighten the

atmosphere. But Diana was not to be distracted.

'How humiliating,' she wailed. 'All those jokes about you being in her pouch!'

Searching high and low

The last two months had been agony for Andrew. After receiving that ominous letter from Ryder St Bartholomew there had been silence: the bastard was letting him sweat it out. Meanwhile Andrew had to get on with his busy and active life as a Royal Navy Helicopter pilot, and with making those tricky adjustments from bacherlorhood to responsible married man. His flame-haired Princess was sweet, loving and understanding, though at times she was perturbed that he seemed preoccupied. But how could he possibly tell her? He could see as clear as daylight how the evidence would look to anyone — a large cheque, signed by him, to a foreign trollop. With his track record, who would believe the truth?

There was no one for Andrew to confide in; not his father, certainly not his mother, let alone either of his brothers. And imagine going to the police! It wasn't just that it would ruin him, the mud would splatter the entire Family. No, this was one mission — however perilous — that he would have to deal with himself.

After fretting, and waiting to hear from St Bartholomew for several weeks, Andrew resolved to take the initiative. He made some discreet enquiries about the Australian: there was precious little information and none of it reassuring. His researches revealed nothing that had not appeared in the newspapers about his activities as the so-called 'Kangaroo King'. The most intriguing fact concerned the opening of his London Casino, the Busted Flush, where the newspapers had reported in lurid detail the squalid fight between Charles's ex-valet and a Palace footman.

Was there a clue here, Andrew wondered? He noted, much to his surprise, that Princess Michael of Kent had opened this gambling den: God, the mystery got deeper and deeper.

That ghastly rag the *Daily Disclosure* ended its account of this notorious evening with a statement from a spokesman for The Busted Flush. 'Two queers stabbing each other? Rivers of blood? Tosh! This is a high-class sporting club,' said society playboy, the Hon Henry Fairlie. 'There was a small incident which has been blown up out of all proportion.'

Henry Fairlie? That name rang a bell. Christ, wasn't that the chap who had once been a greeter at the Mayfair club, A Night in Tunisia? Yes, and then Andrew remembered something that struck him like a shock of a thousand volts. It was at A Night in Tunisia that he had met Ilaria Pucci.

It came back to him clearly now: in his bachelor days he had toddled along with a bunch of chaps from the Squadron, all half cut, to the old Tunisia, one of his favourite haunts before he got married. Lots of lovely crumpet, and dark enough for indiscretions. The host had been Henry, one of those ne'er-do-wells who sponged off their rich friends and held down what they called 'jobs' at nightclubs and the like. In fact, oh God, it had been that lounge-lizard Henry who had introduced him to Poochers, herself one of those pretty girls who hung around such joints in the expectation of hitching their hawsers to the bollards of wealthy patrons.

The picture was becoming painfully clear. When he'd entered the club that night there'd been no photographers, yet when he left, after midnight, with Ilaria in tow, the paparazzi were in waiting. Strewth, it was clear as crystal: Henry and Poochers must have been in league. He thought about all the publicity that had dogged his relationship with the Italian 'starlet' — all those inexplicable leaks when he'd been off frotting in various country houses with the Neapolitan madam. Hell's bells, what else did they have on him? With a sudden stab of panic he remembered that romp at Rollo's place. Oh no! What if that came out?

He realized there was only one course of action: he would have to meet that odious fly-by-night, Fairlie.

So it was that these two unlikely luncheon companions found themselves seated uneasily opposite each other over a glass of Château Cheval-Blanc 1970 at the smart gentleman's dining club, Oliver's in Berkeley Square. Andrew had chosen the club because his presence at this discreet retreat would cause no comment: everything here was comfortable, well-heeled, impeccable, muted, and privacy was guaranteed.

Over the asparagus, and after some brittle pleasantries, Andrew came to the point.

'Look, Fairlie. Won't beat about the bush. We both know what this is about. What's your game?'

Henry wiped away a dribble of butter from his chin. 'Game, Sir?' he said, playing for time. It was a tricky one this; depending on how he dealt his cards this meeting could either advance his social climb or he could end up in the Tower.

'Cut it out, Fairlie. Just what is the score? Put your cards on the table, man.'

Henry, his bluff called, realized that he had a very poor hand. He knew almost nothing. Still, he was getting a free lunch, excellent wine, and the fact that he had been spotted at Oliver's in the company of Prince Andrew would do his social standing no harm at all. He decided to come clean.

'Fact is, Sir, I'm afraid to tell you this dingo Bartholomew has got a cheque of yours made out to a tart.'

'I know that, you clot' spluttered Andrew. 'But what the hell does he intend to do with it?'

'Do with it, Sir?' echoed Henry, with a sinking feeling that he had got himself into something deeper than he had ever bargained for.

'Don't pretend you don't know this Bartholomew bastard is blackmailing me.'

'Beggar me,' exclaimed Henry, appalled. 'Never thought the chap'd go that far. What's he after?'

'Idiot! That's what I want you to tell me.'

'But I didn't know about it, Sir. Cross my heart.'

Henry, realizing he was up to his neck in something criminal, spilled out all he knew about the crazed antipodean with an unlimited bank account and an insatiable ambition to gatecrash English society. Henry was unable to throw any light on Bartholomew's sinister intentions. He was only able to tell an appalled Andrew of the mysterious telescopic surveillance of Buckingham Palace.

'Oh, and there was one other thing he did say before going back to Australia...'

'What?'

'It was when he was talking about you actually, Sir. Something about going for the big one.'

The colour drained from Andrew's face. 'I see,' he said grimly. 'So why has this scum kept silent for two months? Why doesn't he come out and say what he's after?'

'He's a gambling man,' said Henry. 'Must be upping the ante. Making you sweat.'

They fell silent as the waiter carved the boeuf à la mode de chef. As soon as the waiter retreated, Henry, now seeing his only social hope being an alliance with the distressed Prince, volunteered a theory which came to him in a flash of inspiration.

'Christ, I should have thought of that before, Sir!'

'What?'

'Well, the Down Under connection!'

'Don't speak in riddles, Fairlie. You're in hot water, man. Spit it out.'

'Don't you see, work it out! Ask yourself — who opened The Busted Flush?'

'Princess Michael,' answered Andrew.

'And where was she brought up?'

'Australia.'

'Aha! You see — like-you-know-who.'

'What exactly are you suggesting, Fairlie?'

'You don't suppose... gosh, no, well... that von Reibnitz is planning to overthrow the Windsors?'

'Don't be ridiculous, Fairlie. She's one of us now.'

It was clear to Andrew that Henry, true to his wastrel nature, had simply been a dupe. He had only one piece of information which could now be of use to the Prince. The whereabouts of Miss Ilaria Pucci.

The Italian customs officer peered inquisitively at the bizarre figure in the turned-up Burberry raincoat, trilby hat and dark glasses. Strange attire for this weltering Mediterranean heat, thought the officer, but then these English were crazy. 'Jack Brazen,' read the customs man. 'Born February 19th, 1960. Profession: commercial photographer. Physical peculiarities: none.' He looked again at the suspicious figure.

'Please, you take off those glasses, Signor Brazen... you know, you looka like someone... maybe a bit like the young Marcello Mastroianni. Purpose of thees visit?... Ah, to photograph le belle signorine. Bene. Allora, Signor Brazen, enjoy Napoli.'

Andrew looked carefully about him to make sure he was not being followed. It was the devil of a job for a chap in his position to sneak out of the country just for a day. He'd even had to give his own detective the slip. He hailed a taxi, and they sped towards the city, past orange groves, vineyards and donkey carts, while in the background Vesuvius loomed through the heat haze. The sweat tricked down Andrew's collar. God, the temperature must be in the hundreds. He struggled out of his raincoat and even removed his jacket. No one was going to recognize him in the back streets of Naples.

The taxi dropped him at the corner of via Carlo de Cesare, the address Henry Fairlie had given him. It was a narrow, steeply-inclined cobbled street, overrun with urchins playing football and street vendors shouting their wares at full voice. An old lady sat on an upturned fruit box selling contraband cigarettes. Everywhere life was spilling out into the streets in a riot of colour and noise. The mediaeval drains, in this fetid heat, gave off an acrid, sulphurous stench.

'Ciao,' called a sweet, siren voice.

He looked round. Out of a first-floor window leaned a leering hag, her unruly drooping bosom threatening to spill out of her loose-laced bodice. She parted her brightly painted lips.

'Hey, sailor, you wanna have some cheap funtimes?'

Prince Andrew cleared his throat. 'No thanks, jolly nice of you all the same,' he said, checking the piece of paper in his hand. 'Actually I'm looking for er, numero cinquanta sei...'

Lines of washing hid the entrance, disguising the crumbling façade of a once magnificent baroque palazzo. In the courtyard, beside a wilting palm, he found a coughing, wheezing caretaker. Andrew showed him the address and followed the shuffling, muttering old boy up three flights of worn, pitch-black stairs. Taking out a bunch of huge keys, the caretaker unlocked the creaking door and ushered in the anxious Prince.

'Momento,' instructed the ancient as he shuffled off to summon his mistress.

Inside it was shadowy and cool. On the walls were faded portraits of cardinals and noblemen. The suspiciously bare marble-floored room was redolent of past grandeur.

'Principe!' Andrew looked round. 'Andrea, bello. 'Ow nice to see you. Why I 'ave this piacere?'

Andrew was shocked. In the eight months since he had seen Ilaria, she had gone to seed. Under her flimsy white cotton slip, her figure was fleshy, her wild hair entangled and unbrushed. She stood, slatternly, leaning in the doorway, a cigarette dangling between her lips as she spoke.

'We hada some good times, eh baby? You looka hunky.'

She moved towards him, padding on her bare feet, swinging her now heavy hips.

'You're acting as if you've forgotten,' said Andrew, backing off, 'but I got married.'

'Hey baby, so did I!' laughed Ilaria. 'I am now a contessa. I marry the sixteenth Conte Avellino della Croce.' She shrugged. "'E's an old fart.'

'Thing is, Contessa, I need your help.'

'Any time.'

Andrew spelled out his predicament. Ilaria blanched.

'That Ryder, he's merda... evil. You be careful, Andrea,'

She told him all she could. Again, it wasn't much. When St Bartholomew had learnt about the cheque for Andrew's Christmas prank, he had paid her £90,000 for it, and ordered her to get the hell out of town. He had also warned her that if she ever so much as squeaked about what she knew, he had 'friends of friends' in Italy who... wordlessly she drew her forefinger across her throat.

'Oh Andrea,' she said, putting her arms around the Prince. 'I am so frightened...'

The door opened and in hobbled a bent old man, leaning on a walking stick.

'Thees is my 'usband,' announced an unperturbed Ilaria.

Breaking away from her embrace, Andrew extended his hand.

'Hello Count. I'm...'

The first blow cracked down on his head. Andrew stumbled backwards, but the flailing walking-stick continued to beat upon him.

Andrew backed towards the door, his hands held up defensively. The enraged Count Avellino della Croce, rejuvenated by jealousy, drove the Prince out of his home and down the stairs, accompanied by a torrent of rich Neapolitan abuse. Reaching the courtyard, Andrew fled; and as he pelted down the cobbled alleyway he heard behind him, from a window on high, Ilaria's piercing adieu: 'Andrea, I luff you...'

The final hurdle

In the office of the *Daily Disclosure*, for the umpteenth time, Spalding was attempting to write his colour feature for the women's page about life aboard *Britannia* when the shadow of his new editor loomed over him.

'God, not that drivel,' groaned Snitch. 'I can't abide this waffling flimflam. What we need, laddie, is some hard old fashioned exclusives that will sell this newspaper.'

'What do you want, old boy?' asked Spalding. 'The inside story of how the Queen suffers from catrarrh?'

'Don't be disgusting, Spalding, people don't buy our product to throw up over breakfast. Give me something that lifts the lid.'

'What then? How the Queen is as grey as your granny and uses a dye called Chocolate Kiss to give it that lovely chestnut sheen?'

'Acch laddie! When will you learn — we are not here to tarnish their image. We don't want to break the public's illusions — unless it's a very good story, of course.'

'Want a new angle on the Queen's drinking?'

'Now you are talking. Got a wee problem, eh?'

'No. But I heard the other day that in order not to be seen drinking too much, footmen fill her glass with tonic straight from the bottle — only gin has been added to the bottle first.'

'Boring,' said Snitch. 'I'll tell you what I want to know, and our readers want to hear about — the truth behind Princess Anne and this cowboy. We keep hearing these rumours about them riding off into the sunset.'

'You know we tried to stand it up...'

'Yes, and a right arse you made of yourself there,' said Snitch as he ripped the paper out of Spalding's

Remington. 'Enough of this crap. Get back on the trail. I want to know — is it a leg-over situation?'

'But...'

'No buts, laddie. On your bike.'

The Gatcombe Riding team and their grooms were being put up for the duration of the Knowlsborough Horse Trials, held each year at the home of their hosts, Major Nobby Knowlsborough and his robust wife Petronella. The Knowlsboroughs had a magnificent Palladian mansion, with original Adam interiors, set deep in the rolling Yorkshire countryside near Holme on the Wolds. All around the leaves were turning to their autumn russet colours.

After the completion of the first day's competition, the Gatcombe mob were relaxing over supper in the main dining-room where trestle tables had been put up to accommodate the large and rowdy party. Steaming bowls of spaghetti bolognaise had hardly been placed before them when Captain Mark Phillips thought of a jolly wheeze. It was a competition to see who could get the longest strand of 'spag bol' to stick to the finely frescoed ceiling. Soon, to the accompaniment of a twang of forks, pasta was being splattered all over the room.

A splodge of bolognaise landed upon the tight curls of Mrs Knowlsborough, who tried her best to remain amused. Having the Phillipses to stay and patronize their three day event was a social coup.

'Ha! Ha! Ha!' brayed Nobby. 'Bit off-target, Mark.'

'Sorry, Nobbs.'

'Don't apologize to me, old man. Grovel to the wife. Give Pet a pat. Ha! Ha! Ha!'

'All right, chaps,' ordered Princess Anne. 'Simmer down.'

One person had not been taking part in this horse-play. Hal had been shocked by this wanton desecration of the great old house, which was older than America's Declaration of Independence itself. Mark, frustrated, turned his attention to their most brilliant pupil, who had made a pig's ear of the dressage.

'Well, Hal, old bean, you didn't display much grace and deportment today,' said Mark. 'You rode like the cowboy that you are.'

'Sure I lost a few points, but I can't get this itsy-bitsy fiddle-faddle stuff,' replied the young man, not rising to this teasing.

'You're not out on the range in Montana now,' said Mark. 'When you were doing the counter canter you looked more like John Wayne.'

'Captain Mark, maybe I ain't the prettiest rider, but when I get out on that cross-country tomorrow you watch me claw back those points.'

'Absolutely, old bean.' Captain Phillips guffawed at his own joke. Hal Bean was getting sick of this puny pun, which the Captain had used from the moment he arrived at Gatcombe. 'But I wouldn't get too cocky, old bean. Some of those jumps out there, devised by Nobby, are killers.'

'Pipe down, Mark,' said Anne, coming to Hal's rescue. 'If Hal can jump our five-bar gate without a saddle, I'm sure he can look after himself out there.'

Hal smiled gratefully at the Princess. But inside he boiled. He'd sure as hell show them tomorrow.

As Hal was saddling up his bay, Alacrity, he noticed two strangers — one gentleman of unsporting proportions, the other slung with cameras — approaching him in the paddock.

'Morning, Mr Bean,' said the larger one, jovially.

'Hello, howd'ya know my name, sir?'

'Well, you are getting quite a reputation, Mr Bean.'

'But I haven't done anything yet . . .'

The larger man laughed. 'We'll be the judge of that.'

'What can I do for you gentlemen?'

'Spalding, of the *Daily Disclosure*. Wonder if we might have a few words, Mr Bean?'

'You guys covering this event?'

'Absolutely.'

'Well, I guess there's no problem. Shoot.'

Spalding pulled out a notebook, and put on his best I'm-terribly-interested-in-what-you-are-about-to-say look. 'I gather Princess Anne has brought you on?'

'Right. She's one hell of a terrific lady.'

'You're an admirer of hers?'

'Heck, ya. She's a hell of a sportswoman, the Princess.'

'So the two of you have a close relationship?'

'What the deuce is going on here?' They turned round at the sound of a familiar voice. Captain Mark Phillips was standing by Alacrity with his hands on his hips, looking furious. 'Hal, you know damn well you're not allowed to talk to the press.' Then turning to the newsmen he added: 'And you're jolly well not supposed to talk to us.'

Spalding, not to be intimidated, replied: 'Just exercising the freedom of the fourth estate, Captain. And good luck to you, Mr Bean — the very best of British.'

Spalding and Jerry found a vantage point on the top of a Land Rover which gave them a view over most of the course. Five riders had already come in, and Hal Bean had started on his circuit ten minutes ago. They were now waiting for him to appear from the copse at the brow of the hill.

'There he is,' cried Spalding, scanning the course with his field glasses. 'He's out of the wood and coming hell for leather for the Table. Christ, he's approaching that at a lick. The boy's got no fear at all. Phew, look at that . . . beautiful, what grace. He's coming down the hill — belting down — he looks like bloody Lester Piggot the way he's out of the saddle — they are over the Fallen Logs, in . . .' Spalding consulted his Beitmeister multi-dialled watch. 'That's in thirteen minutes fifty . ., shit, Jerry, this cowboy is burning up the course. The others have only clocked fourteen minutes thirty-five at the best. What a rider, look at the way that kid moves in the saddle. Now there's only the Cresta to cope with. Here he comes — he's over ... no Christ ... they are down ... the boy's fallen! Jeez, did you hear that crack — the horse's up. The boy's just lying there. He's not moving.'

With a little shriek, Princess Anne, who had been standing by the last jump, rushed forward. She fell to her knees by the motionless figure. Gently she bent down, the tears flowing freely. She cradled the head of the lifeless rider.

'That's my picture,' said Jerry.

In the distance they could already hear, across the field, the wail of an ambulance. Jerry was furiously shooting and rewinding, shooting and rewinding.

Hal's exhausted horse, Alacrity, wild-eyed and sweating, its flanks heaving, came to a stop by the Land Rover, snorting nervously. Spalding jumped down and

grabbed the reins. The saddle had slipped underneath Alacrity's belly.

It was this, obviously, which had caused the fatal accident. Spalding looked closer at the girth strap.

'Hey, Jerry, come and look at this.'

Jerry examined the tackle. 'Bloody hell,' he murmured. 'That's a suspiciously clean break. You don't think...?'

'What?'

'That he could have been nobbled?'

'Impossible!'

'Just think of the story he could have told. Bloody convenient he's snuffed it right now!'

Spalding looked at his photographer, appalled. 'Forget it, mate — and don't you ever think it!'

Scotch mist

Balmoral, where the Royal Family spent their annual autumn eight week retreat, was a Victorian monstrosity. Designed by Queen Victoria's husband, Prince Albert, in the grandiose Scottish baronial style, it embraced the whole mock mediaeval fantasy of battlements and turrets. The grey Invergelder granite lent a stolid, dour aspect to the exterior of the Royal holiday home, while inside hundreds of stags' head trophies glowered down on what most people would consider a rather spooky and definitely depressing surroundings. But the Royal Family thrived on this kind of wet welly-boots holiday. Their feelings about this gloomy Aberdeenshire homestead had been summed up by Queen Victoria, who had confided to her journal: 'My heart becomes more fixed in this dear paradise and so much more so now that all has become my dear Albert's own creation ... and his great taste and the impress of his dear hand, has been stamped everywhere.'

This underheated, draughty mansion, which was permeated with the smell of wet dog, summed up everything the Windsors held dear: it was a fishing, shooting, stalking, riding, sketching, picnicking, tramping through wet heather, gossiping, singing, climbing, boating, parlour games-playing way of life.

Now and again workaday life intruded. The Queen still had to deal with her State papers, approve the appointment of some new worthy to the Privy Council and sanction the sacking of the odd Cabinet Minister. Then to consider there was her own growing family, children, grandchildren, nieces and nephews, and troublesome daughters-in-law.

There was also the occasional staff problems. Only the other day she had noticed the lethargy of her table attendants, and when she had enquired as to why they always appeared to be so tired, one had boldy replied: 'It's Princess Margaret, Ma'am — she will stay up and play the piano every night till two in the morning, and we can't go to bed before her.' Her Majesty had instantly instituted a new rule: once she had retired, all could withdraw.

Then there was her beloved mother, who did still insist that she would go fishing in the fast-flowing waters of the Dee though she was now heading for ninety. She didn't want a granny floating down the Dee. So, discreetly, she had made sure that six gillies were always hiding behind nearby trees.

And dear Anne. She had been so upset about the death of her young American friend. She did take things so to heart. She seemed almost inconsolable. But nice Mark was being a brick. The bracing air would do her no end of good. She's be all right once she got back in the saddle.

Philip was the one member of the family who did not present a problem up here. He sublimated his frustrations during the rest of the year by restlessly ranging the world, but in Scotland in their fifty-thousand acre estate, he had fish to catch, birds to shoot, stags to stalk.

Diana, however, was a worry. The Queen was pleased Diana had got over her fears and insecurities about 'another woman', and she was delighted that her daughter-in-law had confided in her. But the sweet girl, alas, was beginning to believe some of her own publicity. Fancy ordering all those papers at Balmoral. The Queen made it a point never to read about herself. In Diana's case this had led to her expressing the desire to take a higher public profile, and get more personally involved with one of the great social issues of the day — why, the Queen had even discovered that she had been taking lessons from an actor towards this end.

But it was Charles, her son and heir, who was her real headache.

Diana was right in one respect, though she had drawn the wrong conclusion: Charles had indeed been strange of late. Thoughtful, meditative, introspective, full of doubts, questioning everything. He was so quiet nowadays. And when he did speak it was in riddles. This harping on about caring and love; well, of course, we all believe in that, but one didn't go on about it. And, honestly, that silly protest about not eating meat the other night. The sanctity of life, for goodness' sake! Charles would, somehow, have to be brought back down to earth. It was all very, very odd. The worry sometimes kept her awake at night. As a Head of State she fretted, but as a mother she agonized. What, oh what, was happening to her darling son?

As Andrew and Sarah had come up for the weekend the Queen had planned a special treat for them, an outing for the whole family on the banks of the nearby Loch Muick where they would picnic under the brooding mountain of Lochnagar. When they arrived at the spot, chosen and prepared by the staff, through the light veil of Scotch mist and intermittent drizzle, the purple mass of mountain frowned down on the party, lending a foreboding, rather ominous air to the proceedings.

'Not really picknicking sort of weather, is it?' inquired Princess Sarah as they set out in a fleet of Land Rovers.

'We Windsors, my dear, rather like weather,' replied the Queen, shooing three black labradors into the back of the vehicle.

The Firm loved picnics. They were under the illusion that this was how ordinary people lived. They loved to lay out the tartan rugs (unpacked and de-mothed by the maids), unload the hampers (prepared by the chef), open the bottles of wine (selected and chilled by the butler) and cook their steaks over the barbecue (built and laid beforehand by estate workers).

Philip, wearing an apron stating 'I'm the boss', was in his element. Brandishing a fork he stood in command over the smoking grill.

'Right, how many are we? Eleven. So that's eleven rump steaks and twenty-two sausages.'

'No steak for me, thanks, Dad,' said Charles from behind his book *The Whole Earth Cookbook*.

'Don't be ridiculous. Everyone needs red meat.' Philip threw another raw slab of Aberdeen Angus on to the fire. 'This is the stuff to put hairs on your chest.'

'I don't like men with hairy chests,' said Diana loyally.

'Oh, I don't know,' said Sarah, 'I think hairy chests are rather hunky.'

The ladies of the group laughed.

'Oh dear, do look at what Binkie and Noël are doing,' said the Queen Mother, pointing to the two interlocked black labradors.

'Noël' yelled Prince Philip. 'Filthy dog.'

'Binkie must be in season again,' said the Queen. 'Do separate them, Charles.'

'Are you sure, Mummy? Don't you feel that our Western propensity to intervene in nature has led to some terrible...'

'Oh, Charles,' said the Queen crossly. 'Just do it.'

Philip served up eleven well-done steaks and the family, leaning over them to protect their food from the rain, tucked into their lunch with relish. Charles surreptitiously slid his portion to the chastised Noël, who downed it in one.

Diana was polishing off her soggy salad when she casually announced that a jolly interesting challenge had been put to her by a nice American film producer she had met at Wimbledon.

'He wants me to — what do they call it? — front a docu-drama on the smack problem.'

'Spanking?' asked Andrew.

'Oh God, Andrew, belt up — this is frightfully grown up,' admonished Diana. 'This is really senior. I'm talking about the scourge of heroin. It's a world-wide disaster which knows no boundaries of class, creed or colour.'

'Colour?' echoed the Queen Mother with a start. 'Do you remember Dickie's servant from Jaipur? Never could quite cotton on to English ways. Do you remember the time he...'

'Druggies, ha!' huffed Philip. 'Bring it on their own heads as far as I'm concerned.'

'Well, I've asked Dickie Attenborough and he thinks the idea absolutely darling,' said Diana defiantly. 'The film is going to open with a long shot of me in a poppy field, then pan in for a close-up... yours truly. Thereafter we follow the drugs trail overland to Sicily, and to its final destination in the back streets of Birmingham and the film sets of LA. I feel strongly this will be a major statement.'

The Queen listened, appalled.

By that night the rain was really bucketing down. The wind howled down the glens. The old leaded-light windows rattled. Icy currents swept down the long stone-floored corridors. As the Queen sat before a roaring fire in her private chambers the flames sent dancing shadows over the rough walls, eerily illuminating the prize antlers, the bewhiskered portraits of dour clan chieftains, shields and cross cutlasses. Charles sat opposite his mother in a light grey kilt, with the black and red overchecks of the Balmoral tartan. For a while they stared in thoughtful silence at the crackling fire. Her Majesty, alarmed by what she had heard that afternoon, had come up with a delightfully simple idea that she hoped would kill two birds with one stone: it would divert both Charles and Diana, each from their potentially disastrous courses of action.

'A nightcap?' offered the Queen. 'A Macallan?'

'No thanks, Mummy. Have you got any dandelion coffee?'

'Gracious, no.'

'Oh, well, I'll pass then.'

The Queen cleared her throat. 'Charles...'

'Yes, Mummy?'

'Now, you won't mind my saying this, but you've been a little out of step lately with the Family. This faddy nonsense about food and drink, for example. It's got your father and me most worried.'

'But it's to do with one's organicity, Mother. One is attempting to develop a holistic approach to life. One is trying to get back in touch with...'

'Now now, dearest. Not at this time of night. We don't mind you having hobbies, darling, but it's not very "us" to take them to these extremes.'

'What I am trying to do, you see, Mother, is explore my own inner processes, my own emotions...'

'Emotions, ah.' Her Majesty took a large dram of Macallan's. 'That's rather what I wanted to talk to you about, Diana. She seems a little unsettled of late, not enough to do. It's a tricky period for a woman, believe me. They cast about for things to do, to occupy themselves, and this sometimes leads them into all sorts of mischief.'

'Not sure one follows your drift, Mother.'

'I know Diana is keen to have a daughter, you see — to take her shopping, dress her in lovely clothes, go to the hairdressers and all those nice girlish things. Don't you think that would give her something to do?'

'But she's got something to do. This drugs thing.'

'Exactly, darling, that's part of the worry. It's not us. It's not really a very appetizing subject, is it? And one doesn't want one's daughter-in-law gallivanting goodness knows where with all sorts of unsavoury types.'

The Queen put down her glass firmly and put on that look of hers which spelt Mummy-is-on-the-warpath.

'I do think, Charles, that it is time you had another baby. It's for the good of The Firm. It might bring your head out of the clouds, too.' She was no longer speaking just as a mother; she was speaking as the figurehead of a dynasty. 'So we'll say no more about it. Goodnight.'

The next morning Philip was up before dawn. In the dim light, under a soft drizzle, he stood in the gravel driveway before the castle discussing the day's prospects with his head stalker. A fine stag, a six pointer, had been spotted high in the Grampians. They set out at first light, followed at twenty paces by a second gillie carrying the rifles, telescope and lunch, while bringing up the rear was old McCrumb, the pony-boy, and the sturdy Shetland that would be used to carry the day's trophy back home.

An hour after breakfast Charles wandered in leisurely fashion down to the River Dee in anticipation of a relaxing day's salmon fishing. He loved this highland solitude; up here he could even leave his detective behind.

Only half a mile away on the Ballater to Braemar road a red Ford Sierra cruised back along that same stretch again for the sixth time. Out of the passenger's window Spalding scoured the fir-clad Balmoral hillsides with his binoculars for any evidence of royal life.

Lunchtime at Balmoral was an unusually boisterous affair, for the Queen and Princess Margaret had gone to visit their mother at nearby Birkhall, while Captain Mark Phillips had taken his wife riding.

'The shops in this wilderness are quite a hoot,' said Diana.

'Mediaeval,' agreed Sarah, 'you can't even get stockings with seams down the back.'

'And have you seen the village lasses?' chipped in Edward. 'Real dogs.'

'Well, you should have set something up, old boy,' said Andrew. 'Installed a popsie in a local pub.'

'It's all right for you and your hubby, Carrots,' said Diana to Sarah, 'you only came up for the weekend.'

'Yah, poor Hamster — a whole month more to serve in

Her Majesty's Prison,' commiserated Sarah.

'So don't forget to send a pc back to those of us who didn't make it over the wall . . .'

By three o'clock Spalding and Jerry had located their quarry. On hands and knees they were snaking through the dripping undergrowth. In the distance they could see Charles up to his thighs in the Dee, totally lost in thought.

Prince Philip thoroughly bitten by midges and soaked through, had located the prize stag they had set out to track down. It was a magnificent animal. In order to get downwind of the beast they had to crawl two miles through spiky heather and over rocky outcrops. It was slow, draining, painstaking and ardous. The drizzle turned to rain and a heavy mist was rolling in off the high mountains.

As evening gathered in, Spalding and Jerry, from their lookout in the dripping foliage, watched in frustration for twenty minutes as the Prince of Wales skilfully played a salmon: it was far too murky to get any photos and they didn't dare reveal their hide by using a flash. Charles landed the fish, a fine fourteen-pound salmon. The two sleuths watched, amazed, as the Prince gently released the tired fish back into the dark, rushing waters of the Dee.

The Duke of Edinburgh, after ten hours of foot-slogging, climbing and crawling, was frozen, scratched and elated to have the stag in the sights of his rifle at long, long last. His two stalkers lay hidden twenty yards behind, hardly daring to breathe. Philip's heart pounded in anticipation of the kill; he carefully regulated his

breathing and concentrated his mind. His index finger
began to apply the gentlest pressure upon the trigger.
Suddenly the stag — like a true monarch of the glen —
sniffed the icy wind and with one leap bounded away
over the crag out of sight.

'Hell's teeth, God's death, damn, blast and bloody
shizer!' Up jumped Philip, an entire day's stalking, ten
hours of sheer torture, ruined at the very moment of
victory. 'What in the blazes scared him off?'

'Look Sire,' cried the gillie, pointing a gnarled finger
down the misty valley at two struggling figures in bright
red anoraks scrambling up the mountainside with bulky
rucksacks on their backs.

'I bet those blistering idiots are newspaper scavengers,'
said Philip, raising his rifle to his shoulder again. 'Well
that's the last time they cock up my day's sport.'

'With respect, Sire,' said the Duke's wise old gillie,
'we're noo allowed t'shoot poachers any moor.'

'Right, I'm blinking well going to sort those blighters
out,' said the Duke, striding down the mountainside
purposefully towards the two labouring hikers.

'Hey, *you*!' yelled the Duke. 'Yes, you two idiots in the
red anoraks! Come here!'

Two young startled schoolboys stood before the
bedraggled sportsman, rifle in hand, who bellowed at
them: 'What the hell do you think you are doing up here?'

'W-w-we're d-d-doing a s-s-survival course, Sir,'
stuttered one.

The Duke threw his hands up in frustration. 'Ye gods!
What the bloody hell for?'

'The D-duke of Edinburgh's Award S-scheme, Sir.'

Giving up both victory and defeat

The day the Royal Family made their annual visit to the Braemar Games the weather perked up. There was only the finest of drizzle.

This Highland festival was an archaic expression and celebration of the Scottish soul, Scottish brawn, Scottish dancing and Scottish whisky. The Windsors were the patrons of this colourful folk jamboree, which was a hosanna to swirling tartan, sword dancing, straining muscles and Highland bravado.

It was time for the prize-giving and the Family trooped up on to the podium, all wreathed in smiles and Balmoral tartan. Her Majesty had a slight chill, so it was left to her eldest son to present the prizes and make the valedictory speech. This was a curious rambling discourse, not the easy emollient words the locals had come to expect for what was, after all, only a sporting event. Charles's disquistion on love and truth was more like a sermon.

But watching from the audience Spalding and Jerry were most struck by the Queen's apparent agitation. As her son droned on, her face became set in what they knew as her 'Miss Piggy' look. Her eyes bored into the back of Charles's head as if she was trying to scour out his very thoughts. She continually picked up and put down her handbag, and when he got on to the subject of 'the right way' she began to rotate her wedding ring. The two royal sleuths recognized this mannerism: it was a clear signal that the monarch was very cross indeed.

The homily ended with what sounded like a quotation: 'Conquest begets enmity; the defeated lie down in distress. The peaceful one lives happily, giving up both victory and defeat.'

Spalding, making a rapid note of this epigram, rushed off after the prize-winners to garner some quotes. He found the caber-tossing champion, the huge red-haired, barrel-chested Dermot McDermot.

'What did the Prince say to you?' questioned Spalding, his notebook at the ready.

'It was awful weird. I could'na ken what the mon meant,' said the giant. 'He said — and I can remember it exactly: "How wonderful, how miraculous, chopping wood and carrying water."' He shook his head in bewilderment. 'Chopping wood? And the mon's a Prince!'

Spalding sought out the hammer champion, Iain McPhee. 'And did the Prince have any interesting observations for you?'

'Funny you should say that,' said the sixteen-stone hammer champion. 'I could'na make head na tail o' this.'

'What?' said Spalding, his Parker ballpoint poised eagerly.

McPhee screwed up his face as he struggled to recall the princely words. Then with an enormous effort the champion spake: 'The flesh is only the battlefield — wars are won by the soul.'

'Ang about,' said Jerry excitedly. 'What a story... "Prince of Wales round the twist".'

'Och,' said McPhee, 'it's noo moor than the Prince has had a wee drunk.'

The Royal Party were departing. The farewells and thankyous were being said. Spalding and Jerry hurried over as the Queen was shaking hands with a local clan chieftain, The Maclachlan of Muick.

Next in line was Charles. 'Thank you, Your Royal Highness, for your quite inspiring speech,' said The Maclachlan. 'An address full of meat. But I'm not quite sure I digested it all.'

'Kind of you to say so, Mac,' said Prince Charles. 'Perhaps I can share one final thought with you that I have found particularly illuminating.'

The Prince of Wales paused and looked into the distance.

> 'The right man sitting in his house,
> Thinking the right thoughts
> Can be heard five hundred miles away.'

EPISODE FIVE: WINTER

Back in harness

Winter arrived early.

By the time the leaves had fallen and the swallows departed the Windsors were all back at work. During the month of October Her Majesty the Queen had opened and launched various things, from a new housing estate in Dulwich to the new fleet flagship, *HMS Rampant*. Then at the beginning of November she opened something a little more grand. As every year, she carried out the glittering ceremony of the State Opening of Parliament, the most important constitutional item in her calendar. With the weighty, jewel-encrusted Crown of England upon her head, in the presence of the duly elected Members of Parliament, and their Lordships both spiritual and temporal, she concluded with the age-honoured salutation: 'My Lords, and Members of the House of Commons, I pray that the blessings of Almighty God may rest upon your counsels.'

Prince Philip had just returned from a gruelling fact-finding mission in the Punas mountains of Peru where acid rain was causing skin irritation and baldness to Alpacas, whose wool was vital to the economy of the region. Captain Mark Phillips and Princess Anne buried themselves in work, back at Gatcombe, bringing on new horses. Prince Andrew had been seconded to RAF Lossiemouth to undergo training on a new top secret helicopter prototype. Edward had returned to Cambridge, where Sergeant Harborough was doing very well in their history course. Princess Diana was taking private tuition from a TV newscaster, in Kensington Palace, on presentation and Autocue reading, while the Prince of Wales continued to cause increasing public bafflement.

At the inauguration of the multi-million-pound computer-controlled sewerage purification plant at Clacton-on-Sea, all the Prince had been required to do was cut the ribbon, declare the works open and say half a dozen words. Instead he had attracted some press comment with the remark: 'Man purifies himself by avoiding evil. Purity and impurity depend on oneself. No one can purify another.'

Only a few days later the Prince, in launching a nationwide campaign to erect toad-crossing signs, exhorted drivers not to run over these little creatures as they traversed the road. He had taken as his text the following: 'Whosoever in this world destroys life, speaks untruth, he even in this very life, ruins himself completely.'

Spalding was spurred on by these latest pronouncements. He had a hunch that he was on to a scoop. But over the past month he had been unable to unearth the origin of the remarks jotted down in his notebook at the Braemar Games.

He had even telephoned the Archbishop of Canterbury's man at Lambeth Palace ('not in the Bible, my friend'); he had called the Vatican ('not one of us, yet, Signor'); the Hindus weren't much more help (didn't speak English). Next he tried the Institute for Paranormal Studies ('sorry, can't get any readings'); the United Grand Lodge of English Freemasons was less than helpful ('Free-

masons don't reveal their secrets'), while the Royal
College of Psychiatrists were in two minds ('on the one
hand ... but on the other').

Lastly Spalding consulted the Tavistock Institute of
Human Relations. 'Your friend sounds like he could be in
trouble,' said the spokesman. 'But we never discuss such
delicate matters on the phone. I suggest you persuade
your chum to make an appointment as soon as possible.'

Chopping wood? Carrying water? Lying down in
distress? Spalding reached for his glass of claret. Purity
and impurity depend on oneself? He swirled the rich red
liquid round the bowl of his glass and inhaled the
bouquet. No one can purify another? Spalding tilted his
head back and let the smooth trickle of wine take away
some of the frustration. Damn. The trail had gone cold.

A delicate operation

'Ruddy heck, Harborough, what the bloody hell's been going on?'

'Well, it has been rather a tricky assignment this, Sir.'

'Tricky, Harborough? What about my position? These last two months have been sheer headachesville.'

'Indeed, Sir. But I am sure you will appreciate this was an operation of the utmost delicacy.'

'Quite, Harborough. But did it need to take so long? Time in such matters is pressing.'

'This very factor was uppermost in my mind, Sir. However, the nature of the surveillance undertaken necessitated the utmost discretion.'

'I'll have you know the suspense ruined my hols at Balmoral. It went over and over in my mind. What on earth was I going to tell Mummy?'

'A not uncommon dilemma for a young man, Sir. While your gracious mother is extremely broad-minded, one can see a conflict of interest, seeing as she is Defender of the Faith and all.'

'Agonies I went through. Hateful, hateful. And here I am, Harborough, still on bloody tenterhooks.'

'Ah well, Sir, I think I am now, after extensive investigations, in a position to answer your not unnaturally concerned queries. I have my full report to hand.'

Harborough opened his special security briefcase, the one that contained his full bag of tricks — his long range listening device, his anti-terrorist tear-gas grenade, two gas masks, his armoury of guns and ammunition and a small phial of cyanide pills. He drew out a neat regulation police clip-board, and cleared his throat in preparation for reading the first report.

'Letitia Younger, aged twenty-three, born Bath, previously residing at Cambridge University,' read Harborough.

'Previously?' echoed Prince Edward. 'You've made a goolie already. Should be currently at Cambridge. Nit.'

'I beg you to bear with me, Sir, and not to jump the gun. All will be revealed.'

'Get on with it, man.'

'Father, Dr James Younger, a respected GP and pillar of the local community. No suspicious influences at a formative stage. Miss Younger attended the Divine Heart and Immaculate Conception Convent at Clifton. A report from the said school in my possession shows certain interesting traits which could be germane to our case.'

'School reports and that sort of kit? How did you get hold of them Harborough?'

'Your Roman Catholic nun, Sir, has the interest of the state very much to heart. Aged thirteen, the suspect was apprehended smoking a packet of Marlboros in the staff toilet during a maths lesson.'

'Oh God, Harborough, so what?'

'I think you will find, Sir, that we are building up a picture of a rebellious personality, who is bent upon challenging the established order.'

'Smoking Marlboros in the staff bogs! What's that got to do with her being preggers?'

From across the town they heard the bells of King's College summoning the faithful to compline. It was dark outside. From the quad below came the muffled sound of students' voices and the dull thud of their footfalls across the courtyard.

Harborough smiled indulgently. 'What we are attempting to create is a personality Identikit.'

'Yes, but has she or hasn't she got a bun in the oven, dammit?'

'Well, perhaps we can skip this,' said Harborough,

flicking over on the clip-board several pages of detailed notes, reports and official documents. 'We therefore come to the HCG test, if you would care to verify the evidence with your own eyes, Sir.'

He handed a pink, official-looking slip to the Prince, who stared, baffled, at the formulae. 'This is gobbledegook, Harborough. How am I meant to tell from this whether the damn girl is up the spout?'

The detective's finger pointed to a complex algebraic equation. 'That, Sir, is the nub. It reveals beyond all reasonable doubt that the subject is indeed in a gravid condition.'

'It's as bad as that, is it?' said Edward, not knowing what he meant.

'I am afraid so, Sir. The evidence proves incontrovertibly that the suspect is pregnant.'

A small whimper escaped from Edward's lips. He buried his head in his hands. Oh, the shame! Oh, the dishonour! Gone were the days when kings and princes could spawn any number of bastards and get away with it, why, even make them dukes and earls. Nor would the antics of his namesake, Edward VII, be possible any more; the jackals of the yellow press had seen to that. If those scavengers got hold of this... The bastards.

In a broken voice, Edward croaked: 'Oh Alan, what am I going to do?'

'Well, Sir, I think it best if I elucidate exactly, but briefly, what I have done,' continued Harborough implacably.

Having gone to exceptional and sometimes illegal lengths, and travelled 2,650 miles in his quest to unearth potential evidence, the sergeant was not going to have his endeavours treated lightly. He read: 'Item. Political affiliation. Very interesting. Liberal-SDP sympathies. Pamphlets of this nature were found in her digs, including one demanding the instant introduction of proportional representation.'

Edward slowly raised his head from his hands, and shook it in disbelief. 'Letitia Younger is in the club and you are talking about voting patterns! Christ, Harborough, I'm in trouble.'

'If you will bear with me one moment, Sir, the picture will become all too clear. For subsequently upon interception of her telephone . . .'

Edward looked at him aghast. 'You bugged her phone? Is that, well, legal?'

'I wouldn't worry yourself about such a minor detail at this time, Sir,' said Harborough. 'Merely taking the necessary precautions to protect you.'

'Protect me? Well, you didn't protect me from that female. In fact you jolly well pushed me in her direction.' Edward's anger was mounting. 'All that stuff about Mr and Mrs Swallow . . . and now look where it's got me!'

'To complete my report,' continued the detective imperturbably. 'Having exhausted my enquiries, last week I approached the suspect in person.'

'God, Harbers, what did she say?'

'She was to be found at a remote farmhouse in Northumberland. She did not deny the state she was in. Indeed, this condition was apparent for all to see.'

'Oh no,' moaned Edward, the scandal already looming in his mind.

'She was quite clear. She would not have the operation.'

Edward looked out of the window; on the other side of the Jesus College courtyard he could see the lights in the windows. A Mozart minuet mingled with the anarchic aggression of P60's latest hit. Student life went on. Soon he would be banished from all this, sent down, disgraced.

Harborugh's voice intruded. 'And she is insisting upon marriage.'

So there was no escape. He'd just have to accept his fate and marry below his station. And the baby? Well, they'd simply have to persuade the press it was premature.

'The date of the nuptials has already been fixed,' he heard the sergeant say. 'The venue is to be the Church of

St Peter and St Paul of the Catholic denomination, in the Northumberland village of Blasset.'

Edward sat listening to this litany in a near catatonic state.

'One fact in which you will take a particular interest, Sir,' said Harborough slowly, 'is the bridegroom's name.'

'The bridegroom?'

'Oh yes, Sir, a prerequisite at such events. A very pleasant gentleman, as a matter of fact. A respected local veterinary surgeon. One Mr Percy Roberts.'

'What the hell's this Mr Roberts got to do with it?'

'It is he, Sir, who is the father of the child. Or so Miss Younger says.'

'Yippee! Off the hook! Alleluia,' Edward did a little jig in the centre of the room. 'I thought for a moment it would be back to New Zealand for me!'

Harborough had not finished. 'Miss Younger has discontinued her studies at the university, and wished me to pass on a message to you, Sir.'

Suddenly Edward's relief turned to blazing self-righteous anger. 'I don't think I want anything more to do with that woman. She's behaved despicably.'

'Be that as it may, Sir, she merely wished to say that she was sorry about being unable to speak to you properly at the last meeting aboard *Britannia* and that she would like to extend you an invitation to her wedding.'

'The hussy! I'll be damned.' This bloody business had already made him late for that evening's date. He was taking the delectable Amelia Cumming-Brice to the Eastern Counties Hunt Ball. He scrambled into his dinner jacket.

'What about our essay, Sir?' asked Harborough as the Prince splashed a last dab of Eau Sauvage underneath the armpits of his dinner jacket. 'Exams are but around the corner.'

'Keep up the good work, Harborough,' replied Edward as he dashed for the door. 'I am sure we'll do splendidly.'

Dogged by ill luck

Princess Margaret's lady-in-waiting, Lady Caroline 'Bunny' Berringer, was organizing a series of elegant soirées of baroque music in the home of her mother, the Dowager Pamela Countess Berringer. The concerts would be performed by the Venezia Quartet from Hartlepool in the huge tithe barn on their two thousand acre Berkshire Downs estate (somewhat shrunk since the days when Bunny's great-great-grandfather had been 1st Lord of the Admiralty to George III). The Dowager and her late husband the Earl had never trifled much with music and the like; the fox and pheasant were more their game. Nor for that matter did their prune-faced spinster daughter, Bunny, care much for fluting and piping. Their sudden patronage of chamber music was not, heaven forbid, for their own pleasure but for a Good Cause. The proceeds from opening their sixteenth-century seat to local burghers for the evening were to go to the Venice in Peril Fund. After the concert, included in the price of the £50-a-head ticket, was a glass of sherry, a cold buffet, half a bottle of wine and a raffle ticket. It was to be the social and cultural event of Ogbourne Maizie that winter.

Princess Margaret had been invited to be patron of this grand event. She had accepted on condition that she did not have to attend. She had graciously consented to write a foreword to the programme, a duty which had been conscientiously carried out by her private secretary.

During a committee meeting held in Bunny's rooms at Kensington Palace a small problem was raised by the Hon. Treasurer. What about publicity? Bunny was astonished.

Did one have to have that sort of thing? Wasn't it vulgar? The Hon Secretary rather thought it would give the soirée wider coverage and so help swell the coffers.

'But does one really want the press trampling all over one's house?' wondered Bunny. 'Anyway, one doesn't know any of those types. One tries to avoid them like the plague.'

At that point the representative of the junior committee of the Venice in Peril Fund spoke up. Miss Georgina Wallingford-Giles rather thought she knew someone who might fit the bill. Georgina, who worked as a secretary in the Prince of Wales's office, assured the committee that the chap she had in mind would jump at the opportunity.

Spalding stood outside the daunting Tudor pile. It was the biggest private house he'd ever seen. The much-impressed newsman would have turned round and raced the five miles back to the station if he had known what lay in store for him over that weekend. The rolling Lambourne Downs and the imposing brick and timbered house should have warned him that this was not an auspicious locale for one who, by profession, was a poacher not a gamekeeper.

That Friday evening, everything considered, he manoeuvred the tricky social minefield with some aplomb. He had done Georgie proud; she had extracted a promise from him not to reveal what his true role was, but to say he was the Arts Correspondent of the *Daily Disclosure*. It had not been difficult to impress the doughty old Dowager and her plain daughter with his theories on Vivaldi's influence on Scarlatti, and they were particularly taken with Spalding's observation about the inherent dishonesty behind the facile wit of Vivaldi's *Four Seasons*.

The concert itself had been appalling. The Venezia Quartet were an amateur group whose leader's efforts at the violin resembled a stick insect making music by

rubbing its back legs together. A December gale blew
through the mediaeval barn. Spalding only slightly
blotted his copy-book when he and Georgina Wallingford-Giles got a fit of giggles. The Dowager's middle-
aged son, the bachelor Earl, Willie Berrington, glared and
hissed: 'Have you no reschpect for culschure?'

The buffet, however, had definitely not gone well. As
he mingled with the stuffy local worthies and attempted
to engage some of them in conversation about sheep
prices, sheep dip and sheep tick, he had unwisely drunk
more than his allotted half-bottle of plonk. Spalding was
caught short. The funny thing was that in this vast
house of a hundred and twenty rooms he had not yet
found a bathroom and now he needed one fast. Shy to
ask, uncertain of the correct terminology, he slipped out
a side door. Before him lay two inches of crisp, freshly-
fallen snow. Emboldened by the wine and certain in the
knowledge that country gentlemen did it in the garden,
he relieved himself with a baroque flourish. In the snow,
in rather fine italics, he etched 'SOD SNITCH'. He
returned to the ballroom to discover a group of
disgusted guests clustered around the window, peering
down and tut-tutting at his handiwork.

As Spalding, attempting to cover his tracks, mingled
with the good folk of Ogbourne Maizie, tut-tutting
with the best of them, he felt a sharp nip at his ankle. It
was Maharanee, the Dowager's favourite Chinese
Crested toy dog, a bald, blotchy, rabbit-sized creature
with an absurd back-swept plume of hair on its pin head.
The midget Maharanee grimaced up at him malevolently,
as if she knew his shameful secret.

After the paying guests departed and the ladies had
retired, Spalding and the male house guests withdrew to
the billiard room with the purple-nosed Earl, who by
now was becoming quite belligerent with alcohol. Just as
the corridors of Berringer Hall were crammed with
stuffed wildlife from the Indian sub-continent — wild
buffaloes, leopard, cobras, mongoose — so the billiard
room contained such trophies as tiger skins and bear

rugs, dating from when the Earl's father, Percival, had been a Governor of the North West Frontier. Hollowed-out elephants' feet contained the billard cues.

Over the brandies Willie Berringer turned his venom in the direction of the defensive Spalding, who found it difficult to sustain his cover story when questioned too closely about his pedigree, his public school, his college, his club. After batting manfully for an hour, and taking a few balls in the chest, Spalding retired hurt. And very drunk.

After only half an hour between the damp sheets he was caught short again. He stumbled down the creaking, pitch-black corridors, feeling his way in search of the longed-for but yet undiscovered bathroom. Catching a whiff of what smelled like lavender Air-Wick he opened a door and gingerly felt his way in, running his hands like a blind man over unseen surfaces. Suddenly he froze in horror. Beneath his fingers was what felt like skin, a bony cheek, the long tip of an icy nose, and the faint hint of hair on lip. He fled.

The next morning Spalding was first down to breakfast and was sheepishly picking at his kedgeree when he caught the waft of Air-Wick. He turned. The angular Bunny Berringer stood in the doorway smiling sweetly at him.

After breakfast Georgina took Spalding aside into the Victorian-tiled conservatory full of Benares brass objects and tables. Spalding noticed in the hot house atmosphere of the conservatory that Georgina's complexion took on a most becoming flush. She really was the most decent sort.

'How's that bloodthirsty fiancé of yours?' asked Spalding who had once met the brusque Captain of the Royal Inniskilling Dragoon Guards and thought him odious and entirely unworthy of the lovely Georgina.

'One is a little annoyed with Captain Hackstall-Smith,' she said. 'He jolly well skipped the music but wouldn't dream of missing the slaughter. Incidentally, that's what

I want to talk to you about — today's shoot. How are you
with a gun?'

'Lethal,' said Spalding.

'Oh God,' groaned Georgie. 'You have done so well up
to now. I mean, do you know the difference between a
cock and a hen?'

'Eh?'

Georgina winced. 'Look, if they call for a cocks only
day just aim your shotgun at the creatures with
colourful feathers. They're the chaps. For heaven's sake,
don't pot anything drab.'

'Like Bunny Berringer.'

'Don't you dare! Princess Margaret's ladies-in-waiting
are out of season.'

'You're telling me,' said Spalding. 'Probably don't even
come into it.'

'Nick, stop it.' Georgina tried to put on a serious face.
'Listen this is vital. There are three points of etiquette I
want you to memorize — never call a cartridge a bullet,
never point your gun at anyone and never, never poach
another chap's bird . . .'

Georgina unfortunately had omitted to tell the *Daily
Disclosure's* man the etiquette of dress. When, half an hour
later, the shooting party were mustered on the lawn
with gun dogs, loaders and beaters, they were appalled to
see the resplendent Spalding emerge in what he
imagined were country togs: his favourite claret anorak
(used for many an undercover operation), green city
shirt with white collar, silk Liberty print cravat, and
furry moon boots.

'And we thought the Yeti was in Tibet,' said the
Dowager, rather taken with her unconventional guest.

'Good God, Mummy,' observed her liverish son Willie,
whose magnificent nose matched the colour of
Spalding's jacket, 'looks like we're throwing the place
open to oiks.'

'Too right,' said the idiotic Captain Hackstall-Smith. 'If
that clot scares the birds back to the bearers we should
declare open season on him.'

As the ladies waved off the departing sportsmen in their Land Rovers the Dowager had a parting word for the nice Mr Spalding. 'Very fetching, dear. Most becoming,' she said. 'In India, when out after poor Mr Tiger, we used to wear all sorts of lovely outfits.'

The day's shooting was not, from Spalding's point of view, an unqualified success.

In the event it was the blustering Captain Hackstall-Smith who broke the rules: for some reason the loud military man had taken against the jovial reporter. It was the Captain who poached all Spalding's birds out of the sky.

At midday the ladies arrived in a convoy of Land Rovers bearing what the Dowager called 'tiffin', little lunch boxes for the guns which were comprised of last night's buffet — execrably cooked in the first place. Spalding unhappily nibbled at his cold egg and ham pie, reflecting that for all their wealth, he ate better fare on his expenses. Nor did this stodgy collation help his pressing problem (he had still not worked out the geography of the rambling mansion). While everyone was busily chatting he stole away into the bushes, and after some searching he eventually settled for a particularly discreet spot behind a dense bramble thicket. Spalding settled down with pleasurable anticipation, but no sooner had he taken up his position than there was a shrill yapping from behind. It was Maharanee, the Dowager's hateful Chinese Crested.

'Shhhh,' hissed Spalding. 'Piss off, you little rat.'

Pleased to have flushed out such a prey, Maharanee's barking became even more frenzied.

'Ranee, Ranee,' came the sound of the Dowager's voice. 'What have you found there, sweetie?'

His position betrayed, Spalding had no option but to emerge from the undergrowth. Thwarted and flustered, he found himself faced with a dozen curious stares.

'Just exploring,' said Spalding, lamely. 'Thought I saw a grouse.'

'Odd,' said Hackstall-Smith with glee. 'Must have

flown off course from Yorkshire. No one's seen them this far south — ever.'

Spalding's luck changed dramatically.

On his return to the house, cold, deafened and with a throbbing headache, the hapless royal sleuth found waiting in store for him one of the greatest thrills of his life. He had spent fifteen years in this dedicated quest. He had risked his neck, ruined clothes, caught chills, even missed lunches, in pursuit of this very cause. Now here he was at last, in the same party, in the same house, in the same room, face to face with Royalty. Spalding, for once, was speechless.

Princess Margaret, now that the music was over and the local dignitaries departed, had decided it was safe to visit Berringer Hall. She looked so relaxed and at ease as she sat in the creased old Chesterfield armchair, a stiff glass of whisky in one hand and the ubiquitous tortoiseshell cigarette holder in the other. The Princess expressed delight to meet the Arts Correspondent of the *Daily Disclosure*.

'Arts Correspondent? I didn't know they had one. But they do have a loathsome little royal man.., do you know him?'

'Quite, Your Royal Highness, dreadful little man,' muttered Spalding.

'All of you, do sit down,' said Margaret, waving her cigarette holder like a magic wand.

Spalding, awestruck and overcome with excitement, simply plumped down into the nearest armchair without looking where he was sitting. It felt lumpy and uncomfortable, but he turned all his concentration on to Princess Margaret, desperate not to miss a single syllable. Goodness knows what royal secrets might pass her lips. He had looked forward to such a moment, he'd had imaginary conversations, even dreamed about it, and yet now that it had come to pass he found himself as awkward and tongue-tied as any alderman in a presentation line, laughing loudly, mirthlessly, and making idiotic, inane interjections.

Spalding was trapped by his own duplicity: how could an arts correspondent ask the kind of questions that he, as a royal reporter, was dying to pose? Spalding was in an agony of frustration, for he also knew that it was not form to ask questions of a Royal personage. One simply had to wait to be talked to. He squirmed in his lumpy chair. And Prince Charles — Margaret would almost certainly have the key to that riddle. If only he could ask.

Spalding was not going to let his golden opportunity slip. Unable to ask a question, he resolved to take the full frontal approach.

'I saw your nephew fishing last week, Ma'am,' he said casually, as if he had been hobnobbing with the Prince himself.

'One has never understood piscatorial pursuits. Did you catch anything?'

'Indeed, Ma'am,' lied Spalding. 'A healthy fifteen-pound salmon. But the Prince of Wales, in his infinite wisdom, decided to throw the whopper back.'

'Curious boy,' said Margaret. 'Did he explain why?'

'No. We didn't discuss that. The Prince does seem to be becoming a mite alternative of late.'

Hackstall-Smith chortled. 'Odds bods, Ma'am, if one is to believe what one reads in the public prints he's even given up shooting.'

'Oh well,' said the Princess, taking a swig. 'Charles is thinking about life.'

'Too much ponderin' never did anyone any good,' growled the Earl. 'What nexsht? A King of England whoshe a vegetarian!'

'Charles would certainly have something to say about your drinking, Willie,' said Margaret. 'He's even taken me to task. And about my smoking, too. D'you know, he said something really extraordinary the other day.'

Spalding, hoping he was appearing nonchalant, strained to hear every word. He wished he had a tape recorder as the Princess attempted to recall the epigram.

'It was something like this . . . "If one holds himself dear to himself, let him diligently watch himself".' She took a puff of her Sobranie. 'One supposes he meant herself. Or oneself.'

From down the corridor they heard the distant, muffled reverberations of a Goan gong, which was familiar to all those who had dined at Berringer Hall. It was the summons to dinner.

The dozen guests, led by Margaret, rose from their seats. Spalding followed suit, though somewhat stiffly for he had pins and needles in his bottom. His seat had been most unaccommodating; like most things in this rickety old house, just not designed for soft living. Nevertheless, the chair had been uncommonly hard and unpleasantly bumpy. Spalding looked down to see what had been causing this discomfort.

What he saw in the ancient, creased leather-upholstered, wing armchair appalled even that hardened reporter. Between the two frayed, tapestry cushions, almost hidden under them, lay a small inert lump. It was bald and mottled with pink and liver-coloured spots. It was the crushed and lifeless body of Maharanee the Dowager's pedigree Chinese Crested.

Spalding, aghast, looked away and closed his eyes. Please, please, oh God just let it wake up and trot away. Spalding opened his eyes. Maharanee still lay there, lifeless.

He panicked. There was no doubt where the guilt lay. The candle of its brief existence had been snuffed out by his large bottom. Oh death, where is thy sting? Not only had he murdered the Dowager's favourite companion — but in the presence of the Queen's sister!

He had to act quickly. Spalding glanced round; they were all heading for the door, led by the Dowager herself. He perched on the edge of the chair and swiftly scooped the dead dog into the inside pocket of his tweed sports coat. Never had the royal sleuth imagined that this so-called poacher's pouch would be used to conceal such evidence. Casually putting his left hand in the pocket to try and bolster up the weight he sauntered after the other guests towards the dining-room.

Dinner was agony. All he could think about was his horrendous crime and how to dispose of the body.

It was after dinner that the Dowager first noticed her beloved Maharanee was missing. No amount of its owner's urgent calling could summon the absent pet. Nor could the butler find the tiny Chinese Crested. A search was mounted. The guests combed the corridors, searched the numerous rooms and even hunted in the cellars. Margaret also joined in, and was to be found on hands and knees looking under the sagging sofa. Secretly she was rather enjoying this little drama. The ancient house echoed with whistles and calls. 'Coo-ee, Maharanee...'

Spalding hunted energetically. He searched hither and thither, though careful to prop up the bulge on the left side of his jacket. So keen was Spalding to display his innocence that he proceeded to look under all the cushions on the chairs, including his own.

Hackstall-Smith glared at him resentfully. He really did not see why his fiancée found that scribbler so amusing.

'I bet Spalding sat on it,' he said.

'Oh, do shut up,' snapped Georgie. 'Why can't you put your military mind to finding Ranee.'

Suddenly Spalding hit upon a solution. 'I tell you what,' he announced. 'I'll go and look for the poor little thing outside.'

'Kind of you, Mr Spalding,' said the Dowager, looking in the coal scuttle. 'Ranee's a house dog really. The sweet darling wouldn't go out at this time of night.'

'Well, you never know,' said Spalding, feeling the carcass in his jacket getting heavier and heavier. 'Someone should go and have a look.'

The corpse was beginning to feel like a boulder, and just about as conspicuous. Hand casually in pocket, he sauntered out into the cold night air. Standing on the threshold, so that everyone inside might hear, he shouted: 'Ranee, Ranee — coo-ee...'

Quickly he bent down, and under the myrtle bush by the side of the door he frantically scraped at the snow and the hard earth until he had scooped a shallow grave. Urgently he stuffed the troublesome Chinese Crested into this little hollow and shovelled several handfuls of earth back over the limp cadaver. Taking two fistfuls of fresh snow Spalding sprinkled it over the departed doggie. He did so carefully, reverentially, as if carrying out the final rites. The snow now concealed the last resting place of Maharanee.

Spalding woke at first light. He had hardly been able to sleep, wracked with guilt and the fear of the social disgrace which threatened to descend upon him. What if his crime were discovered tomorrow — in front of Princess Margaret herself? It was too much. The shame and humiliation were unthinkable. Spalding could not face this appalling possibility. At six o'clock he rose and packed quietly. He scribbled a note:

'Sorry, gone. Urgent recall to office. Bolshoi ballet defection. Must write story. Thanks mostest. Cheerio, Spalding.'

Carrying his Gucci shoes in one hand, and his Vuitton suitcase in the other, Spalding sneaked down the creaking stairway on tiptoe. Gingerly he raised the cast iron lock on the heavy sixteenth-century wooden front door and slowly eased it open. Oh my God!

There on the doorstep stood the grim-faced Dowager. Beside her was a black labrador, its tail wagging furiously. In its mouth, limp and frozen, was the pathetic little pink body of Maharanee.

Spalding gawped, speechless, into the flinty, unforgiving eyes of the Dowager.

'I have only one thing to say to you, Mr Spalding,' she said in a steady, unemotional voice. 'Whosoever in this world destroys life, speaks untruth, he even in this very life, ruins himself completely.'

Spalding grabbed the startled Dowager by the arm. 'What? What did you say? His grip on her arm tightened. 'Where did you hear that? That phrase?'

The phlegmatic Dowager, who had fearlessly once faced riot and rape in Peshawar, looked into the burning eyes of the *Daily Disclosure's* correspondent with terror. First he had murdered her little Ranee, and now ... She winced as Spalding's grip clamped harder still. 'Where did you hear that phrase?' he repeated fiercely.

'In Tibet,' she gasped, fearful for her safety. 'It's a Buddhist saying.'

The Dowager was taken aback by the transformation her words wrought upon this unpredictable man. For suddenly he had thrown his arms around her.

'That's it,' he cried ecstatically. *'He's a Buddhist!* HE'S A BUDDHIST!'

A rude awakening

The news that hit Britain the next morning was a political and constitutional time-bomb. The shock waves reverberated round the world.

But already, while the nation slept during that historic freezing December night, as gales blew in from the Russian steppes bringing with them an unusually heavy snowfall, the key figures in the kingdom had been woken, wherever they were, at whatever hour they could be found, in order to be informed of the astonishing revelation.

Across London in the grey early hours of an unforgiving dawn a number of blue official Rovers emerged from their respective garages and raced across town with the VIP passengers, who would have been easily recognized had there been anyone about at that time of morning in the blizzard-blown streets. From a number of ministries in Whitehall despatch riders, wrapped heavily in leathers and oil capes, sped through the silent city with their sealed boxes. And a helicopter took off from Battersea Heliport to fetch the Home Secretary from King's Lynn where he had been making a speech.

The Cabinet Secretary, the most powerful civil servant in the land, had been up all night with his assistants desperately contacting ministers. As he tracked down each one he tersely informed them that there would be an emergency cabinet meeting at ten the following morning. They were to make no statements to the press. The Minister for Trade and Industry, the last one to be crossed off the list, was finally located at the Clapham home of his mistress.

The Home Secretary, when he eventually managed to persuade his neurotic wife Prunella that this emergency call from Number Ten was not a nuclear alert, put on his Liberty-print satin dressing-gown and padded downstairs to telephone the Commissioner of Police, who in turn alerted the head of Special Branch. An invisible extra security cordon was thrown around Buckingham Palace, Clarence House, Kensington Palace and St James's Palace as a precaution against any possible civil unrest. Finally, one of the most important characters, who would play perhaps the crucial role in this drama, the Archbishop of Canterbury, was located when he returned to Lambeth Palace in the early hours.

The Prime Minister, after a brief and agonized audience with the Monarch before dawn in Buckingham Palace, began working feverishly with the Downing Street staff to prepare a strategy for the storm that was about to break.

The Queen, although she'd had premonitions, was the most shocked of all. At one thirty-five precisely her Press Secretary woke her with a call at Buckingham Palace. She had received the news with stoic calm, but as soon as she replaced the receiver Her Majesty broke into uncontrollable sobs. In the silence and solitude of her bedroom she cried into her pillow for a full ten minutes. She so wished that her husband was with her now. But, alas, he was on his travels again. She would have to face the crisis alone. Totally alone. That was the burden of being the monarch.

One person, the subject and cause of this excitation, could not be located. It was Prince Charles. He had been in Wales addressing a seminar at Branwyth Abbey, a converted monastery now used for conferences and retreats. The subject of the two-day conference was 'Hands Across Religion: A Trans-Denominational Approach to Life — The Hope for the Future of Mankind?'

The ancient abbey, fifteen miles north-east of Aberystwyth, did not have modern amenities like the

telephone. The Lord Lieutenant of Dyfed was instructed
to inform the Prince of the crisis that he had precipitated
— and that an Andover of the Queen's Flight would be
waiting to take him to London at first light.

When the news of the revelation was broken to him
the Prince of Wales, while all around him raged, was
curiously tranquil.

But the greatest uproar was in Fleet Street. When, at
ten forty-five pm, the first edition of the *Daily Disclosure*
hit the streets there was mayhem. Night news editors
screamed for follow-ups to this astonishing world
exclusive. Editors returned to their offices and began to
oversee the complete rewriting of their papers.

The *Daily Disclosure* that day sold more copies than ever
before in its history. All across the kingdom radio and
television stations flashed this sensational news. It was
Spalding's finest hour.

Breakfast reading

Princess Sarah first learned of these astonishing developments when she opened her copy of the *Daily Disclosure* over breakfast. Sarah stopped chewing her Sugar Puffs in mid-mouthful. When she saw the sensational story, under screaming headlines, by Nicholas Spalding (Court Correspondent) she nearly choked.

'Andrew,' she gasped.

'Not so loud, Buttons,' groaned the Prince. 'I've got a really senior hangover.'

'Wow. I don't believe this.'

'Do you have to read that trash, Sarah?' said Andrew, pouring a strong black coffee. 'They say such beastly things about us.'

'Oh, my giddy aunt! What's your mother going to say?'

'Do pipe down, Buttons, there's a good chap. My head's splitting.'

'But, sweetie, look what Charles has gorn and done!'

'Gorn and dropped us in it, has he?'

'Telling me.'

Andrew sighed. 'Probably isn't true. But give us a dekko.'

Sarah held up the front page with its blockbuster, four-decker headline. Andrew blinked in disbelief. The bold black slabs of print yelled at him —

GLOBAL EXCLUSIVE:
THRONE DRAMA...
CHARLIE SPURNS GOD!
Can we have a Karma King?

Countdown to crisis

The Queen sat alone, stiff-backed and with her hands folded on her lap. The drapes of her Buckingham Palace day-room were half-drawn, allowing only a faint hint of the dull December day outside to filter in. She had been sitting in this position for two hours, ever since the Prime Minister had left. Their tense meeting had resolved nothing. The PM was rattled and clearly, though not admitting so, had no idea how to handle this faradiddle. Nor, frankly, had she. However, of one thing the Sovereign was certain: just as Winston Churchill had said that he was not prepared to preside over the dissolution of the Empire, she was equally determined that she, Elizabeth II, would not watch over the dismantling of the Monarchy.

It was an institution which had lasted in Britain for over a thousand years, apart from that unpleasant little interlude with Mr Cromwell. A millennium, and by God she wasn't going to have the whole magnificent edifice torn down by some wretched difficulty over a question of religious denominations.

Her face betrayed no emotion. She had given vent to all her personal heartache in the privacy of her own bedroom. Now she had taken on the resolute façade of the Head of State. It was up to her to show that she had no doubts about the Rights of Kings and the solidity of the institution. Only by her example could this crisis be resolved. But she wished Philip were by her side to give her strength; thank goodness he had phoned that morning to say he would be jetting straight back from Northern India — where, much to the consternation of the local villagers, the Duke had been helping to save the man-eating tigers.

Hardly a mile away in Number Ten Downing Street the cabinet was in full emergency session. The Prime Minister had opened the meeting with a terse summation of events. The Prime Minister was quite clear on one point: they had a full constitutional crisis on their hands.

Quite simply, it was untenable to have a non-believer as the future king of England. It just wasn't on. The law said so quite clearly. Thanks to Henry VIII and his bloody gonads it was mandatory for all kings and queens of England to be Protestant.

'Having a Prince of Wales who is a Buddhist is as impossible as having a Prime Minister who is a crook,' said the Premier.

There was a silence round the oval table.

'So the point is, to get to the bottom line,' said the Foreign Secretary finally, 'this government's faced with the old heave-ho.'

'In a word, Foreign Secretary,' replied the Prime Minister, 'yes.'

'Don't mind being brought down by massive inflation, galloping unemployment, or a rollicking good sex scandal,' said the Minister for the Environment. 'But I'm damned if we're going to be brought down by ruddy religious squabbles.'

'Quite,' agreed the Secretary for Trade and Industry. 'The boy can believe what he wants as long as he does it in private.'

'All institutions are based on hypocrisy, for heaven's sake,' said the Chairman of the Party. 'The point is — as long as the boy is seen to be a Protestant then everything's hunky-dory.'

'If the Prince appeared on television singing carols in Westminster Abbey the whole crisis would disappear.'

'Hear, hear. A few shots on prime time, with that most acceptable wife, singing "O, Come All Ye Faithful". Bloody hell, be an election winner.'

'Excellent,' said the Home Secretary. 'One phone call

to the Chairman of the Beeb will fix that up. *Pas de problème.'*

'Incidentally,' asked the Lord Chancellor, 'the Beeb are being responsible about this reprehensible business?'

'Oh heavens, yes,' said the Home Secretary. 'Maintaining radio silence.'

'Can't say the same for the rest of the media. The vultures are hovering. Anyone would think that the fabric of British society was about to collapse.'

'It is,' said the Prime Minister gravely.

The meeting broke up an hour later in some acrimony. No decisions had been reached or solutions proffered. The worried ministers left Downing Street, attempting to smile for the large contingent of press photographers and television cameras that had set up a permanent camp outside that famous front door.

'How are you coping with the crisis, Home Secretary?' shouted an American correspondent.

'What crisis?' replied the Home Secretary, attempting to maintain his insincere smile under the heat of the TV arc lights.

Across the river from the secular furore of the cabinet an altogether more dignified, though no less fraught, meeting was taking place at Lambeth Palace, the London home of the Archbishop of Canterbury. The convocation of these elders of the church could no more come to a solution. So the Archbishop fell back on a last desperate resort. He prayed.

The Archbishop was a greying, scholarly gentleman, more noted for his learned discourses on St Thomas Aquinas or the Albigensian heresy than for extricating himself from the thickets of such twentieth-century conundrums. He made his way, with mitre on head and staff in hand, to the private chapel, where he eased himself down arthritically on to a duck-down hassock, lovingly made for him by the nuns of St Dorothea's convent in Barnstable.

Here, eyes heavenward, he began an agonized personal conversation.

'My dearest friend, I know you work in mysterious ways, but I was just wondering if you felt it absolutely necessary to take from us our second most important soul. Yes, yes, I know that all men are equal in your eyes, but this one, for us silly old mortals, is rather more equal than others. Fact is, there's a frightful old houha down here and the Queen, it has to be said, is horribly upset and the Prime Minister absolutely hopping mad. Actually, the Prime Minister's in an absolute bate and seems to blame this whole rumpus on me. What am I to do? Honestly, I'm quite stumped on this one. It's a thorny old bramble patch. One can't tell the blackberries from the brambles. Yes, I know I've got to bring the wayward boy back to the fold — that's what the PM keeps telling me. But how?' The Archbishop strained as if to hear something in the silent chapel. 'What's that? Pardon? Job, chapter 22, verse 28...'

The Archbishop creaklily rose to his feet and shuffled over to the lectern nearby, upon which lay the magnificent early copy of the King James version of the Bible. He flicked over the pages till he found the Book of Job, chapter 22, verse 28. He read the words out loud to himself: '"Thou shalt also decree a thing, and it shall be established unto thee; and the light shall shine upon thy ways."'

The Archbishop banged his staff irritably on the ancient stone flagging. 'Blast,' he muttered. 'Left in the lurch again.'

The crisis grows

Day two of the crisis saw the world's attention focused upon the Windsors. The gravity of the situation had sunk home to everyone. Extra security, this time of a more visible kind, was thrown around the royal London residences. The Windsors stayed indoors. Indeed they could hardly have gone out: they were besieged by a huge ragtaggle regiment of international newsmen who camped outside their palaces like an army about to breach the walls. The Queen Mother had considerable difficulty in being conveyed the five hundred yards or so through that throng from Clarence House to Buckingham Palace. She brought solace to her daughter, and several cups of strong Darjeeling tea.

This state of siege was also being conducted around the other royal palaces. A particularly large contingent was positioned outside Kensington Palace, covering all exits. All windows were closed and curtains drawn. There had been no sighting of Prince Charles. Indeed, there was no sign of life within Kensington Palace. From behind the curtain, however, Charles was spying on them.

'Goodness me, there's more and more of those types every day. Haven't they anything better to do?'

'Now darling, do come away from that window,' said Diana soothingly.

'This is all so silly,' said Charles. 'If only I could go out there and have a chat with the chaps. Then we would clear up all this absurd misunderstanding.'

'You know jolly well that the Queen has issued orders to all the family. Mum's the word.'

'Yes, I know. But if I could only pass on this thought from the *Dhammapada* ...'

'Sounds like an Indian take-away to me,' said Diana, who was irritated at not being able to go out shopping.

'You see, dear, the *Dhammapada* says: "If one speaks or acts with a pure mind happiness follows him, like a shadow that never leaves him."'

'Now, you know what I've told you about repeating those silly sayings, dear. If you're not careful, they'll take you away to the funny farm.'

Diana had obeyed the Queen's instructions to the letter: she had kept him inside the Palace, mothballed from the crisis. She had successfully subverted his every attempt to go out and explain himself to the waiting newsmen, she had even managed to hide him away from their prying cameras. Diana had cancelled all the newspapers, removed the radio and even tampered with the television to ensure a total news blackout.

Never had she felt so protective. Funny that, how in recent years their roles had slowly changed. She remembered how when she had first joined The Firm what a shy, gauche creature she had been. What a rock, what a tower of strength Charles was during those early, testing years. She'd been a child really, and with the thirteen-year difference between them Charles had been able to guide her through the maze of public life with such fatherly assurance. Now she was a woman, and it was Charles who needed her motherly protection.

She looked pityingly at her husband as he peeked out from behind the curtains. He certainly cut an eccentric figure.

But she was only following orders — even to the extent of removing the Prince's trousers.

Blackmail in the air

As the crisis deepened the Royal Family kept their heads firmly down. The Queen remained ensconced in Buckingham Palace, receiving a constant flow of senior advisers and ministers. The sealed red dispatch boxes, containing state papers for Her Majesty's attention, arrived with a greater and more urgent frequency.

The Queen Mother, who herself had been through such a dire emergency during the abdication crisis, was the only member of the Family that the government considered advisable to be allowed out in public. It had been resolved at the Cabinet meeting that in order to play down this whole business at least one Windsor should be seen to be carrying on with normal life. The old lady, so experienced and wily a campaigner, took upon herself all the Family's official engagements. She was surrounded by such a huge posse of policemen and pressmen that the people could get nowhere near her, and to any of the reporters who managed to get close enough to shout an impertinent question, she merely replied with a benign smile: 'Very well indeed, thank you.'

Princess Margaret, by good fortune, was away in Mustique with Lord Rubberton and the usual crowd, topping up her tan for Christmas. Princess Anne and Captain Mark Phillips were busy behind firmly locked wrought-iron gates, exercising their horses in the Gatcombe indoor training school. Prince Edward remained cloistered away from the world in his rooms at Cambridge (attended by Amelia Cumming-Brice) with the excuse that he was swotting intensively for his post-grad exams.

Sergeant Harborough fortunately maintained a ceaseless twenty-four-hour vigil outside the Prince's door at Jesus College, for on the third day of the crisis he spotted what appeared to be the Vice-Chancellor of the University of Cambridge shinning up the drainpipe attired in the distinctive crimson gown and black mortarboard of his office. Harborough hesitated, for academics in such elevated positions tended to be distinctly eccentric. It was only when the Vice-Chancellor swung perilously on the guttering and his cloak parted to reveal the telescopic sights of a long lens camera that the detective realized this was not simply another manifestation of academic irrationality. Harborough apprehended the Vice-Chancellor, who turned out to be an enterprising Italian paparazzo. Rinaldo passed the next week neutralized in the cells of the local police station.

Prince Andrew and his wife were also shut away in their apartments, with strict instructions from the Sovereign not even to poke their heads outside the front door. As a young, active, outdoorsy couple, not much given to reading or other more reflective pursuits, Andrew and Sarah were soon impatient and fidgety with this enforced captivity. By day four of the crisis, their entire video library having been exhausted, they began to bicker. Prince Andrew had casually expressed the opinion, in his usual forthright naval manner, that his elder brother had obviously gone completely off his rocker. Sarah, loyally sticking by her chum Diana, pointed out: 'It's probably only a passing phase. Hamster says it's because he wasn't allowed an adolescence, so it's some sort of mid-life crisis.'

Then the tedium was broken by the arrival of a letter.

It was hand delivered, marked STRICTLY PRIVATE AND CONFIDENTIAL. Andrew recognized that strangely precise italic script.

The letter was brief and to the point:

'Your Royal Highness. I trust you enjoyed your trip to Italy, and that

the Honourable Henry Fairlie picked up the tab for your luncheon at Oliver's! The time has come, I think, for us to meet at last.

'*I would be indebted for your presence aboard my good ship,* The Busted Flush *which will be hove-to off Gravesend tomorrow at noon. This invitation, sir, is extended to you and you alone.*'

Instructions were attached for how Andrew was to reach the boat, which would be moored out in the estuary. It was signed with a flourish:

'*I remain, sir, as ever, your respectful and obedient servant, Ryder St Bartholomew.*'

Leaving for this assignation was no easy matter. Prince Andrew got out the dressing-up box which he had inherited from his brother when he had married Diana. At the time Charles had said with a wink that he had no more need of it. Andrew was delighted that it had completely slipped his mind to pass on this priceless heirloom, as had been his intention, upon the occasion of his own marriage.

He looked at himself with satisfaction in the mirror. He saw before him a smarmy Italian waiter. With his Brylcreemed wig, waxed moustache and mascaraed eyes Andrew looked rather like Rudolph Valentino in *The Cheater*. As he drove into the street in his batman's Fiat Uno his way was inevitably barred by the clamouring newshounds. Television arc lights were switched on and questions hurled at him in half a dozen languages.

'What's going on in there? Is it true that the Royal Family are thinking of going into exile? *C'est la fin de la famille royale Britannique*? What branch of the Buddhist faith has Prince Charles embraced? Is it true that the Queen has had a nervous breakdown? Can you confirm that Prince Andrew has been designated heir to the throne?'

Andrew looked straight at the television cameras and gave what he thought was a Neapolitan shrug. 'Donta ask me. I only the cook,' said Andrew, doing his best to imitate Ilaria Pucci's fractured English.

'Perhaps you can tell us then,' said an aggressive woman from ITN, 'have they been put off their food because of the crisis?'

'Eh no. Whata crisis? They eata lika kings.'

So saying, Andrew put his foot on the accelerator, leaving the reporters to rush away with this morsel of a quote which duly appeared on front pages all over the world next day.

Andrew sped east towards the mouth of the Thames. It was freezing, and Andrew concentrated hard on the icy road. Large flakes of snow splattered the windscreen.

The weather had worsened by the time he reached Gravesend and the snow was driving hard. The docks were deserted and he found, as instructed, a small dinghy with outboard motor tethered to the pier.

Somewhere out there in the choppy estuary was *The Busted Flush*. As he navigated through the swell, bucketed and drenched by the spray, he heard the unusual sound of a Mississippi paddle-boat whistle. The next moment, through the flurries of snow, he saw the dark outline of the floating casino. Andrew wondered if he had made a terrible mistake. The mascara had begun to run down his face. The Prince presented a wild and dishevelled sight as he climbed up the swinging rope ladder and on to the heaving deck of *The Busted Flush*. But there was no one to see him. The ship creaked and groaned. Andrew looked about him in alarm.

A lone light shone in the main saloon. Andrew pushed through the swing doors and found himself in a hazy gambling den, silent and deserted now, the green baize tables covered in calico sheets. The room appeared deserted.

'G'day, Your Royal Highness.'

Andrew swung round. There, in the corner, under a swinging gas-lamp, sat an extraordinary figure with his feet up on the roulette table. Dressed incongruously in a tropical white suit, and with his face almost hidden by a wide-brimmed felt hat and a pair of dark granny glasses, the man calmly puffed at a huge Havana cigar. Andrew noted, with a shiver, the sardonic smile.

'Siddown, Sir,' said the man waving his cigar expansively towards a velvet upholstered chair.

'St Bartholomew, I presume,' said Andrew stiffly.

'Spot on, Highness,' grinned Ryder. 'Take a pew and have some bubbly.'

'No, thank you,' replied Andrew. He remained standing, his legs splayed apart to balance himself against the uneven rolling of the paddle-steamer.

'Suit y'self, Sir, mind if I do?' said Ryder, who had obviously already had a few. 'Not exactly jolly boating weather, eh, Highness?'

'Look, I didn't come here to talk about the bloody weather,' snapped Andrew.

'Sorry to hear about your bro's spot of bother,' said Ryder amiably. 'Tell me, has old Charlie really flipped?'

'None of your damned business.'

'Don't get me wrong, Prince. I'm with the Windsors one hundred per cent. Flamin' disgraceful, some of the press comments. I don't know why you let those Pommy newspapers get away with it. Bleeding reds, most of 'em. Monarchy's the finest bloody institution we got, I say.'

'Keep your cheek to yourself,' said Andrew angrily. 'Just who the hell do you think you are?'

For a moment St Bartholomew seemed genuinely taken aback. 'Don't be like that, mate. I think you might have got me wrong. Jeez, you won't find a more true blue subject than me, cross me heart and hope to die.'

'Look here, Bartholomew, stop beating about the bush. What the deuce do you want from me?'

'Put it this way, Your Royal Highness, you are in a position to help me achieve a life-long ambition.'

'I don't care about your blackmail, Bartholomew. I shall not do anything which harms Her Majesty in any way.'

'Last thing on my mind, sport. But there are some things which all my money, power and influence can't buy me.'

'You rotter,' said Andrew, barely able to restrain himself from thrashing the insolent fellow there and then. 'A fine moment you've chosen to crawl out of the woodwork. Very clever.'

'You're saying some very hurtful things, Andrew.'

'Alright, Bartholomew, I know you've got me over a barrel. Stop stringing it out. Tell me exactly what it is that you want.'

'Fair do's, Prince. There are three pre-conditions. Firstly, privacy. Secondly, I want your word as a man of honour that I will have absolute security. And finally, a personal invitation.'

'Come on, man, spit it out. What precisely do I have to do to get that cheque back?'

'OK, here's what I want.' Ryder paused, drew deeply on his Havana and blew out a puff of blue smoke.

'Tea with the Queen.'

The crisis, what crisis?

A protracted crisis, just as the Chancellor of the Exchequer had feared, meant that confidence in sterling collapsed. The pound dropped to its lowest level since the war; there was a rush to withdraw investments from the City, billions were wiped off the stock exchange, the share index tumbled, and as with all such panics, gold went through the roof. The Cabinet was in almost permanent session and it was announced that Parliament would soon be recalled from its Christmas recess.

In Kensington Palace all was tranquillity. Prince Charles, for once free from the pressing tyranny of his official engagements, played happily with his children in the nursery. Charles's favourite game was Blind Man's Buff.

Diana was becoming concerned. The Prince of Wales was enjoying this enforced freedom all too much: no hands to shake, silly questions to answer, things to open, countries to visit or stiff and starchy uniforms to wear.

'It's so cosy here,' he said, as he lay sprawled out before the blazing log fire during one of those long December evenings, listening to a Bach cantata. 'This is what I love — time to reflect, think about life, ruminate, get to know the children, and above all to spend time with you, darling. Isn't this just simply wonderful?'

Diana could not believe her ears. 'Charles, you really must pull yourself together. Do you realize the seriousness of this situation?'

'Well, I suppose it depends on what one thinks is serious in life,' replied Charles thoughtfully. 'As the *Dhammapada* says — "Happy is the practice of virtue during one's whole life; happy is confidence firmly rooted; happy is the attainment of wisdom..."'

242

Diana gave a little shriek. 'Charles, this cannot go on. You've got to snap out of it. Darling, do you realize that some people are even saying you are not fit to become king?'

'Let each man first establish himself in what is proper, then let him admonish others.'

Diana bit her lip. She must remain calm. After all, it was clear that it was up to her to guide Charles through this funny phase. What he needed was heaps of TLC — Tender Loving Care — and a proper job.

'Darling, petal,' said Charles, after a meditative silence.

'Yes, darling?'

'Actually darling, I'd quite like my trousers back. I feel a bit foolish in this kaftan.'

'But, darling, you know perfectly well Mummy says you can't go out.'

'I don't see why not, darling.'

'Because quite simply, darling, some people think you are bonkers.'

Charles digested this information for a moment. Then quietly he said: 'Let the wise man guard his mind. The guarded mind brings happiness.'

Coup de grace

Week two and the crisis was reaching a crescendo. But Andrew had his own worries. Despite all the other comings and goings at Buckingham Palace he had arranged for Ryder St Bartholomew to be let in. He had duly sent the requested official invitation. When the white chauffeur-driven Rolls with its all-round smoked glass windows arrived at the gates it was ceremoniously waved through. The frozen pressmen peered in vain to see who this visitor was, but the curtains in the back windows were firmly drawn.

A footman met Ryder at the side entrance with a formal bow. 'Follow me, sir.'

After walking down miles of confusing corridors, Andrew was waiting for them in a small ante-room. Andrew dismissed the footman. The two men were alone.

'It's most gracious of your mother to receive me, Your Highness,' said Ryder, with a deferential bow. For once the towering Australian was dressed in a sober grey pin-stripe suit, most appropriate for the occasion. There was only one detail out of place. He was still wearing dark glasses.

'I assume you have got the cheque with you,' said Andrew brusquely.

'Some place you've got here,' said Ryder, looking around admiringly at the room. 'Quite a stack of paintings, eh? Must have been collecting for a few years.'

'Can we get to business, Mr Bartholomew?'

'Of course, Your Highness, only too pleased to oblige. No hard feelings I hope.' Ryder reached inside the pocket of his well-tailored suit and produced a Coutts cheque.

'There y'go sport — too old to cash anyway!'

Silently Andrew took it. There was the incriminating evidence: £1,500 made out to Ilaria Pucci, with his signature. He tore it into shreds.

'Sorry I had to do it this way, Andrew. But you know how it is — a man like me has got to get what he wants.'

'Quite,' said Andrew. 'And I shall guarantee that you do.'

'Gee, thanks,' said Ryder, quite overcome. 'You know, this is the greatest moment in my life. Jumping roos! Tea with the Queen!'

'This way,' said Andrew curtly.'Through that door,'

Ryder eagerly obeyed. Abruptly he found himself outside in Buckingham Palace gardens. Behind him he heard the door slam. Ryder swung round to find Prince Andrew facing him with set jaw and raised fists.

'What the hell's going on, son?'

'You're about to get what you've been asking for,' said Andrew through gritted teeth. 'A bloody good lesson.'

'Wait a mo', Andy,' gasped the startled Ryder. 'Don't lose your rag.'

'Fists up, Bartholomew,' ordered Andrew. 'Queensberry rules. Seconds out!'

The first blow struck Ryder savagely on the chin, knocking his head back and his dark glasses on to the grass. The bulky Australian let out an involuntary whimper. There was an expression of sheer terror in his weak, watery pink eyes. As he tried to make a run for it, the second blow sent him spinning backwards into a thorny rose bush.

The Prince hauled his adversary up again by his lapels, swung him round and with a powerful right fist doubled him over. A stiff left upper-cut straightened Ryder abruptly, and a series of swift, sharp blows sent him cowering for cover behind the stone statue of Aphrodite.

'Come out, you swine, and take your punishment like a man.'

With a desperate final effort Ryder hurled the Aphrodite through the air. Andrew ducked and the stone ornament shattered against the wall behind him.

'Queensberry rules, you cad,' said the Prince, squaring up again. 'I am now going to thrash you within an inch of your life.'

He proceeded to do so ...

All the Queen's men

The inner cabal of the Privy Council had already been closeted in emergency session for three hours with Her Majesty in her ornate music room at Buckingham Palace. So secret, and so select, was this meeting that the Sovereign had invited only five people to attend: her husband, the Prime Minister, her most distinguished ex-Prime Minister and the Archbishop of Canterbury. It was to this coterie of trusted personal advisers that she turned in her hour of great tribulation. But the obstacles posed by the constitutional dilemma seemed insurmountable and the meeting had become bogged down in bitter bickering between the present Prime Minister and the former premier, who took the rather lofty view that such a damaging situation would never have been allowed to develop in his day.

The Archbishop of Canterbury, who always found human discord most distressing, took this opportunity to stretch his arthritic limbs. He wandered over to the window with its magnificent view of the Palace gardens below. The forty acres were covered with a picturesque sprinkling of snow. Verily, a Christmas scene, thought the Archbishop, momentarily transported from the disharmony behind him; yea, a time of peace and goodwill towards all men. But what's this? He peered down over the gold rim of his pince-nez. In a corner of the garden by the wall were two intertwined figures.

'Good gracious,' he exclaimed. 'Why, bless me.'

'Oh for heaven's sake, do pay attention, Canterbury,' barked Prince Philip.

'Something most odd happening on your lawn,' Sir,' muttered the Archbishop, shaking his head, bemused.

'There, there, my dear, do come and sit down,' said the Queen gently. 'This is a frightful problem, and we do need your help.'

'Yes, Ma'am, but there appears to be a bout of fisticuffs taking place down there. Most distressing.'

'Do sit down, Canterbury,' said Philip loudly, adding sotto voce to the others: 'Bloody old fool, completely gaga.'

So important was the decision that they had to arrive at that not even the full Privy Council could be called. All Councillors swore the Oath of Confidentiality which dated back to 1250, a year after the first English parliament came into existence. Despite this ponderous weight of history and precedent, the Queen preferred to consult only this tiny band from the Council, which was the guarantor of the British constitution. She could be sure that whatever they discussed that afternoon, however difficult or painful, would never be revealed outside the music room.

'Right, this is getting nowhere,' said Philip decisively. 'I think I'd better take over the helm.'

He rose and, hands behind his back, strode back and forth as if on the bridge of his wartime destroyer. Suddenly he stopped and pointed to the Prime Minister.

'Right, you, let's have some concrete ideas. Enough shilly-shallying. Enough of your fine words, we're not in parliament now, y'know. Let's hear what's really on your mind.'

The Prime Minister had been waiting for the opportune moment to present the position paper which had been drawn up by the Cabinet. It was so tricky dealing with a Head of State who wasn't really head of the whole caboodle; it did necessitate a great deal of 'shilly-shallying', for form had to be followed, protocol observed, precedent paid tribute to, and egos assuaged. The Prime Minister and the Cabinet of course had the first and final say; but after all the Queen was still the Queen.

'Thank you, Your Royal Highness, as a matter of fact

the Cabinet has isolated what, in the last analysis, seems to us to be, everything taken into account, three possibilities ... among others,' said the Prime Minister, in that familiar tone of insincere gravitas adopted for television pronouncements to the nation. 'Get on with it,' said Philip.

'First,' said the Prime Minister, taking the position paper out of a smart red leather briefcase, 'we have what I and my colleagues have tentatively called the Mountbatten Project.'

'Wasn't that to do with the atom bomb?' asked the Archbishop, appearing to wake up, rather like the Dormouse at the Mad Hatter's tea party.

'That's the Manhattan project,' said the Queen tactfully.

'Do pipe down, Canterbury,' growled Philip. 'Carry on, PM.'

'The Mountbatten Project, so named after your uncle, Sir, who successfully handed over India to the Indians ...'

'History, history,' said Philip.

'The Cabinet felt that it might swing public opinion if your son was seen to be following in the glorious, imperial footsteps of the late Earl. It would be a major political test, worthy of a true Prince of Wales. The idea would be for him to hand over Hong Kong to the Chinese.

Philip was appalled. 'Handing over Honkers? To the Chinks? Not bloody likely!'

'One doesn't really know if it would be all that helpful sending Charles out East,' said the Queen gently. 'Aren't they all Buddhists there?'

The Prime Minister reddened. 'Ah, I see what you mean, Your Majesty.'

'Coals to Newcastle,' boomed the voice of the ex-Prime Minster, who never let slip an opportunity to embarrass the present incumbent of the office he had not willingly relinquished.

'So we come to the second option,' continued the Prime Minister hurriedly. 'The Fiji Factor.'

'Sounds like a bloody cosmetic,' said Philip.

'Rather well put, Your Royal Highness, that's exactly what it is — cosmetic. The idea would be to send the Prince to Fiji in a plumed hat to cool his heels for a few years while all this business blows over.'

'You sure Fiji's still one of ours?' asked the ex-Prime Minister.

'Yes,' said the Queen curtly.

'He would be Governor-General,' explained the Prime Minister. 'Lots of pomp and ceremony. But out of sight out of mind.'

'Out of mind,' echoed Philip. 'Let's not beat about the bush, PM. That's what you're thinking, isn't it? That our eldest son is out of his bloody mind.'

'Good heavens, no, Sir. Never entered my head.'

'Balls,' said Philip. 'And quite frankly that's what I think too.'

'Philip, please,' said the Queen quietly.

'Must be said, dear. The boy's been bloody odd for a long time. First it was food, then it was natural cures and alternative whatsits and now it's naked fakirs. Where's it all going to end? Can't possibly send him off in ostrich feathers to some South Sea atoll. The boy'd come back thinking he's a ruddy teapot.'

'Tea?' said the Archbishop.

'Y'know what the problem is,' continued Philip, 'fresh paint. Fumes everywhere. Lead poisoning. Fuddles the mind.'

Everyone else round the table looked at each other uncomfortably. It was difficult to stop the Duke of Edinburgh once he had started.

'Then we come to the final option,' said the Prime Minister hurriedly. 'The Stonewall. We bluff it out.'

'Oh, you mean the political solution,' said the Queen. 'To do absolutely nothing at all and to pretend nothing is amiss.'

'Exactly, Your Majesty.'

'Oh, I don't think that'll do at all,' said the Archbishop worriedly. 'Not sure I can sell that one to my flock.'

Philip turned on him. 'What's the matter, Canterbury?'

'Well, the next Defender of the Faith has got to believe in God, really.'

'Don't be such a knocker, Canterbury. Come up with something positive, man.'

The Archbishop looked startled. 'Ah, well... I'm seeking divine guidance.'

'Much good that's done us,' muttered the Prime Minister.

'In fact,' continued the Archbishop with gathering enthusiasm, 'I've instructed all my bishops to pray publicly this Sunday, and to ask their congregation to intercede with the Almighty for the return of this lost soul.'

'Not so much lost,' remarked the Queen. 'Merely mislaid.'

'Sorry, Canterbury,' said the Prime Minister. 'No can do. That would give the whole game away.'

'Oh dear, will it?' quavered the Archbishop.

'It would blow the whole gaff. We can hardly go on putting out press statements that there's no crisis when you go broadcasting the opposite from your pulpits.'

The ex-Prime Minister, summoning up all the huge reserves of pomposity at his disposal, noisily cleared his throat. It was a clear sign to Her Majesty that he was about to make one of his enormously ponderous and self-important declarations.

'Yes, my dear?'

'Your Most Gracious Majesty,' he began. 'I feel it behoven upon me, as one now above the cut and thrust of everyday party politics, indeed some might say an elder statesman...'

'Crack on with it,' said Philip.

'...who has served you with unstinting devotion for many a year, and thus is perhaps in a privileged position, with nothing to lose, save Your Majesty's approbation...'

'Come to the point, man,' interrupted Philip.

'Oh yes, do,' pleaded the Archbishop.

'...and thus I feel it my bounden duty to mention the

fourth and final option,' continued the ex-Prime
Minister. 'I refer to the Elba Solution.'

'Eh?' said Philip. 'What are you getting at, man?'

'I think he is referring to the Emperor Napoleon, dear.'

'Napoleon?'

'Yes, dear,' said the Queen. 'I think you will find that
the ex-Prime Minister is referring to his exile.'

'Exile!'

'Now don't lost your temper, dear,' said the Queen
soothingly. 'I know your family have been down that
road before. But leaving Greece wasn't the end of the
world.'

'Hell's teeth, you're not taking that idiotic suggestion
seriously are you, Lilibet?'

'One must consider all the options, dear.'

'But the House of Windsor in exile? The idea's
unthinkable!'

The Sovereign turned to her ex-Prime Minister. 'I
assume you are not saying this as a joke, my dear?'

'It has to be said, Ma'am, there is a growing body of
radical opinion that this *crise* could be simply solved by the
installation of a Republic. And, at the other end of the
spectrum, among certain High Tories, there's a growing
swell of support for the other Hanovers — the branch
that didn't change their name.'

'Bloody Germans,' muttered Philip.

'Well, if the Windsors are to go into exile,' said the
Queen, 'where on earth could we go?'

'There's always friendly Switzerland,' suggested the
ex-Prime Minister. 'Or, of course, Monte Carlo.'

'Wouldn't be seen dead,' said the Queen.

'Fiji?' piped up the Archbishop helpfully.

'Enough of this bloody nonsense,' thundered Philip.
'We're not abandoning ship. Everything's under control.
No need to panic. Main thing is to keep Charles under
wraps. Thank God Diana's doing a damn fine job keeping
him in jankers.'

The hot line rang. The Queen picked up the red phone
at her elbow. She listened in silence for a moment.

Slowly she replaced the receiver. She had gone pale.

'Something up, Lilibet?' asked Philip.

The Queen looked grim.

'It's Charles,' she said. 'He's escaped.'

Never-Never Land

Kensington Palace had been under siege for more than a week now by the massed cohorts of the world's press. Nevertheless the Prince of Wales simply wandered out of a small side door into Kensington Gardens. All before him in the public park, as dusk gathered, was a shimmering white, and the frosted snow glinted like crystals. Under the glow of the park lanterns a group of laughing children were building a snowman and they had given him a glowing red nose and merry, beaming face.

The frozen and bored pressmen were clustered round the brazier at the two main exits on the other side of Kensington Palace. Streetwise traders had set up business to cater for all the needs of this scavenging army: hamburger stalls, pizza runners, coffee vendors and one ice-cream van which had been rapidly transformed into a mobile bar. Thus the waiting reporters were unaware that the object of their attentions had slipped away, and shortly afterwards they were disquieted by the sudden evidence of police activity and the clatter of two helicopters overhead, their powerful searchlights scanning the park.

The reporters were further unsettled when the official black Rover of the Police Commissioner shot through the Palace gates. London's top policeman had come to interview Princess Diana. This was a tricky business, as he could not go about it like any ordinary cop cross-questioning a member of the public. The Police Commissioner's debriefing had to be respectful and diplomatic. Diana, however, proved to be somewhat bashful.

'Sorry to put you through this ordeal, Ma'am,' said the Police Commissioner. 'But we must be in possession of all the facts if we are to apprehend, er, locate and ascertain the whereabouts of your missing husband.' The Police Commissioner consulted his notes. 'To recapitulate, Ma'am, at the time of the incident you were under the hairdryer...'

'Yes, you see, normally I go to the salon on Monday and Thursdays, but now we are prisoners, my dressmaker, my hairdresser and pedicurist have to come to me. It's such a fag.'

'My sympathies, Ma'am. But to get back to the very important missing person, what we need to know is the full details of his apparel.'

'But surely, Commissioner, even your men know what the future king of England looks like!'

'All the same, Ma'am, respectfully, every element of identification could be vital to the success of our operation. If I may enquire, what type of jacket was the Prince wearing?'

Diana hesitated. 'Actually, He wasn't.'

'I see, even on this frosty night your husband exited without a jacket. Trousers?'

Diana blushed. 'Not those either, actually.'

'No trousers,' noted the Commissioner. 'Aha!' May I deduce from your testimony, Ma'am, that Prince Charles was wearing a kilt?'

'Not exactly.'

'I see, no trousers, no jacket.'

'That's correct, Commissioner. He was wearing a kaftan.' The policeman looked baffled. 'Kaftan, Commissioner, it's a loose-fitting, ankle-length, flowing garment.'

'Oh, I have you, Ma'am — a frock! Pray, don't be embarrassed. We meet all types of taste in our line of business. One of your lovely outfits was it, Ma'am?'

When it had been explained to him that the Prince was in fact wearing nothing more bizarre than a thin cotton Indian garment of a cool eau-de-Nil green, the

Commissioner remarked: 'Speed is of the essence. His Highness must be freezing. Never fear, Ma'am, teams of my very best and most trusted men are at this very moment scouring the capital. I expect that even now he has been apprehended, er, found.'

On the contrary.

The Prince of Wales, unconscious of the wind biting through his thin kaftan, was wandering meditatively through the winter landscape of Kensington Gardens. He skirted the edge of the Round Pond, where in summer young boys sailed their toy boats. A heavily muffled courting couple sitting on one of the park benches broke off from their embrace to stare at this curious figure. Their interest was aroused not by who he was, but by what he was wearing: like many well-known faces out of context he was simply not recognized. All that the courting couple saw was an eccentric Englishman in a long flowing green dress and leather thong sandles. They snickered.

Unaware, Charles passed by the ornate bandstand and padded over the crisp snow towards the monumental statue called 'Physical Energy' by the now forgotten Victorian artist, G. F. Watts. It portrayed a ludicrously perfect, muscled man in heroic pose astride an absurdly majestic horse. But Charles, deep in his thoughts, failed to notice this huge bronze tableau. He continued on till he reached the banks of the Serpentine.

Here he found a small group of children, accompanied by their mothers and nannies, feeding the ducks. Charles joined them. From under his kaftan he produced a small cottage loaf of freshly baked home-made wholemeal bread. 'Come on, quackers,' he sang softly, dividing the bread and casting it upon the frozen waters. 'There, my friends, share my humble meal.'

One or two of the nannies moved their children away quickly. Charles turned to the four remaining children, a boy and three small girls, all under ten years old.

'Have you seen this?' he said, indicating the Peter Pan statue behind him. 'Do you know what it represents?'

'Yes,' piped up one of the little girls. 'It's Peter Pan. The boy who never grew up.'

'And lived in Never-Never Land,' added another girl.

'Where there were pirates and Red Indians,' said the boy.

'That's right, it sounds like magic, doesn't it?' said Charles. 'Only it could be real. You see, we can make magic exist.'

The mothers and the remaining nanny looked uneasily at each other, but the children found nothing odd at all in this man dressed so strangely. They listened rapt as he described to them how the statue represented Peter Pan summoning with his flute all the tiny woodland creatures, the dormice, rabbits and squirrels so charmingly depicted here in bronze.

'The story of Peter Pan is really about how the world would be a better place if we could remain as nice as you children,' explained Charles. 'And if only we could believe hard enough, Never-Never Land could really exist. But you see, when people grow up they often stop dreaming about nice things and so of course they simply don't exist. That's why Peter Pan ran away from home.'

'Why did he run away from home?' asked the boy.

'Because,' explained Charles, 'he heard his parents discussing his future as a grown-up.'

Overhead, there was the clatter of a low-flying helicopter. Its searchlights swept the opposite bank.

'So, if you really want, does that mean you can fly like Tinkerbell?' asked a girl.

'Well, in a way. If you really, really want you can — in your imagination. In your imagination, if you really believe, you can make anything happen.'

'Even Never-Never Land?'

'Yes, some people call it Never-Never Land, other people call it Nirvana. You might know it as heaven.' In the shadows behind them loomed half a dozen dark figures, who lurked in a semi-circle around this small group.

Charles continued softly, almost as if talking to himself: 'You see, people don't believe in these things because they are so frightened. They laugh at things they don't understand.'

The semi-circle of policemen moved in closer.

'But, please, mister, where is Never-Never Land?' asked the little boy.

Charles smiled at him wistfully. 'Never-Never Land? It's a long journey, and quite a difficult one, but you'll always find it if you look hard enough.'

'Excuse me, Your Royal Highness,' said a firm voice at his ear. 'Would you be kind enough to step this way?' Two large plain-clothed detectives lifted him under the arms.

There was the incomprehensible babble of another

policeman talking into his two-way radio. Nearby the helicopter landed.

The two silent policemen bore off an unresisting Charles. From behind came the urgent voice of the little boy: 'But, please, please, *where* is Never-Never Land?'

Though wedged tightly between his two captors, Charles managed to twist around. He smiled serenely. 'Why, my child,' he called, 'it's inside you.'

Order, order

Though the precipitator of this mayhem was gently returned to the enveloping arms of his princess, and the secure and safe haven of Kensington Palace, the crisis continued inexorably on its course towards a major political showdown. Increasingly, alarmingly, it began to look as if the majestic ship of state was heading for the rocks.

Charles, to ensure his continued incarceration, was allowed only an oversized pair of Winceyette pyjamas. Even his Indian sandals were taken away. The kaftan was quietly burned. The guard outside was doubled. This time, however, it was not to keep the press out; it was to keep the Prince in.

By mid-December this crisis came to a head. The Establishment had stonewalled as only it knew how. But despite its centuries of experience of maintaining silence and secrecy, the glowing embers of rumour and speculation could not be dampened down. The unquenchable desire for information lit up the land, spreading from one end of the kingdom to the other, like beacons upon every hill, till the nation was ablaze with the demand for truth.

It had become clear that the once durable fabric of British society was in the gravest danger of simply disintegrating. The Chief Constable of Liverpool, in a top secret memorandum, had gone so far to suggest that such was the ferment in his city that he could not rule out a popular insurrection.

After a hurried consultation with the Queen, the Prime Minister finally made a statement. The communication from Downing Street was terse: 'The House of

Commons will be recalled from its Christmas recess on Monday when the Prime Minister will make a statement.'

The nation waited.

'Order, order,' yelled the Speaker of the House of Commons ineffectually. There was bedlam. The debate was getting totally out of hand.

Six hundred order papers were waved angrily in the air. All around there were animal noises, rowdy interjections, furious accusations and uninhibited abuse.

'Order, order,' shouted the Speaker again, his face quite puce under his wig. 'I must insist that the Honourable Members refrain from the use of unparliamentary language.'

'Bugger off, you old fool,' yelled a Tory from the back benches.

The Speaker surveyed this rowdy scene with dismay. It was quite beyond his control.

The proceedings had disintegrated after the delivery of the Prime Minister's statement. It was a masterly display of political backsliding and fence-sitting. During the evasive five-minute statement, which teams of civil servants had worked on word by word over the weekend, the Prime Minister managed to deliver a gratuitous and entirely irrelevant attack upon the Opposition, and just at the end managed to slip in: 'While the Prince has, as is the right of every citizen of this land, a certain interest in Eastern religions and philosophies, it in no way compromises, in the view of the government and all right thinking persons, his position as the future Defender of the Faith and Head of State.'

The Leader of the Opposition sprang to his feet. 'All the country wants to know, Prime Minister,' he bellowed, 'is this — is he or is he not a Buddhist?'

'It's not as simple as that . . .' began the flustered Prime Minister.

This was greeted with Opposition jeers. From the back

benches came a concerted chorus of 'Baa-baa' and 'Resign!'

'Order, order,' bleated the Speaker.

'Toadies.'

'Lickspittles.'

'Creeps!'

'Crawlers!'

The insults flew back and forth across the Dispatch Box. The Mother of Parliaments was at work.

'Scumbag.'

'Godless sinners,' sang out a Welsh voice from the Government benches. 'This nation will not tolerate a king, surrounded by naked fakirs, sitting cross-legged before the graven image of a heathen deity. It's ... un-English.'

Behind this bedlam two poles of opinion began to emerge. On the far right of the traditionalist side it was argued that in order to save the glorious institution of the monarchy it was imperative that the Prince of Wales should stand down in favour of a suitable Protestant candidate — whether from the House of Windsor, or even from the House of Hanover if needs be. At the other end of the spectrum the radical view was unequivocal: the monarchy must be dissolved and a republic instituted.

'The symbol and reality of monarchy is what has not only saved this great country from anarchy and revolution for nigh on a thousand years,' said Anthony Cruickshank, the right-wing MP from East Anglia, in his most Churchillian tones. 'In this dark hour we must not falter in our steadfast adherence to ...'

'Twatface!'

'Dickhead!' riposed Sir Anthony.

For another uproarious five minutes this sophisticated badinage and rapier-like wit, for which the Commons was so justly famed, traversed the House.

'Order, order,' cried the Speaker, but his voice was drowned out.

'Centuries of monarchial tyranny are about to be torn

down, the oppressors trampled underfoot as the peoples shoulder to shoulder, march towards their inevitable and glorious destiny,' shouted Doug Fletcher, the fiery left-wing orator from Humberside, employing his most rabble-rousing rhetoric. 'This decadent, corrupt and obsolete institution, so long the opium of the British people, must be swept aside by the tide of the proletariat . . .'

'Chickenshit!'

Suddenly, on the floor of the House, Sir Anthony Cruickshank and Doug Fletcher were at each other's throats. They exchanged a flurry of punches and then, in a blind fury, to the cheers of their respective supporters, they wrestled each other to the ground.

'I suspend this sitting,' cried the Speaker. But no one heard.

The Home Secretary, who had borne much of the pressure over the past two weeks, cracked. With a demented cry he lurched forward from the Government front bench and seized the mace. Whirling the gilt staff of office above his head, he launched himself at the Leader of the Opposition. There was a sharp crack as he brought the mace down upon that shining pate. From all sides MPs leapt over the benches and joined the fray.

Anarchy.

Hark to the new born king

As Christmas approached, and the snow continued to fall gently over the troubled kingdom, the Windsor clan gathered together once again within the comforting encirclement of the twelve-foot thick granite walls of the castle that bore their name. This year the Family were particularly grateful for those massive battlements and ramparts. Although Windsor Castle had not been under attack from arrow or cannonball since 1215, the time of bad King John, the Royal Family were at bay. The walls of the Windsor dynasty shuddered under the onslaught from the besieging forces without; battering rams of ideology and catapults of invective produced alarming cracks in the mighty edifice, while a long war of attrition threatened to force them to relinquish their stronghold and flee into exile.

From all over the kingdom the beleaguered Family had come together, closing ranks for the traditional Royal Christmas. Whatever tempests or battles raged beyond the walls, within all was calm. The regimen remained resolutely unchanged. The Christmas tree, as ever, stood in the corner of the Queen's pink day-room, which the Family liked to use for their informal afternoon tea ritual. The room was festooned with Christmas cards, while from the ceiling hung loops of colourful streamers and glinting tinsel. As a special treat for the children, the fairy on the top of the tree had already been lip up, and her wand twinkled merrily.

'Isn't this lovely?' said the Queen. 'So cosy.'

'Mmmmm,' agreed Princess Sarah. 'Really homey.'

'Right, darling,' said Andrew, putting his arm

affectionately round his wife. 'Christmas is great. It brings families together.'

Half a dozen footmen bore in the tea, a sumptuous affair, with sardine and cucumber sandwiches, home-made cottage loaf bread (still warm from the Windsor ovens), buttered crumpets, hot muffins, brandy snaps filled with clotted Devon cream, mince pies, and a special almond and cherry fruit cake.

'Yummy,' said Diana.

'Glad to see you've got an appetite for once,' said Philip.

'Yah,' laughed Edward. 'I'd noticed you'd been stuffing your face of late, sister-in-law dear.'

Diana blushed. 'Actually, I have been putting on some weight.'

The Queen looked up sharply. 'Good.' She picked up a silver teapot in either hand. 'Now, shall I play mummy — Darjeeling or Earl Grey?'

The door opened, and in swept a flustered Princess Michael of Kent. Her husband shuffled in embarrassedly behind her. Princess Michael curtsied to the Queen.

'We had no idea you were having tea,' said Princess Michael.

'Oh, didn't we tell you?' said the Queen Mother innocently.

'No,' said Princess Michael, a trifle petulantly.

'How remiss,' remarked Margaret, drawing deeply on her cigarette.

Princess Michael had overdressed for tea. Her two-piece Dior suit was a vivid cherry-blossom pink, a startling contrast to the casual formality of the rest of the family — save Charles. While his brothers wore pressed corduroys and sports jackets, the Prince of Wales had not conformed to the convention that even for afternoon tea the Windsors made an effort and put on a tie. Charles was all in white.

He wore a smart, starched white Nehru jacket, with loose-fitting white cotton trousers, held up by a drawstring waist, and on his feet he had a pair of open-toed sandals. From the Prince's neck hung a hologram

pendant, the size of a fifty pence piece, which, if caught in
the right light, reflected the 3-D image of Buddha
Gautama.

In the three days that the Royal Family had been
together at Windsor no one had mentioned Charles's
new and unusual adornment, nor indeed had anyone
remarked upon the Prince's singular apparel. The fact of
his conversion to Buddhism, and all the fuss that it had
entailed, had gone entirely unremarked. The Family
carried on, quite as usual. Never once was the crisis
mentioned. While out there in the real world mayhem
raged, here in Windsor all was talk of mistletoe, holly,
Christmas presents and the seasonal weather.

'Why, I do believe it will be a white Christmas,'
remarked the Queen.

'Who's going to play Santa?' demanded Philip, who still
felt entitled to the part.

'Bags I,' said Andrew.

'But it's my turn, Mummy,' complained Edward.

'Now, now, boys,' said the Queen, casting her eyes
meaningfully in the direction of Charles. She was
determined to make her son snap out of his reverie: for
the last three days he had been in meditative retreat and
all they had heard from him was a low chanting sound
from the other side of his bedroom door. She had
resolved to make the Prince come out of himself. 'I
think Charles should play Father Christmas,' she said
loudly.

'Humph,' said Philip testily. 'Well, he likes dressing up.'

A footman entered with a stack of mail on a silver
salver. 'The afternoon post, Ma'am, said the attendant.
There were a dozen Christmas cards and a letter from
Cambridge for Edward.

The Family scrabbled to get a pick of the cards: there
was nothing the Windsors loved better than opening
things.

'One for you, Megs, from that island of yours,' said the
Queen, putting on her spectacles and squinting. 'From
someone called... Croissant.' She peered closer. 'It's

with lots of love and . . .' Princess Margaret snatched the card out of her sister's hand.

'Xmas Greetings from Zanzibar here,' said Philip. 'Oh dear. The poor old woolly-tailed marmoset is on his uppers again.'

Sarah tore a card in half and tossed it on the fire.

'What are you doing, Buttons?' asked Andrew.

'Just some Christmas kisses for you, poppet,' said Sarah coldly. 'From a Miss Stark.'

'I've got one from that nice President Waldheim,' trilled Princess Michael.

'Here's "Noël Felicitations" with a picture of an elephant from the President of Sri Lanka,' said the Queen Mother. 'Look, he didn't put enough postage on.'

'Christ,' swore Philip, 'and the chap's not even Christian.'

Everyone looked up in alarm. But Philip, unaware that he was treading on dangerous ground, continued: 'Bloody heck, I mean just tell me — how can a chap send Christmas greetings when he's a bloody Buddhist?'

The Queen gave him one of her looks. Philip shut up.

Edward let out a little whoop of delight. 'Listen all,' he announced. 'Some rather please-making news. You know that last paper I wrote, "The Fall of the Romanovs — a family tragi-comedy or the victims of the locomotive of history?"'

'Well?' said the Queen. 'Tell.'

'Blimey,' preened Edward, 'I just happen to have come top.'

'Show-off,' said Andrew, who always found talk of academia intensely irritating.

'Edward, I thought I told you something this time last year — not to draw attention to yourself,' said Philip. 'Just not on. Don't do it again.'

'Sorry, father. I shall make sure it never happens again,' said Edward contritely. He'd have to bollock Sergeant Harborough for being too clever by half.

From below stairs came the sound of singing. The footmen and kitchen staff were practising for their carol service on Christmas Day.

> 'Hark the herald angels sing,
> Glory to the new born king!'

The Queen began humming her favourite festive tune.

'Oh, that reminds me,' remarked Diana casually. 'I won't be able to do my little tele project after all.'

'Why's that, dear?' asked the Queen.

Diana blushed. 'Actually, I haven't even told Charles yet,' she said shyly. 'There's something I think you should all know — we're expecting another baby.'

The Queen beamed. Her plan had worked. 'Well done, my dears,' she exclaimed. 'Well played.' It was the first bit of good news for weeks.

Below, the singing reached a crescendo:

> 'Hark the herald angels sing,
> Glory to the new born king!'

The inner cabinet was closeted in emergency session at Chequers, the Prime Minister's official country residence in the Chiltern Hills. Here there was no Christmas spirit, only a smoke-filled room, and the politicians certainly did not have goodwill unto their fellow men. They were locked in a battle for survival. The Prime Minister, the Foreign and Home Secretaries, the Chancellor of the Exchequer and the Lord Chancellor had faced the facts: their days were numbered. They knew that if they could not find a swift solution to this crisis by Christmas Eve the Prime Minister would simply have to resign — with incalculable consequences for the country.

At last, at midnight, they came to a decision.

The Queen had noticed that Prince Philip had been more restless than ever since their Christmas incarceration.

She put it down to the fact that the unmentioned business was getting to him. The next morning, after breakfast, while Her Majesty was busy with her State papers she noticed her husband striding up and down his dressing-room.

'Phil, you look like a caged tiger,' she called.

'As a matter of fact, Lilibet,' confided Philip, 'quite frankly I'm worried stiff.'

The Queen put down a secret service report. 'I know, dear,' she said comfortingly. 'It is a worry, isn't it? You can tell me.'

The Duke of Edinburgh looked out at the three-mile avenue of elms towards the Henry VIII gate. 'It's the hook-billed, bob-crested shag,' he said.

'I beg your pardon?'

'They're in real trouble. Poor blighters, that spillage from the North Sea oil rig has really messed about with their feathers. They want me up in the Shetlands.'

'Who? The shags?'

'Don't be silly. The wildlife people.'

The Queen was baffled. 'But why do they need you?'

'To save the shag.'

'Couldn't you do that after Christmas, dear?'

'And then there's the bumble-bee bat. Encroaching civilization has destroyed their habitat. Now there's nowhere for them to hang upside down.'

'Oh dear.'

'The whole world's gone stark staring mad,' barked Philip. 'Guess what our Australian friends tell me? The old koala's gone and got VD.'

'How disagreeable,' said the Queen. 'But honestly, darling, there's nothing you can do about it right now. We need you here.'

'Right now I'm desperately needed in Malaya,' said Philip. 'The miniature flat-headed tapir is set bang on course for extinction. Such are the wonders of evolution that the silly little buggers have forgotten how to mate. They could be wiped out by the New Year.'

'So could we,' replied the Queen sternly. 'As far as I am

concerned there is only one endangered species — the Windsors.'

That afternoon in the green velvet card room Diana, Sarah, Andrew and Edward were whiling away the long hours by playing Monopoly. 'I suppose I might as well buy Bond Street — as under prevailing conditions one is not allowed to go there,' said Diana.

She slapped down the paper money. It was the only cash she ever handled these days.

'Isn't it a drag not being able to shop?' said Sarah, who so far had only managed to acquire the Old Kent Road (wherever that was).

'Talking of presents, folks, we guys wouldn't mind a microwave oven for Chrissie,' said Andrew, who had not succeeded in buying anything at all, not even a waterworks.

'Could do with an umbrella stand, too,' added Sarah.

'Or a fridge-freezer,' prompted Andrew. 'But we've decided the most useful thing really would be the micro. They're so convenient. Indispensable really for modern living.'

Princess Margaret, who had been idly picking out a Scott Joplin rag on the piano between puffs of her Sobranie, could not believe what she was hearing. Philistines, Sloanes, Yuppies. Oh Gawd. What prince was going to take *her* away from all this?

In the deep armchair the Queen Mother snored softly.

Hamster, do you want a boy or girl?' asked Sarah, who had just acquired Pall Mall.

'A girl,' said Diana emphatically. 'Someone to play dollies with, take shopping and to teach make-up to. I am sick of playing cowboys and Indians and kicking footballs.'

'Blast,' said Andrew, who had landed on a penalty square. 'Go back to jail!'

'Bit like being here,' observed Edward.

'Feeling a bit horny, ha ha,' laughed Andrew. 'Time

you got hitched, old man. You should have made provision. Put a popsie in the pub.'

'I did actually,' said Edward. 'Thing is, with all those jackals prowling around outside a chap just daren't risk sneaking out.'

'Oh goodie,' squealed Sarah, 'I've just bought Fleet Street.'

'Yuk,' said Diana, 'isn't that where the reptiles come from?'

'I say, old son,' said Andrew with a conspiratorial wink towards his brother, 'so who is this bit of fluff?'

'The lovely Amelia Cumming-Brice.'

'Come across, has she?'

'I'll say. But because I can't get out there I am racking my brains as to how I can smuggle Amelia in here.'

Andrew paled. 'Christ, Eddie. Don't be crazy. If there's one thing I have learned this past year, old man, it's that that would be most unwise. In fact, catastrophic. Let me impart one piece of fraternal advice, be it from a happy married man — let sleeping dogs lie.'

'But she's no dog,' said Edward missing the point.

From down the corridor they heard a low repetitive murmur. It got louder and the group pretended not to hear as the sound passed outside the door and receded down the corridor. But the words could be clearly picked out.

> 'Om-mane-pedme-hum,
> Om-mane-pedme-hum.'

As dusk fell on the Chiltern Hills the Archbishop of Canterbury's white Vauxhall Cavalier came to a stop outside Chequers. He had been summoned urgently to the Prime Minister's country seat.

The Prime Minister did not mince words. 'You have had three weeks to come up with a miracle, Canterbury, and all you can produce is a silly text from the Bible. So you'll probably know this one. "By your works shall ye be judged".'

'That's not exactly in the Christmas spirit, PM,' said the old Archbishop.

'Blow Christmas,' said the Prime Minister. 'No votes in that. But it does mean we have only two days to pull the rabbit out of the hat.'

'How on earth are we going to do that?' quavered the Archbishop.

'Not we, Canterbury, *you*.'

'Oh dear.'

'The Cabinet and I have decided that you must go before the nation and explain everything.'

'But, but..'

'To this end we have arranged that you shall be interviewed by the BBC on the main news tomorrow night. You will resolve the crisis once and for all. You will explain to the British public why there is absolutely nothing incompatible about being a Buddhist and a Christian at the same time.'

'But, PM, no one will believe that.'

'Nonsense, Canterbury. You underestimate the power of television,' snapped the Prime Minister. 'A word of advice. Just keep smiling, and for heaven's sake don't answer the interviewer's questions. Say what you have to say but don't spell it out too clearly. Look confident and very holy. Believe me, they'll swallow it.'

'But, PM,' wailed the Archbishop, 'what am I going to say?'

'God knows, Canterbury,' shrugged the Prime Minister. 'I suggest you seek higher guidance. And keep smiling for heaven's sake.'

Dinner at Windsor Castle was rather less festive than usual despite the fact that the Queen tried valiantly to cheer the troops. Her Majesty, going against her normal frugal habits, had instructed the butler to open at least a dozen bottles of the potent and extremely expensive Château Leoville Barton 1964. They ate a terrine of game, with a port sauce, followed by stuffed partridge shot on the Sandringham estate. Charles ate only his Brussels sprouts. Diana had two portions. The Queen lived up to her reputation as an excellent mimic by delivering a wicked impersonation of her Prime Minister and then, quite out of character, desperate to jolly everyone up, she cracked three risqué jokes.

'I heard rather a good one in Verona recently at the Wildlife Conference,' said Philip, chuckling to himself in anticipation. 'Why is an owl, so much smarter than a chicken?'

'Don't know,' said the Queen, 'give up.'

'Simple. When did you last eat Kentucky Fried Owl? Ha! Ha! Ha!'

There was little laughter around the table.

'I don't get it,' said the Queen Mother. 'What is a Kentucky Fried Owl?'

The Queen signalled the end of dinner. As they filed out of the room Princess Michael sidled up to Her Majesty.

'Your Majesty, I thought I'd better tell you,' confided Marie-Christine. 'I have been offered the position to be guest host of the Johnny Carson television show in Los Angeles. Naturally I have turned it down.'

'But why?' asked the Queen. 'You'd be most suited. Right up your alley, one would have thought.'

'Surely it is not compatible with my position as a Royal?'

'You think so?' said the Queen lightly.

Marie-Christine hesitated. 'But I rather thought, Ma'am, that you would not approve.'

'On the contrary,' said the Queen. 'You should go. In fact, I insist.' Her Majesty smiled warmly at the baffled Princess Michael. 'Well, that's decided then, Marie-Christine. You *must* go.' The Queen rubbed her hands together gleefully. 'Capital!'

This put the Queen in an excellent mood, and she thoroughly enjoyed the family cabaret, which Philip kicked off by impersonating an amorous orang-utan, while the Queen Mother had them all falling about with her unregal impression of Elizabeth II winning the Derby. Her mood took a dip when it came to Charles's turn, for he elected to entertain them by demonstrating a few of the more recondite yoga poses. But the mood plunged when her sister took to the floor. Margaret chose to sing a little blues number, accompanying herself on the piano.

'This little lyric is kinda special to me,' she drawled between puffs of her Sobranie, 'it's dedicated to all young lovers ... who long for microwaves.'

She began to sing in a husky smoke 'n' whisky voice. The Queen's face grew steelier and steelier.

> 'If I give my man my last nickle
> And it leaves me in a pickle
> 'Taint nobody's business if I do.'

Margaret half rose from her piano stool and slowly, suggestively rotated her pelvis.

> 'I'd rather my man hit me
> Than jump up and quit me.'

The Queen coughed loudly.

> 'I swear I won't call no copper
> If I'm beat up by my poppa.'

The Queen rose purposefully and swept out of the room. As she strode down the corridor Her Majesty was followed by the raucous refrain:

> "Taint nobody's business if I do,
> 'Taint nobody's business if I do.'

The headlines of the newspapers on the morning of Christmas Eve announced that the Archbishop of Canterbury would be interviewed on prime time television that evening. *The Times* announced: 'CRISIS RESOLVED TONIGHT — ARCHBISHOP MAKES STATEMENT.' The *Guardian*'s headline was more speculative: 'END OF THE LINE FOR MONARCHY: THE WINDSORS INTO EXILE?' The racy *Morning Chronicle* had a more startling front page: 'EXCLUSIVE — CHARLES STEPS DOWN, RETIRES TO TIBET.' The *Daily Disclosure* had a different story: 'QUEEN STANDS FIRM, CHARLES TO STAY.'

The morning papers lay strewn over Her Majesty's bed. When Philip came in from his adjacent bedroom, to join his wife for morning tea, he found her engrossed in the front page report of the *Daily Disclosure*.

'Oh, Lilibet, do ditch that tripe,' said Philip. 'It'll only upset you.'

'Listen to what this Mr Spalding has to say,' said the Sovereign, reading out aloud. '"The constitutional crisis, which I exclusively exposed a month ago, I can now reveal has been resolved in an amazing behind-the-scenes deal..."'

'Reptile!'

The Queen let the *Daily Disclosure* fall to the floor. 'It's nice to know that they know more than we do. Indian or china tea, dear?'

'Well, it's all in the hands of God, now. And that idiot Canterbury.'

'Gosh, I've got the collywobbles,' said the Queen.

'Nothing we can do any more. Just pray, I suppose.'

'What about, dear?'

'That Canterbury doesn't go and make a balls-up. The man's a complete clot.'

The Queen began to pour from the ornate William IV silver teapot. 'Darling,' she said tentatively, 'suppose, just suppose, that it all goes wrong tonight and we have to go... where would you fancy, darling?'

'What's this? Defeatist talk!'

'Well, Philip, I know I've never said this before, darling, but I realize that over these more than thirty years while I've been on the throne it hasn't all been easy for you, not having a proper job, being number two and so on. I just wanted to say — you've been a brick.'

'Oh, do cut it, old girl,' said Philip, embarrassed.

'I must say this, darling. I couldn't have managed this Queen business without you. And that's why if — just supposing — we have to go abroad, well, I'd like you to choose where. I want you to be happy. I mean, would you like to go back to Corfu?'

'Lilibet!' roared Philip. 'This is treasonable talk and I won't have it on my bridge.'

'Well, one does have to plan ahead. What would happen to the staff, my horses, the corgis?'

'Snap out of it, Lilibet. We have got to find something to occupy ourselves. Keep busy — that'll keep the butterflies at bay. I'm off to shoot some pheasant.'

The other members of the family also found distractions to keep their minds off the impending resolution of their fate. Princess Michael of Kent was on the line to Hollywood, sorting out the details of her contract.

'... is that net or gross? Well done, Mort! And what about the budget for my frocks? Then we come to the billing — one is not at all happy about the size of one's name in the credits...'

Charles was the only member of the family who was totally clam. Indeed, he had achieved inner peace. He was in his room meditating.

Diana and Sarah had arranged for Harrods to come to them, and a dazzling display of the store's goods was laid out on the state banqueting table. Princess Sarah held up a fluffy angora sweater. 'Isn't it lovely, Hamster?' she cried. 'Would you like this for Christmas?'

'Terrif, but that's frightfully expensive,' said Diana. 'And you know the Queen's rule? Nothing more than fifteen pounds.'

'B-o-r-i-n-g,' sang Sarah. 'I suppose I'll just have to buy it for myself then.'

The most elaborate diversion had been organized, with some secrecy, by the Queen Mother. She had arranged some racing. Princess Margaret, the Princes Andrew and Edward (who had sworn not to tell Her Majesty) assembled in the long, marble-floored Carolean corridor for what the Queen Mother had promised would be prime sport. Already gathered they found half a dozen footmen who were going to act as stewards. Five servants held a corgi under their arm, the sixth clutched a live chicken.

Each barrel-like little body of the royal corgis was encased in specially cut-off shooting sockings of different colours. This was to be a corgi race, announced the Queen Mother, to be called The Socks Memorial Doggie Derby Stakes. The procedure was simple: the Queen Mother would act as bookie, while the fleetest-footed servant would race down the corridor with the chicken, pursued along the two hundred yard 'track' by the pack — and the first dog past the Bernini statue would be declared the winner.

Although the race was supposed to be discreet, in the event it was a rowdy affair. The yaps of excitement and the yells of encouragement reverberated through the castle as Smokey, Sparky, Jolly, Myth and Fable scampered down the marble corridor after the squawking chicken. Smokey was first past the Bernini,

winning £50 for Prince Edward. However Andrew
lodged a strenuous objection, claiming that Smokey had
bitten his fancy, Fable. While the footmen adjudicated,
Jolly set off again in pursuit of the chicken, which was
last seen flying out of the castle windows.

Thus the Windsors amused themselves.

That evening at nine o'clock, after a frugal supper, the
Family gathered before the twenty-six-inch screen in the
television room. There was a scraping of seats and
nervous coughing as the family settled down to watch
the BBC news. Charles calmly squatted on the floor, legs
crossed in the lotus position, as the broadcast which
would decide the fate began. The Queen kept her fingers
crossed.

'I have with me in the studio tonight the Archbishop of
Canterbury, who we hope will throw some light on the
constitutional crisis which has rocked the country,' said
the news announcer, enunciating carefully, in modu-
lated BBC tones conveying the gravity of this
momentous occasion. 'Now, Archbishop, the question
seems to be — is it compatible for a future Defender of
the Faith to be a Buddhist?'

'Ah, I'm glad you asked me that,' replied the
Archbishop, smiling in accordance with the Prime
Minister's advice. 'Theologically, a most interesting
question. The Buddha said: "I teach but two things —
suffering and the release from suffering." Not so
different from our "Vale of Tears", eh? Oh yes, there are
any number of opportunities for a reconciliation
between these two great religions.'

'People might say, Archbishop, that it was not up to
Prince Charles, as our future king, to effect such a
reconciliation. Indeed, is it not irreconcilable for the
Prince to have taken such a position?'

'What's important here is to remember that both
faiths bear witness to the reality of a spiritual dimension.
They have Nirvana and we have Heaven.' The
Archbishop beamed. 'Different ticket. Same destination.'

'So if I understand you correctly, Archbishop — it is

perfectly possible to be a Christian and a Buddhist?'

'I think perhaps I can best answer that by quoting the New Testament, Luke, chapter 8, verse 10. It's the parable of the sower. The disciples ask Jesus the meaning of it all. Jesus explained that he liked to convey his message in parables. Jesus shared this little thought with them: "seeing they may not perceive, and hearing they may not understand". This, said Jesus, is the meaning of the parable.' The Archbishop beamed. The Prime Minister would be pleased with him.

The BBC news announcer looked totally bemused. 'You're saying — the conversion of Prince Charles is really a parable?'

'Did you know that Buddha was listed among the saints by mediaeval Christians? Of course, he was never officially canonized.'

'With respect, Archbishop, I must press you on this point. Are you advancing the theory that Buddha could be a Christian saint?'

'Goodness me. Do you know the story of Buddha? Prince Gautama, who lived in the sixth century BC, came from an enormously wealthy family. Young Gautama did what all rich and privileged young chaps do — played sport, chased the girls. Then in his mid-thirties, when he saw some of the tragedies of this life, he decided to change his ways and seek enlightenment.'

'Archbishop,' interrupted the news announcer aggressively, 'I can't quite see what all this has got to do with Christianity.'

'Ah, well, you see, the Buddha's story is taken up in the mediaeval Christian legend of the Saints Barlaam and Josaphat, whom we Christians celebrate on November 27th. Josaphat was a rich young fellow who chucked up his wealth and privilege and went in search of truth.'

'I see,' said the interviewer, now thoroughly lost.

'And he was accompanied by Barlaam!'

'So... Josaphat was the Buddha in disguise?'

'Exactly, dear boy!' The Archbishop was now warming to his sermon. 'Josaphat is an adaptation of the title

Bodhisattva, which means "The Englightened Being".
There are so many parallels. All the Buddha was really
saying was — cease to do evil, learn to do good and purify
your own mind. No quibble there.'

'Quite, Archbishop, but the law of this land specifically
requires that the King of England be a Protestant. The
question I must put to you, and I must press you for a
brief and frank reply, is — can Prince Charles, as a
Buddhist, also be a Protestant and therefore be entitled
eventually to sit upon the throne?'

'Why bless you, yes.' The Archbishop smiled
beatifically. 'The Prince of Wales is still one of us, you
know.'

'Thank you, Archbishop,' said the announcer, turning
back to face the camera. 'Well, there you have it. The
Archbishop of Canterbury has given his blessing. But
the final verdict, of course, will be up to the British
public. Goodnight.'

The Windsors rose and filed out of the TV room, and
the only recognition of what they had just been watching
came from the Queen, who remarked to no one in
particular: 'That went rather well.'

The Family went to bed early that Christmas Eve,
because tomorrow was a Very Important Day.

Christmas Day

Her Majesty was awoken by the hubbub of a huge crowd gathered outside Windsor Castle. When she looked out of the window she was astonished and alarmed to see that the high street of Windsor town was thronged with a multitude of people, and there were more and more of them filling the side streets and alleyways down the hill, as far as the eye could see. It was a frightening sight. From this vast gathering rose a low, ominous rumble.

As the family gathered for the traditional Christmas Day procession to attend Matins at St George's Chapel the Queen addressed them briefly: 'Now don't be frightened. Walk slowly, backs straight, eyes ahead, and keep smiling.'

At a slow, steady pace they set out on the hundred and fifty yard walk to the Chapel. The snow lay crisp and even. The only sound that could be heard was that of their own footsteps, crunching on the frost. The crowd has fallen totally silent.

The Windsors had formed a discreet phalanx around Prince Charles, who alone showed no signs of apprehension. For the rest of the family each step of the way to St George's was an agony. To cover that short distance seemed to take forever.

Suddenly, when they were only ten yards from the Chapel entrance, Charles broke away. Before anyone could restrain him the Prince was striding towards the barriers behind which the crowd had been restrained. The Family watched appalled, rooted to the spot, horrified.

Not a sound came from the waiting mob. A tense, expectant hush hung over Windsor.

Charles faced the crowd.

The Windsors held their breath.

The Prince placed his hands together, in an act of supplication, and bowed. The crowd roared its approval. Hats were thrown in the air.

A chant began: 'Karma king, karma king, karma king . . .'

The cry was taken up; the sound grew, swelled, and became a deafening tumult that some later said they could hear as far away as London.

Karma king? Good God. The Queen blinked in wonderment. He'd been accepted! The line of succession was guaranteed. Back in the driving seat. *Dieu et mon droit.*

The Family Firm was safe.

THE END